PUBLISHED

Poetry of the First World War

A CASEBOOK

EDITED BY

DOMINIC HIBBERD

M

Selection, editorial matter and Introduction © Dominic Hibberd 1981

First published 1981 by
THE MACMILLAN PRESS LTD
London and Basingstoke
Associated companies in Delhi Dublin
Hong Kong Johannesburg Lagos Melbourne
New York Singapore and Tokyo

Printed in Hong Kong

British Library Cataloguing in Publication Data

Poetry of the First World War. – (Casebook series).
  1. English poetry – 20th century – History and
criticism – Addresses, essays, lectures
  2. European War, 1914–1918, in literature –
Addresses, essays, lectures
  3. War poetry, English – History and criticism –
Addresses, essays lectures
  I. Hibberd, Dominic   II. Series
821'.9'12093   PR605.W65

  ISBN 0–333–26120–8
  ISBN 0–333–26121–6 Pbk

CONTENTS

ACKNOWLEDGEMENTS

The editor and publishers wish to express thanks for permission to use the following copyright material: John Bayley, article 'But for Beaumont Hamel . . .' in *Spectator* (4 Oct. 1963) reproduced by permission; Bernard Bergonzi, extract from *Heroes' Twilight* (1965) by permission of Constable & Co. Ltd; Edmund Blunden: (a) article 'The Real War' in *Athenaeum* (10 Dec. 1920) by permission of A. D. Peters & Co. Ltd, and (b) Introduction to Frederick Brereton (ed.), *An Anthology of War Poems* (1930) published by William Collins Son & Co. Ltd; William Cooke, extracts from *Edward Thomas: A Critical Biography, 1878–1917* (1970) by permission of the author; Donald Davie, article 'In the Pity' in *New Statesman* (28 Aug. 1964) by permission of The Statesman and Nation Publishing Co. Ltd; T. S. Eliot, extract from article 'Reflections on Contemporary Poetry IV' in *Egoist* (July 1919) by permission of Mrs Valerie Eliot and Faber and Faber Ltd, copyright © Valerie Eliot 1980; Paul Fussell, extracts from *The Great War and Modern Memory* (1975) by permission of Oxford University Press; D. W. Harding, article 'Aspects of the Poetry of Isaac Rosenberg' in *Scrutiny*, III, 4 (1935) reprinted in *Experience into Words* (1963) by permission of the author and Chatto and Windus Ltd; Philip Hobsbaum, article 'The Road Not Taken' in *Listener* (23 Nov. 1961) by permission of the author; John H. Johnston, extract from *English Poetry of the First World War* (1964) by permission of Princeton University Press; C. Day Lewis, extract from *A Hope for Poetry* (1934) by permission of A. D. Peters & Co. Ltd; John Middleton Murry, articles 'Mr Sassoon's War Verses' in *Nation* (13 July 1918) and 'The Poet of the War' in *Nation and Athenaeum* (19 Feb. 1921) republished in *The Evolution of an Intellectual* (new edition 1927) by permission of the Society of Authors as literary representatives of the author's estate; Margaret Newbolt, extract from *The Later Life and Letters of Sir Henry Newbolt* (1942) by permission of Faber and Faber Ltd; Wilfred Owen, extracts from letters in Harold Owen and John Bell (eds), *Wilfred Owen: Collected Letters* (1967)

by permission of Oxford University Press; David Perkins, extract
from *A History of Modern Poetry* (1976) © 1976 the President and
Fellows of Harvard College, by permission of Harvard
University Press; John Press, article 'Charles Sorley' in *Review of
English Literature* (April 1966) by permission of the Editor and the
author; Isaac Rosenberg, extracts from *Collected Works of Isaac
Rosenberg* (1937; new edition 1979) by permission of the author's
literary estate and Chatto and Windus Ltd; Timothy Rogers,
extract from Introduction to *Rupert Brooke: A Reappraisal and
Selection* (1971) by permission of Routledge & Kegan Paul Ltd;
Siegfried Sassoon: (a) extracts from Introduction to *Poems by
Wilfred Owen* (1920) by permission of G. T. Sassoon, and (b)
extract from *Siegfried's Journey, 1916–1920* (1945) by permission of
Faber and Faber Ltd; Jon Silkin: (a) article 'Keeping the Home
Fires Burning' in *Stand* IV, no. 3 (1960) by permission of the
author, and (b) extract from *Out of Battle* (1972) by permission of
Oxford University Press; Dylan Thomas, extracts from *Quite
Early One Morning* (1954) by permission of David Higham
Associates Ltd on behalf of the trustees for the copyrights of the
author; Arthur Waugh, extract from *Tradition and Change* (1919)
published by Chapman and Hall Ltd, by permission of
Associated Book Publishers Ltd; Dennis Welland, ch. 4 from
Wilfred Owen: A Critical Study (1960) by permission of the author
and Chatto and Windus Ltd; Virginia Woolf, extract from article
'Two Soldier Poets' in *Times Literary Supplement* (11 July 1918)
reprinted in 'Mr Sassoon's Poems' in Mary Lyon (ed.), *Books and
Portraits* (1977), reproduced here by permission of the author's
literary estate and The Hogarth Press; W. B. Yeats; (a) extract
from Introduction to Oxford Book of Modern Verse (1936) and
extract from *Letters on Poetry from W. B. Yeats to Dorothy Wellesley*
(1940) by permission of Oxford University Press, and (b) 'On
Being Asked for a War Poem' in *Collected Poems of W. B. Yeats*
(2nd edn 1950) by permission of A. P. Watt Ltd on behalf of
Michael and Anne Yeats.

GENERAL EDITOR'S PREFACE

The Casebook series, launched in 1968, has become a well-regarded library of critical studies. The central concern of the series remains the 'single-author' volume, but suggestions from the academic community have led to an extension of the original plan, to include occasional volumes on such general themes as literary 'schools' and genres.

Each volume in the central category deals either with one well-known and influential work by an individual author, or with closely related works by one writer. The main section consists of critical readings, mostly modern, collected from books and journals. A selection of reviews and comments by the author's contemporaries is also included, and sometimes comment from the author himself. The Editor's introduction charts the reputation of the work or works from the first appearance to the present time.

Volumes in the 'general themes' category are variable in structure but follow the basic purpose of the series in presenting an integrated selection of readings, with an Introduction which explores the theme and discusses the literary and critical issues involved.

A single volume can represent no more than a small selection of critical opinions. Some critics are excluded for reasons of space, and it is hoped that readers will pursue the suggestions for further reading in the Select Bibliography. Other contributions are severed from their original context, to which some readers may wish to turn. Indeed, if they take a hint from the critics represented here, they certainly will.

A. E. DYSON

INTRODUCTION

There were thousands, probably millions, of poems written in
English during the First World War; critical opinion has never
taken more than a very small number of them into account, and
the choice of poems has varied with the changing tastes of the age.
Most critics are now agreed that Owen and Rosenberg are the
two principal poets of the war, but in 1918 both of those writers
were unknown; other poets who were famous then are now
forgotten. Readers of this Casebook must not expect to find
settled opinions and general agreement. The record is one of a
long and still unfinished debate.

The critical extracts which follow are grouped into three Parts,
the first being of material written during or soon after the war, the
second presenting a selection of comment from the 'thirties and
'forties, and the third containing some of the more interesting
criticism published in the last two decades. Each Part begins
with a few articles which deal with First War poetry in general or
with the work of several writers. These general sections are
followed by studies of individual poets. Nine poets (Blunden,
Brooke, Nichols, Owen, Read, Rosenberg, Sassoon, Sorley and
Thomas) are represented in this way; but they and others are
discussed in some of the general pieces, and so the reader is
advised to make use of the Index. The nine are not selected
according to any theoretical definition of the category 'war poet';
they are simply those authors whose poetry about the war seems
to have attracted most critical attention.

The term 'war poet' has an irreplaceable practical value for
course organisers and general discussion, but a precise definition
has never been agreed for it. Owen wrote his best poetry about
the war; Brooke was more successful with other subjects. Thomas
wrote almost all his poetry during the war but before he saw the
trenches, and his work is highly admired; Nichols is remembered
only for his trench poems and they are often considered to be
embarrassingly bad. Read was an Imagist, Sassoon was a
Georgian. The common factor is the war, but not merely as

subject-matter; critics find these poets interesting not only for what they said about the conflict but also for the way in which they were themselves affected by war experience. Do we see them as in some way representatives, voicing, however clumsily or skilfully, the consciousness of the people as it developed from 1914 to 1918? Some critics might say so, thereby giving the phrase 'war poet' a meaning a little akin to its significance in 1914. Others see the true war poet more specifically as a rebel; he must be expected to protest that war is exploitation and that social reconstruction is its essential aftermath. Other critics again take a literary rather than a literary-political approach to individual poets; one result of this can be that the war loses some of its central importance, and then the label 'war poet' may seem an unnecessary limitation. It has been suggested that English literature might have taken a different road after the war if Thomas, Owen and Rosenberg had survived. But that returns us to the representative quality of these poets and 'the undone years, the hopelessness' which they knew to be their part.

In 1914, the war poet was certainly expected to be a representative – a 'prophet . . . , champion and consoler', as the preface to the first of the war anthologies puts it. He had to speak for the nation and steel its heart for battle. There had been many such poets during the Boer War;[1] Edward Thomas remembered this when, in an article on 'War Poetry' that was remarkably sane for 1914, he drew a distinction between 'verses' and 'poems' and said that the writer of 'poems' would be regarded as 'pro-Boer' by the contemporary public. 'Verses' were what was wanted. As William Cooke points out (in Part Three below), the article is of particular interest because Thomas himself wrote 'poems' during the war which conform with his belief that the true poet does not deal with the raw material of public events. He was no patriotic 'war poet' in the crude 1914 sense, but Cooke argues the connection between his few years as a poet, his love of the English countryside and his readiness to serve in the trenches.

With the notable exception of Yeats, whose attitude to war poetry has become a standard reference point for critics, the established poets 'did their bit' for the national effort in 1914 by turning out patriotic verse for the newspapers. The Government quietly but actively encouraged such writing and within a few months there were more than enough 'verses' to fill an anthology

(*Songs and Sonnets for England in War Time*). The pre-war success of
Georgian Poetry, the anthology launched by Edward Marsh and
Rupert Brooke in 1913, had made anthologies popular and the
war spawned a great many of them. Critics were not slow to
remark, however, that the leading poets of the day had not
outshone themselves in their war verses; in 1915 public attention
turned to the work of the 'soldier-poets'.

   The vogue for poetry by the men who were actually doing the
fighting was given force by Brooke's death in 1915; in his *1914*
sonnets he seemed to have come closer than anyone to speaking as
the national war poet. Although some people were privately
sceptical about his achievement, his public image was defined
by Winston Churchill in an eloquent obituary in *The Times*.
Hundreds of soldier-poets were discovered in the middle years of
the war, and often introduced to the public in extravagant terms,
although the verse in their slim volumes was rarely of the smallest
literary merit. A typical introduction to one of these books – that
for *The Undying Splendour* (1917) – is given (p. 33) in Part One
below; fulsome rhetoric of this kind made serious criticism almost
impossible, and the more responsible critics felt obliged to hold
their peace. Nevertheless, the researcher can find a good many
essays on poetry and the war in the periodicals of the time, and
the work of the soldier-poets was given ready attention, particularly if the poet concerned was known in literary circles. The
principal contributors of war verse to *Georgian Poetry* were
Siegfried Sassoon, Robert Graves and Robert Nichols; it was not
difficult to see them as Brooke's heirs and fellow-Georgians,
writing poems like those he would have written if he had lived.
The modern habit of sharply contrasting Brooke and Sassoon is
not altogether accurate. Sassoon's war poems aroused adverse
criticism but fewer hostile reactions than we might expect. Some
critics suggested that this young officer had suffered too much to
be able to write without bias, and Edmund Gosse commented
that such verse would tend to weaken the war effort. There was
general respect for Sassoon's burning honesty, but also agreement that, whatever he had written, it was 'not poetry'. In
making this complaint, most reviewers seem to have meant that
Sassoon's subject-matter was too violent and his rhythms too
prosaic. (Such objections shed some light on Owen's famous
phrase, 'Above all I am not concerned with Poetry'.) Similar

complaints had been made against the work of the early
Georgians, particularly that of Masefield and Brooke. However,
Harold Massingham sensibly pointed out (in 1917) that Sassoon
had not intended to write 'poetry' and that his war poems had to
be judged as epigrams. Sassoon was fairly widely read and by the
end of the war was, with Nichols, probably the best known of the
post-Brooke war poets.

Public reviews of the soldier-poets tended to praise them for
their heroism and self-denial; private comment, on the other
hand, sometimes accused them of excessive self-concern. The
contrast may be seen when one sets Churchill's article about
Brooke against Charles Sorley's remark in a letter that Brooke
had been sentimental and too interested in himself, or the *Times
Literary Supplement's* rash enthusiasm about Nichols against
Wilfred Owen's objection to Nichols' egocentricity. The distance
between the poet and his subject-matter was (and is) a central
question. In a forceful article in 1918, John Middleton Murry
pressed the opinion that Sassoon had written 'verses', the raw
data for poetry but not poetry itself; and this time 'poetry' meant
more or less what Edward Thomas had meant by it in 1914.
Murry said that Sassoon lacked 'intellectual remoteness' or, as
Thomas might have put it, his thoughts had not receded far
enough from 'daily events'.

Writing in the *Egoist* in December 1916, John Gould Fletcher
had said that there had so far been no war poetry of value because
no poet had been prepared to respond honestly to feeling and
experience; there was a need for a poetry that would put 'the
reader face to face with the imaged reality, perplexing, horrible,
and yet at times curiously beautiful'.[2] In an *Egoist* review of
Read's *Naked Warriors* in 1919, T. S. Eliot said that the book
contained the best poetry about the war he had seen; it was
honest, it had 'a version of things seen' (Fletcher's 'imaged
reality'?) and it was 'neither Romance nor Reporting'.
Presumably, 'Romance' was sentimentality like Brooke's and
'Reporting' was realism like Sassoon's. However, Eliot's claims
for Read were made with noticeable moderation. A number of
critics concluded sadly in 1919 that the war had produced no
poetry at all that was likely to endure. More mildly, members of
the older generation such as Arthur Waugh and Edmund Gosse
maintained that the chief literary effect of the conflict had been

not so much an improvement in poetry as an improvement in the poets themselves. Young men who had been self-centred and anti-social before the war had been taught to feel a deep and unselfish compassion for humanity. By a nice irony, Sassoon's anti-heroic stance was taken as evidence that he himself had been turned into a hero; Waugh compounded the irony by quoting 'Absolution' as proof, presumably unaware that it had been one of Sassoon's first poems about the war and one which was very far from representing his final attitude. However, Waugh also said that the soldier-poets had succeeded in reporting modern warfare as 'an unspeakable horror'; never again would anyone be able to imagine fighting as a glorious adventure. Subsequent criticism has broadly agreed with this view of 'Reporting', although some early reviewers of Owen remarked that by 1918 everybody knew what war was like and hardly needed poets to tell them about it; but one or two modern critics, notably Jon Silkin, have wondered whether some supposedly anti-war poems do not in fact have the effect of casting a halo on death in battle.

A group of Owen's poems was published in Edith Sitwell's anthology, *Wheels*, in 1919 and Murry at once acclaimed 'Strange Meeting' as the finest poem of the war.[3] In a further review in 1921, he declared Owen to be 'the greatest poet of the war. There have been war-poets; but he was a poet of another kind. He was not a poet who seized upon the opportunity of war, but one whose being was saturated by a strange experience, who bowed himself to the horror of war until his soul was penetrated by it, and there was no mean or personal element remaining unsubdued in him.' (Murry cannot then have known of Rosenberg's words in 1916: 'I will not leave a corner of my consciousness covered up, but saturate myself with the strange and extraordinary new conditions of this life.') Murry went on to say that in Owen's poems there was 'no more rebellion, only pity and regret, and the peace of acquiescence'. Edmund Blunden, however, who had reviewed these poems in 1920, found rebellion present in them as it had been present in the minds of almost all soldiers; Owen was 'first and foremost the witness of the war's effect on the spirit of man'. Murry's essay was idiosyncratic but his championing of Owen, following as it did his criticism of Sassoon, was courageous and influential.

Owen's poems did not gain a wide readership for many years

but they were enthusiastically received by the younger generation, particularly by writers. Older people were more doubtful,
perhaps not surprisingly in view of his attacks on 'old men' and
the views he had imputed to them. Whereas Sassoon's poems
were acceptable to such militarists as Henry Newbolt and
Churchill (it was a soldier, not a poet, who first said 'War is hell'),
Newbolt voiced an 'old man's' feelings when he remarked in 1924
that Owen's pity was really only self-pity. The complaint of self-
centredness, which had been made by Sorley about Brooke and
by Owen about Nichols, was now brought against Owen himself.
There was a much more notorious condemnation of Owen and
others by an elderly poet in 1936. Yeats, from his great eminence,
announced that he had excluded the work of all the First War
poets (except Read's *The End of a War*) from his edition of the
Oxford Book of Modern Verse, 1892–1935, on the grounds that
'passive suffering is not a theme for poetry'; the poets concerned
had identified themselves too closely with the sufferings of their
men to have been capable of a detached, impassive view of the
war.[4] Privately, Yeats described Owen's poems as 'all blood, dirt
& sucked sugar stick': a provocative phrase which has since done
useful duty in many an essay title. Part of his animus may be
explained by his description of Owen as 'a revered sandwich-
board Man of the revolution'. Yeats's sympathies were strongly
at odds with those of the left-wing poets of the period who were
expressing warm admiration for Owen. One of them, C. Day
Lewis, said then and later that the literary ancestors of his
generation were Owen, Hopkins and Eliot. Day Lewis and
Stephen Spender both devoted chapters to Owen in their books
on modern poetry, though Spender had reservations about the
usefulness of 'pity'.[5] In the next decade, another young poet,
Dylan Thomas, gave a fiery broadcast talk about Owen; and a
poet of our own time, Philip Larkin, has described Owen as 'the
only twentieth-century poet who can be read after Hardy
without a sense of bathos' (*Listener*, 10 October 1963).

Whereas Owen's reputation grew fairly rapidly in the two
decades after the war and Brooke's declined faster still,
Rosenberg remained almost entirely unknown. Blunden,
perhaps the most prolific writer on First War poetry, almost
never mentioned him. Rosenberg's collected poems, with some
prose pieces and extracts from his letters, were not published until

1937. D. W. Harding's perceptive article in *Scrutiny* (1935) was
the first substantial study of his work and it has had few
successors. Rosenberg's knowledge of contemporary art and his
lack of a middle-class education had enabled him to think and
experiment more freely than any of the other war poets; his
poems seemed, and to many readers still seem, unfamiliar, raw-
edged and obscure. His handful of critics have observed,
however, how his ideas shape his language and how profitably he
pondered on the relationship between poetry and experience.

   The poets of the Second World War had read their Owen and
Sassoon, and in some cases their Rosenberg, and went into battle
with few illusions. The surviving poets from the previous war did
not speak out against its successor; some of them at least believed
it to be necessary and inevitable, and no one supposed that it
would be glorious. Afterwards, the horrors of war seemed best
forgotten and there was little discussion of war poetry until the
1960s; then, changes in outlook, and the Vietnam war, stimu-
lated a renewed interest. In recent years, there has been a steady
increase in the critical attention paid to the First War poets as
well as in sales of their verse.

   Philip Hobsbaum suggested in a talk broadcast in 1961 that
Thomas, Owen and Rosenberg, had they survived, would have
taken English poetry in a direction more natural to its true
development than that imposed after the war by the cosmopolitan force of Modernism under the leadership of the Americans
Eliot and Pound. Hobsbaum claimed that the three poets shared
'a recognition of the need to adapt the old forms to express new
experience' and an impersonal mode akin to that of fiction. The
current re-evaluation of Modernism has led some observers to
think that the mainstream of modern literature runs, not through
Eliot but, from Hardy through Edward Thomas to contemporary poets such as Larkin. Thomas thus acquires a
particular importance, and the relationship between the war and
his poetry seems a secondary issue (some excellent studies of him
make no mention of the war and have therefore been excluded
from this Casebook).

   The first book-length academic study of the leading war poets
was John H. Johnston's *English Poetry of the First World War*
(1964). One may guess that the book originated earlier as an
American doctoral dissertation; its bibliography seems out of

date for its time of publication, and its 'thesis' – that the only fit medium for poetry about war is the epic – is heavily overstressed. Johnston attempts to show that none of the war poets succeeded in achieving the epic vision: an approach which has since been derided as irrelevant, excessively literary and based on an esteem for war which the war poets do not wish their readers to feel. However, Johnston's book deserves respect as a pioneering study; he drew attention to the war poets as a group worthy of particular consideration and he gave prominence to several neglected writers, particularly David Jones.

A spirited British response to Johnston came from Donald Davie, who said that the war poets had to be understood in terms of British social history and not in those of aridly academic criticism. Overstating his case in a necessarily brief review ('as a poem in any strict sense "Dead Man's Dump" is indefensible'), Davie bluntly insisted on the shortcomings of the later war poets but said that such inadequacies were a necessary part of the myth; Sassoon and Owen, the incoherent amateurs protesting from the heart, had to be set against Brooke, the gilded Edwardian professional. (Johnston himself had said that Owen was 'actually a symbol rather than a prophet'.) The war poets represented the appalling damage done to the national consciousness by the Somme.

The way in which the war was seen through myth and symbol by the men who fought in it has recently been studied in fascinating detail by the American scholar, Paul Fussell, in *The Great War and Modern Memory* (1975). Drawing on a wide range of written records, from poetry and fiction to diaries and newspapers, Fussell shows how writers of the time could not use images such as roses and poppies without evoking a complexity of literary allusions. Some of Fussell's suggestions may seem a little far-fetched, including his claim that the full expression of the war's loathsomeness is only to be found in certain modern novels, but he reminds us of a dimension of First War literature which the modern reader has tended to overlook.

The social, 'political' significance of the war poets has been discussed by a number of British critics, particularly Jon Silkin and some of the writers associated with him through the literary magazine, *Stand*. In his *Out of Battle* (1972), and more recently in his introduction to the *Penguin Book of First World War Poetry*

(1979), Silkin gives the work of war poets some of the most extended consideration that it has as yet received. His shortcomings
are not hard to see: he is difficult to read and sometimes inaccurate in matters of fact, and on occasions his 'political commitment' emerges in its practical effects as little more than left-wing
prejudice. He is unjust to Brooke, the public-school officer, and
perhaps too generous to Rosenberg, the working-class private. In
his dogged analyses, he sometimes wrenches poems into strange
shapes. Nevertheless, at his best Silkin is capable of valuable
insights, and his work on Rosenberg in particular is more
illuminating than anything else that has been written on that
poet. He writes from certain strongly held assumptions, one of
them being that all war is utterly evil and that true poetry must
not say, or even seem to say, anything in its favour. The value of
Rosenberg is guaranteed, for example, by the rat's grin in 'Break
of Day in the Trenches': a grin which forces the reader to perceive
the absurdity of war and man's responsibility for it; no war-
monger, Silkin suggests, could make use of such poems. Owen, in
contrast, has a weakness for the 'haloesque' in language; some
of his poems, such as 'Anthem for Doomed Youth', seem to shed a
glow of sacrificial holiness on death in war. Owen's best poetry is
powered not only by pity but also by anger; Silkin thus stresses
the satirical element in Owen's work and Sassoon's influence on
him, and is suspicious of his tendency towards universal or elegiac
statement. The old critical belief that a poet should distance
himself from 'daily events' seems to be largely abandoned, as in
Marxist criticism. Silkin admires the immediacy of Rosenberg's
poems and has expressed a preference for the cancelled line in
Owen's 'Strange Meeting' ('I was a German conscript, and your
friend') over the final version ('I am the enemy you killed, my
friend'). He finds the second version literary, generalised and
even slightly portentous. Among the advantages of the first are,
he suggests, its specific nature, the word 'German' (which
prevents the 'psychological' reading, proposed by Dennis
Welland, that the dead man may be seen as the poet's *alter ego*),
and the word 'conscript' (with its hint of class-exploitation).[6]

It could be argued that detailed criticism of the kind which
Silkin attempts is even now a little premature. Our factual
knowledge of the war poets is still by no means complete. It is
difficult to say anything very useful about a poet's developing

attitude to war unless one knows what order his poems were written in; and it is risky to consider the precise wording of a poem until one is sure that one has an accurate text. In the case of Owen, for instance, the C. Day Lewis edition of the *Collected Poems* was described as 'definitive' when it was published, yet three-quarters of the poems in it contain some kind of textual error and the few dates which it ascribes to them are manifestly unreliable. There has been a casualness about accuracy by publishers and critics alike in the field of First War poetry and one must warmly welcome contemporary signs of change. George E. Thomas's scholarly edition of the *Collected Poems of Edward Thomas* (1978) is due to be followed by Jon Stallworthy's carefully researched and complete edition of Owen. Ian Parsons has re-edited the *Collected Works of Isaac Rosenberg* and added valuable new material; this volume, published in 1979, contains poems, letters, prose pieces and reproductions of paintings and drawings. The *Poems and Selected Letters of Charles Hamilton Sorley*, edited by Hilda D. Spear (1978), makes Sorley's poems available again.

The establishment of facts about First War poetry requires biographical as well as textual research. Timothy Rogers's brief but informative reappraisal of Brooke (1971) helps to disentangle the poet from the legend. John Press (1966) has looked again at Sorley and shown that some common assumptions about him are off the mark. No fewer than three biographies of Rosenberg came out in 1975, and Jon Stallworthy's beautifully produced life of Owen (1974) gives much new information. Owen's *Collected Letters* (1967) provide a remarkably detailed record of their author, who is probably the best documented of all the war poets except Thomas.

Studies of First War literature as a whole have tended to be of an introductory nature. Bernard Bergonzi's *Heroes' Twilight* (1965) is a swift, incisive and helpful survey of both poetry and prose. Until quite recently it was common for histories of modern literature to make little or no mention of the war poets, but now a chapter on them seems to be more or less obligatory. The chapter in David Perkins's *A History of Modern Poetry* (1976) is longer than most; in his section on Owen, he examines the Romantic element in that poet and suggests that it was a strength rather than a weakness. There is ample scope for more literary criticism of this kind, but so far there have been very few book-length studies of individual poets. Dennis Welland's *Wilfred Owen: A Critical Study* (1960, enlarged but perhaps not improved by a long postscript in 1978) gives perceptive and well-informed accounts of various aspects of Owen's work; and Welland's examination of the manuscripts resulted in some very welcome emendations to the texts of the poems.

Clearly, there is more work to be done. The essential task of establishing texts and dates is not yet finished. There is no biography of Sassoon and no full-length critical study of Rosenberg. Some of the lesser poets need to be brought back into print. No doubt these and other labours will be undertaken in future years. No doubt also, changing tastes and politics will have their effects on literary judgements.

NOTES

1. For an account of Boer War verse, see M. van Wyk Smith, *Drummer Hodge: The Poetry of the Anglo-Boer War (1899–1902)*, Oxford (1978).

2. J. G. Fletcher, 'On Subject-Matter and War Poetry', *Egoist* III, xii (December 1916), pp. 188–9.

3. J. M. Murry, 'The Condition of English Poetry', *Athenaeum* (5 December 1919), pp. 1283–5.

4. Despite the statement in his Preface, Yeats in fact put a few war poems into his anthology, including W. W. Gibson's 'Breakfast' and Sassoon's postwar 'On passing the new Menin Gate'.

5. Stephen Spender, *The Destructive Element* (1935), ch. XII.

6. Jon Silkin, introduction to the *Penguin Book of First World War Poetry* (1979). One must add that Silkin's preference here is as misleading as his curious (and unexplained) printing of 'The Dead-Beat' in its first rather than its final version; Owen's final intentions are ignored in favour of Silkin's own convictions.

PART ONE

Comments and Reviews
1914–1924

1. ON POETS AND POETRY
IN WAR TIME

Edward Thomas (1914)

If they also serve who only sit and write, poets are doing their work well. Several of them, it seems to me, with names known and unknown, have been turned into poets by the war, printing verse now for the first time. Whatever other virtues they show, courage at least is not lacking – the courage to write for oblivion. No other class of poetry vanishes so rapidly, has so little chosen from it for posterity. One tiny volume would hold all the patriotic poems surviving in European languages, and originally written, as most of these are today, under the direct pressure of public patriotic motives. Where are the poems of Marlborough's wars? Where are the songs sung by the troops for Quebec while Wolfe was reading Gray's *Elegy*? But for the wars against Napoleon English poetry would have been different, but how many poems directly concerning them, addressed to Englishmen at that moment, do we read now? One of the earliest, I believe, was Coleridge's 'Fears in Solitude: written in April, 1798 during the alarm of an invasion'. But no newspaper or magazine, then or now, would print such a poem, since a large part of it is humble. He admits that abroad we have offended, and at home

> All individual dignity and power
> Engulf'd in courts, committees, institutions,
> Associations and societies,
> A vain, speech-mouthing, speech-reporting guild,
> One benefit-club for mutual flattery,
> We have drunk up, demure as at a grace,
> Pollutions from the brimming cup of wealth. . . .

He believes that

(Stuffed out with big preamble, holy names,
And adjurations of the God in heaven),
We sent our mandates for the certain death
Of thousands and ten thousands. Boys and girls
And women, that would groan to see a child
Pull off an insect's leg, all read of war,
The best amusement of a morning's meal . . .

When he wrote this at Stowey, Coleridge was a solitary man who, if at all, only felt the national emotions weakly or spasmodically. He was writing poetry, and the chances against the reading as against the writing of poetry early in a great war were overwhelming. The poem, one of the noblest of patriotic poems, has been omitted from most of the anthologies. Another odd thing is that a poem included in several anthologies, and perhaps the finest of English martial songs – I mean Blake's 'War Song to Englishmen' – was written in or before 1783, by one who became a red-capped Revolutionary and cared nothing for Pitt's England. What inspired him? The war with the American colonies? More likely, the history of England as he felt it when he saw the kings in Westminster Abbey and Shakespeare's plays. He wrote from a settled mystic patriotism, which wars could not disturb.

Another poet, touched by the outbreak of war, will be disturbed for some time: he will be more fit for taking up work from the past, if only for relief, though it is possible for a mature man who has seen other wars and is not shaken from his balance to seize the new occasion firmly. Mr Charles M. Doughty might have done so: Mr Hardy has done. The period of gestation varies, but few younger men who had been moved to any purpose could be expected to crystallise their thoughts with speed. Supposing they did, who would want their poems? The demand is for the crude, for what everybody is saying or thinking, or is ready to begin saying or thinking. I need hardly say that by becoming ripe for poetry the poet's thoughts may recede far from their original resemblance to all the world's, and may seem to have little to do with daily events. They may retain hardly any colour from 1798 or 1914, and the crowd, deploring it, will naturally not read the poems.

It is a fact that in the past but a small number of poems

destined to endure are directly or entirely concerned with the public triumphs, calamities, or trepidations, that helped to beget them. The public, crammed with mighty facts and ideas it will never digest, must look coldly on poetry where already those mighty things have sunk away far into 'The still sad music of humanity'. For his insults to their feelings, the newspapers, history, they might call the poet a pro-Boer. They want something raw and solid, or vague and lofty or sentimental. They must have Mr Begbie to express their thoughts, or 'Tipperary' to drown them.

A patriotic poem pure and simple hardly exists, as a man who was a patriot pure and simple could not live outside a madhouse. Very seldom are poems written for occasions, great or small, more seldom for great than for small. But verses are, and they may be excellent. Virtually all hymns are occasional verses. They are written for certain people or a certain class. The writer of hymns or patriotic verses appears to be a man who feels himself always or at the time at one with the class, perhaps the whole nation, or he is a smart fellow who can simulate or exaggerate this sympathy. Experience, reality, truth, unless suffused or submerged by popular sentiment, are out of place. What we like is Mr J. A. Nicklin's city clerk (*And They Went to the War*, Sidgwick & Jackson, 6d net) singing:

> When the air with hurtling shrapnel's all a-quiver
>   And the smoke of battle through the valley swirls,
> It's better than our Sundays up the river,
>   And the rifle's hug is closer than a girl's.

Mr Arthur K. Sabin's sonnet called 'Harvest Moon at Midnight', and dated September 8th (*War Harvest, 1914*, Temple, Sheen Press, 6d), is equally the thing, though nearer truth – it ends:

> Ah, underneath this Moon, in fields of France,
> How many of our old companionship
> Snatch hurried rest, with hearts that burn and glow,
> Longing to hear the bugles sound *Advance!*
> To seize their weapons with unfaltering grip,
> And for old England strike another blow.

It reminds us all of what we thought or heard said during that moon. Here and there I have met a poem that I liked more than others, such as Mr Justin Huntly McCarthy's 'Ghosts at Boulogne':

> One dreamer, when our English soldiers trod
> But yesterday the welcoming fields of France,
> Saw war-gaunt shadows gathering, stare askance
> Upon those levies and that alien sod –
> Saw Churchill's smile, and Wellington's curt nod,
> Saw Harry with his Crispins, Chandos' lance,
> And the Edwards on whose breasts the leopards dance:
> Then heard a gust of ghostly thanks to God
> That the most famous quarrel of all time
> In the most famous friendship ends at last;
> Such flame of friendship as God fans to forge
> A sword to strike the Dragon of the Slime,
> Bidding St Denis with St George stand fast
> Against the Worm. St Denis and St George!

But this is not great poetry, nor is it what is wanted. It is the hour of the writer who picks up popular views or phrases, or coins them, and has the power to turn them into downright stanzas. Most newspapers have one or more of these gentlemen. They could take the easy words of a statesman, such as 'No price is too high when honour and freedom are at stake', and dish them up so that the world next morning, ready to be thrilled by anything lofty and noble-looking, is thrilled. These poems are not to be attacked any more than hymns. Like hymns, they play with common ideas, with words and names which most people have in their heads at the time. Most seem to me bombastic, hypocritical, or senseless; but either they go straight to the heart of the great public which does not read poetry, or editors expect them to, and accordingly supply the articles.

There is a smaller class of better or more honest work which can hardly last longer. I mean the work of true poets which has been occasioned by the war. A few men are in an exceptional position: Messrs Newbolt and Kipling belong to a professional class apart, and may be supposed to suffer less drastic modifications from the war. It was their hour, and they have not been silent. They have written as well as in times of peace. The one silence which can be felt is Mr Charles M. Doughty's. But it might easily have been forecast. He has lived through this time long ago, and *The Cliffs* (reissue: Duckworth, 3/6 net.) and *The Clouds* show that modern warfare and German politics had no surprises for him. Other men who stood on old foundations of character and tradition were not suddenly transported out of themselves. Mr Bridges, Mr de la Mare, Mr Binyon, among others, remained themselves. Years before this they had proved themselves English poets. They have not done more now. Their private and social emotion does them credit, but with few exceptions, such as Messrs Binyon, Chesterton, and John Freeman, they have fallen various distances below their natural level. Nor am I surprised. I should have expected the shock to silence them, had it not been counterbalanced by a powerful social sense genuinely aroused. I have not liked any of these poems, but fancy tells me that they do for persons with more social sense than I, what the noisy stuff does for the man who normally lives without poetry. They are suddenly made old-fashioned: Mr Chesterton's 'Hymn of War', for example (*Lord God of Battles: A War Anthology*, compiled by A. E. Manning Foster, Cope & Fenwick, 1/- net), is archaic and Hebraic, after this fashion:

> O God of earth and altar,
>   Bow down and hear our cry,
> Our earthly rulers falter,
>   Our people drift and die;
>
> The walls of gold entomb us,
>   The swords of scorn divide,
> Take not the thunder from us,
>   But take away our pride.

They revert, and they may be right, though I cannot follow them if I would. They seem excellent only by comparison with 'C. W.', a serious and well-read but ungifted versifier, who tells us (*1914*, Heffer and Sons, 1/- net) that 'his offer of active service for his country being rejected on account of his advanced years, and not being able to turn his thoughts away from the tragic events of the

day, he has put, in a more or less poetic form, his own thoughts on
the circumstances which led to this war, and the consequences it
may and ought to have'. At the same time the poets of whom I
speak have done things not inferior to the similar work of men
more famous. Of six *Patriotic Poems* by Tennyson (Macmillan, 1d)
not one is worthy of him or would have survived without his
name. They have one distinction, that they are the work of one
who had the right, and felt it, to address his countrymen as from
an eminence. Two living men besides Mr Doughty might do the
same, Messrs Hardy and Kipling. Mr Kipling has hardly done
more than speak in echoes of himself. Mr Hardy has written an
impersonal song which seems to me the best of the time, as it is the
least particular and occasional.[1] He may write even better yet. I
should also expect the work of other real poets to improve as the
war advances, perhaps after it is over, as they understand it and
themselves more completely.

SOURCE: 'War Poetry', *Poetry and Drama*, II, No. 8 (December
1914). For a modern insight into the relevance of this article to
Thomas's own poetry, see William Cooke's study in Part
Three below.

NOTE

1. [Ed.–Hardy's 'Song of the Soldiers' or 'Men Who March Away'.
With Thomas's view compare those of J. G. Fletcher (*Egoist*, 16 Nov.
1914), who describes the poem as 'inane driveltry'; and of Charles
Sorley, who said in a letter of the same month that the poem was 'arid'
and 'untrue of the sentiments of the ranksman going to war: "Victory
crowns the just" is the worst line he ever wrote – filched from a leading
article in *The Morning Post*, and unworthy of him who had always
previously disdained to insult Justice by offering it a material crown like
Victory.']

Anonymous (1914)

. . . In the stress of a nation's peril some of its greatest songs are born. In the stress of a nation's peril the poet at last comes into his own again, and with clarion call he rouses the sleeping soul of the empire. Prophet he is, champion and consoler.

If in these later times the poet has been neglected, now in our infinite need, in our pride and our sorrow, he is here to strengthen, comfort and inspire. The poet is vindicated.

What can so nobly uplift the hearts of a people facing war with its unspeakable agony as music and poetry? The sound of martial music steels men's hearts before battle. The sound of martial words inspires human souls to do and to endure. God, His poetry, and His music are the Holy Trinity of war.

Not always the greatest songs that have sent men on to victory. Sometimes it has been a modest verse that has found refuge in the heart of the soldier ready for the ultimate sacrifice, cheered on his way by the lilt of a humble song. Who else, indeed, can take the place of a poet? . . .

SOURCE: extract from the Introduction to *Songs and Sonnets for England in War Time, being a collection of lyrics by various authors inspired by the Great War* (London, 1914), pp. v–vi. (This was the first of the war anthologies.)

W. B. Yeats (1915)

ON BEING ASKED FOR A WAR POEM[1]

I think it better that in times like these
A poet's mouth be silent, for in truth
We have no gift to set a statesman right;
He has had enough of meddling who can please
A young girl in the indolence of her youth,
Or an old man upon a winter's night.

SOURCE: *The Collected Poems of W. B. Yeats* (London, 1933; 2nd edition 1950), p. 175.

NOTE

1. [Ed.] This poem was written on 6 Feb. 1915 and first published in 1916 as 'A Reason for Keeping Silent'. Yeats said of it in 1915: 'It is the only thing I have written of the war or will write, so I hope it may not seem unfitting. I shall keep the neighbourhood of the seven sleepers of Ephesus, hoping to catch their comfortable snores till bloody frivolity is over'; quoted in A. N. Jeffares, *A Commentary on the Collected Poems of W. B. Yeats* (London, 1968), p. 189.

Isaac Rosenberg (1916)

i To Gordon Bottomley

Simple *poetry* – that is where an interesting complexity of thought is kept in tone and right value to the dominating idea so that it is understandable and still ungraspable. I know that it is beyond my reach just now, except, perhaps, in bits. I am always afraid of being empty. When I get more leisure in more settled times I will work on a larger scale and give myself room; then I may be less frustrated in my efforts to be clear, and satisfy myself too. I think what you say about getting beauty by phrasing of passages rather than the placing of individual words very fine and very true.

ii To Edward Marsh

I was most glad to get your letter and criticism. You know the conditions I have always worked under, and particularly with this last lot of poems. You know how earnestly one must wait on ideas (you cannot coax real ones to you) and let as it were a skin grow naturally round and through them. If you are not free, you can only, when the ideas come hot, seize them with the skin in tatters raw crude, in some parts beautiful in others monstrous. Why print it then? Because these rare parts must not be lost.

III To Laurence Binyon

I am determined that this war, with all its powers for devastation, shall not master my poeting; that is, if I am lucky enough to come through all right. I will not leave a corner of my consciousness covered up, but saturate myself with the strange and extra-ordinary new conditions of this life, and it will all refine itself into poetry later on.

IV To Mrs Cohen

The Poetry Review you sent is good – the articles are too breathless and want more packing, I think. The poems by the soldiers are vigourous [sic] but, I feel a bit commonplace. I did not like Rupert Brookes begloried sonnets for the same reason. What I mean is second hand phrases 'lambent fires' etc takes from its reality and strength. It should be approached in a colder way, more abstract, with less of the million feelings everybody feels; or all these should be concentrated in one distinguished emotion. Walt Whitman in 'Beat, drums, beat' has said the noblest thing on war.

SOURCE: extracts from G. Bottomley and D. Harding (eds), *The Collected Works of Isaac Rosenberg* (London, 1937), pp. 371, 310–11, 373, 348. See also I. Parsons's new edition (1979).

Galloway Kyle (1917)

[Kyle, editor of the *Poetry Review*, is discussing the poems of a typical 'soldier-poet'.] . . . Here the soul of young England is revealed. Here we see the wakening to duty and the Vision Splendid which led noble spirits by a horrible road to the redemption of a world grown grey with doubt and timidity and evils too grievous to be longer borne. Here is an epitome of the stern, resolute temper with which the crisis was met and the inevitable questionings faced. Here the Kitchener's men become articulate, and in passionate sincerity a son of the people, with that perfect utterance and intensity of emotion which distinguishes poetry above all literature and redeems from decay the speech of the Divine in man to men, concentrates in a few sonnets the feelings, experiences, aspirations of the youth who have marched through death to the moral and material salvation of Europe. Here is one of the finest of the countless examples of the heroic in literature provided by the war – literature translated into action, action infused with calm seriousness and interpreted into poetry. . . .

These sonnets were accompanied by an illuminating letter, in which Streets explained:

They were inspired while I was in the trenches, where I have been so busy I have had little time to polish them. I have tried to picture some thoughts that pass through a man's brain when he dies. I may not see the end of the poems, but hope to live to do so. We soldiers have our views of life to express, though the boom of death is in our ears. We try to convey something of what we feel in this great conflict to those who think of us, and sometimes, alas! mourn our loss. We desire to let them know that in the midst of our keenest sadness for the joy of life we leave behind, we go to meet death grim-lipped, clear-eyed, and resolute-hearted.

SOURCE: extracts from the Preface to *The Undying Splendour* by Sgt J. W. Streets (London, 1917), pp. v–vii.

Arthur Waugh (1918)

. . . so much cant and humbug has been written and spoken concerning the spiritual influence of the war, that any reasonably cautious man has long since determined to keep clear of such generalisations altogether. Nevertheless, one single impression is beginning to be borne in with reiterated emphasis upon all lovers of poetry, and that impression seems to leave it indisputable that the young rebels of individualism, who have actually experienced the horrors of warfare, come back to their old environment in a spirit radically different from that with which they set out. Individualists they do indeed remain; but their individualism, purged by revelation, has ceased to be introspective, and now directs its activity steadily outwards. One after another, they went out to fight in a mood of exalted self-consciousness; one after another, they return with their sympathies extraordinarily widened, and with half the barriers of prejudice and false distinction swept away. This very broadening of sentiment is perhaps only a development of their revolt against popular sentimentality. The Victorian poets wrote of war as though it were something splendid and ennobling; but as a matter of fact they knew nothing whatever about it. The Georgian poets know everything there is to know about war, and they come back and report it to us as an unspeakable horror, maiming and paralysing the very soul of man.

'Now, God be thanked Who has matched us with His hour', sang Brooke; but that was before he had made trial of the kind of enemy that Death upon the battlefield really is. 'It's a Queer Time', rejoins Captain Robert Graves, and forthwith unfolds one corner of the manifold map of warfare, crowded with movement, and dizzying with confusion. 'War is Hell', he concludes; and Mr Siegfried Sassoon takes up the parable with interest. The whole purpose of his war poems is apparently the stripping of the tinsel from the robes of Bellona, the revelation of the stark and clattering skeleton beneath. All the younger poets who have turned soldiers owe to the tendency which Brooke embodied, their passion for painting war in its true colours; but the most interesting thing about their work is the change which comes over it, when once they have lived the life of a combatant. Their sense of personality breaks the bonds of self and becomes a living human sympathy. Individualism, by one of nature's paradoxes, expands into a passion for companionship.

Take Brooke's poetry almost where you will, and the prevailing impression is one of a brilliantly attractive personality, absorbed in the contemplation of itself. Take the average poet-turned-soldier, open him at random, and the atmosphere is almost always warm and tender with a sense of the suffering of others, and the comradeship of endurance and of pain. It is even possible to trace the change in the work of the same poet. The young soldier in Mr Robert Nichols's 'Farewell' bids good-bye to his home with his thoughts still centred on his own emotions:

> And now tears are not mine. I have release
> From all the former and the later pain,
> Like the mid sea, I rock in boundless peace
> Soothed by the charity of the deep-sea rain . . .
> Calm rain! Calm sea! Calm found, long sought in vain.

This is introspective enough; but Gates, the subaltern, who in the same writer's vivid and poignant 'Comrades' struggles back to die with his own company in the trenches, is thinking only of the men for whose safety he is responsible, and not for one instant of himself.

And Mr Siegfried Sassoon, the most unsparing realist of them all, finds in just the same spirit the only possible antidote to the horrors of war in the knowledge of high companionship in a great cause [quotes 'Absolution']:

> The anguish of the earth absolves our eyes
> Till beauty shines in all that we can see.
> War is our scourge; yet war has made us wise,
> And, fighting for our freedom, we are free.

> Horror of wounds and anger at the foe,
> And loss of things desired; all those must pass.
> We are the happy legion, for we know
> Time's but a golden wind that shakes the grass.

> There was an hour when we were loth to part
> From life we longed to share no less than others.
> Now, having claimed this heritage of heart,
> What need we more, my comrades and my brothers?

There is no need to labour the point; it can be traced in almost every volume of poetry published during the last two or three years. The realistic movement has had its full chance, and it has given us in poetry the most lurid panorama of war that any art has ever achieved. Cheap patriotism and Jingo-verse may henceforth be possible to the music-hall singer; they will no longer be tolerable in the poet. And with this realism has grown a wide-winged sense of individuality, stretching outwards to embrace all fellow-sufferers, even in an alien cause. War, which makes so little of the individual life officially, has suddenly taught the callous that the individual life is the only thing which matters. And since it was officialdom throned in high places which made this war possible, the completion of the struggle between officialdom and individualism begins to draw in sight. But the victory will not be a victory for self. The most self-centred generation in history is to be transformed into the most sympathetic and humane.

SOURCE: extract from 'Rupert Brooke and the Influence of War on Poetry', *Book Monthly* (Autumn 1918); reprinted in *Tradition and Change* (London, 1919), pp. 149-53.

2. ON RUPERT BROOKE

Winston Churchill (1915)

Rupert Brooke is dead. A telegram from the Admiral at Lemnos tells us that this life has closed at the moment when it seemed to have reached its springtime. A voice had become audible, a note had been struck, more true, more thrilling, more able to do justice to the nobility of our youth in arms engaged in this present war, than any other – more able to express their thoughts of self-surrender, and with a power to carry comfort to those who watch them so intently from afar. The voice has been swiftly stilled. Only the echoes and the memory remain; but they will linger.

During the last few months of his life, months of preparation in gallant comradeship and open air, the poet-soldier told with all the simple force of genius the sorrow of youth about to die, and the sure triumphant consolations of a sincere and valiant spirit. He expected to die: he was willing to die for the dear England whose beauty and majesty he knew: and he advanced towards the brink in perfect serenity, with absolute conviction of the rightness of his country's cause and a heart devoid of hate for fellow-men.

The thoughts to which he gave expression in the very few incomparable war sonnets which he has left behind will be shared by many thousands of young men moving resolutely and blithely forward in this, the hardest, the cruellest, and the least-rewarded of all the wars that men have fought. They are a whole history and revelation of Rupert Brooke himself. Joyous, fearless, versatile, deeply instructed, with classic symmetry of mind and body, ruled by high undoubting purpose, he was all that one would wish England's noblest sons to be in the days when no sacrifice but the most precious is acceptable, and the most precious is that which is most freely proffered.

SOURCE: obituary note in *The Times* (26 April 1915).

Charles Sorley (1915)

. . . I saw Rupert Brooke's death in *The Morning Post. The Morning Post*, which has always hitherto disapproved of him, is now loud in his praises because he has conformed to their stupid axiom of literary criticism that the only stuff of poetry is violent physical experience, by dying on active service. I think Brooke's earlier poems – especially notably 'The Fish' and 'Grantchester', which you can find in *Georgian Poetry* – are his best. That last sonnet-sequence of his, of which you sent me the review in the *Times Lit. Supp.*, and which has been so praised, I find (with the exception of that beginning 'These hearts were woven of human joys and cares, Washed marvellously with sorrow' which is not about himself) overpraised. He is far too obsessed with his own sacrifice, regarding the going to war of himself (and others) as a highly intense, remarkable and sacrificial exploit, whereas it is merely the conduct demanded of him (and others) by the turn of circumstances, where non-compliance with this demand would have made life intolerable. It was not that 'they' gave up anything of that list he gives in one sonnet: but that the essence of these things had been endangered by circumstances over which he had no control, and he must fight to recapture them. He has clothed his attitude in fine words: but he has taken the sentimental attitude. . . .

SOURCE: extract from letter of 28 April 1915, in *The Collected Letters of Charles Sorley* (Cambridge, 1919).

3. ON ROBERT NICHOLS

Anonymous (1917)

. . . Nothing can prevent poetry like this from taking its place among those permanent possessions of the race which will remain to tell the great-grandchildren of our soldiers to what pure heights of the spirit Englishmen rose out of the great war's horror of waste and ugliness, noise and pain and death! . . .

> SOURCE: extract from 'Poetry, War and a Young Poet', *Times Literary Supplement* (12 July 1917), p. 330.

Wilfred Owen (1917)

. . . He is so self-concerned and *vaniteux* in his verse. . . .

> SOURCE: extract from letter of 27 November 1917 in Harold Owen and John Bell (eds), *Wilfred Owen: Collected Letters* (Oxford, 1968), p. 511.

Edmund Gosse (1917)

. . . Lieut. Nichols never smiles. . . . He has no military enthusiasm, no aspiration after *gloire*. Indeed, the most curious feature of his poetry is that its range is concentrated on the few yards about the trench in which he stands. . . . We might read his poems over and over again without forming the slightest idea of what all the distress was about, or who was guilty, or what was being defended. This is a mark of great artistic sincerity; but it points to a certain moral narrowness. . . .

SOURCE: extract from 'Some Soldier Poets', *Edinburgh Review* (October 1917); reprinted in *Some Diversions of a Man of Letters* (London, 1919), p. 279.

Douglas Goldring (1920)

. . . Among the younger men, Mr Robert Nichols, who had the advantage of a fair technical equipment, achieved a popular success with his much-praised *Ardours and Endurances*. After his experiences in the trenches he tried nobly to rise to the occasion, and his poem 'The Assault' is the principal result of his efforts. Considered in cold blood, however, it is an empty and pretentious piece of work, too laboured, too patently worked out in accordance with some brand-new 'stuntist' theory to be at all impressive. The dabs and splashes of colour, the onomatopœic rendering of gunfire, fail to interest, because the thought underlying the poem is commonplace. (In a year or two, if the human race is to continue at all, let us hope it will have become an absurd memory.)

> Ha! Ha! Bunched figures waiting.
> Revolver levelled quick!
> Flick! Flick!
> Red as blood.
> Germans. Germans.
> Good! O good!
> Cool madness.

It was characteristic of our war-time criticism that this masterpiece of drivel, instead of exciting derision, was hailed as a work of genius and read with avidity. On the whole Mr Nichols is much more sincere and more effective when he is writing about other things than war, and occasionally, as in his poem 'The Tower', he achieves beauty of atmosphere and description.

SOURCE: extract from 'The War and the Poets' in *Reputations: Essays in Criticism* (London, 1920), pp. 110–11.

4. ON SIEGFRIED SASSOON

H. W. Massingham (1917)

. . . Mr Sassoon has really had no presentable excuse for not writing what was expected of him, except one, and that is the excuse of the truth. And by truth we do not mean realism. Realism is not objectionable; on the contrary, it is fashionable. But truth, and truth about the actual conditions of the war, is objectionable, because of the deadly criticism that, like the dagger under a cloak, underlies it. Realism in modern English letters has been one of the supreme artistic failures of this generation. This is not the place to go into the causes of that failure; but one of them surely is just this lack of intense, explosive criticism that truth, drawn into the sovereign allegiance of art, carries as its inevitable passenger. Realism paralyses art, because its very hypothesis prevents the artistic leaven from working upon and transforming the bare material. Truthful art, on the other hand, has the utmost liberty of imposing its own laws and its own methods upon the raw and helpless substance that it shapes.

It is necessary to make this distinction, because in every review of Mr Sassoon's verse that the present writer has seen, he has been labelled as a realist. And he is nothing of the kind. That he has worked his subject-matter into the serene and beautiful form of literature, would certainly be an exaggeration. But the point is that that has patently never been Mr Sassoon's intention. It is no reflection upon him to say that these war-verses are not poetry, that they have nothing to do with poetry, because we dare venture that he would probably agree with us. Nor are they (to go to the other extreme) simply a convenient instrument for vehement rhetoric and declamation. In a word, they are epigrams – modern epigrams, thrown deliberately into the harsh, peremptory, colloquial kind of versification which we have so often mistaken for poetry. And, to our mind, Mr Sassoon is quite right to select this method to fulfil a purpose in which every line throbs and of which every line is acutely conscious. For into this epigrammatic content he is able to discharge the hot fluid of honest rage and scorn, heartfelt bitterness and indignation, which must read so very unconventionally, so very disagreeably, to those civilians who have been comfortably nurtured upon the war-poem of the past. And how well this developed and adapted form of epigram bears the weight of its author's individual driving-force! . . .

SOURCE: extract from unsigned review, 'Indignation', *Nation* (16 June 1917), p. 278. [The authorship is derived from an unpublished letter of Sassoon's–Ed.]

Wilfred Owen (1917)

. . . I have just been reading Siegfried Sassoon and am feeling at a very high pitch of emotion. Nothing like his trench life sketches has ever been written or ever will be written. Shakespeare reads vapid after these. Not of course because Sassoon is a greater artist, but because of the subjects, I mean. I think if I had the choice of making friends with Tennyson or with Sassoon, I should go to Sassoon. . . .

SOURCE: extract from letter of 15 August 1917, in Harold Owen and John Bell (eds), *Wilfred Owen: Collected Letters* (Oxford, 1968), pp. 484–5.

Edmund Gosse (1917)

. . . The bitterness of Lieut. Sassoon is not cynical, it is the rage of disenchantment, the violence of a young man eager to pursue other aims, who, finding the age out of joint, resents being called upon to help to mend it. His temper is not altogether to be applauded, for such sentiments must tend to relax the effort of the struggle, yet they can hardly be reproved when conducted with so much honesty and courage. Lieut. Sassoon, who, as we learn, has twice been severely wounded and has been in the very furnace of the fighting, has reflected, more perhaps than his fellow-singers, about the causes and conditions of the war. He may not always have thought correctly, nor have recorded his impressions with proper circumspection, but his honesty must be respectfully acknowledged. . . .

SOURCE: extract from 'Some Soldier Poets', *Edinburgh Review* (October 1917); reprinted in *Some Diversions of a Man of Letters* (London, 1919), pp. 283–4.

Virginia Woolf (1918)

. . . It is natural to feel an impulse of charity towards the poems written by young men who have fought or are still fighting; but in the case of Mr Sassoon there is no temptation to indulge in this form of leniency, because he is so evidently able-bodied in his poetic capacity, and requires no excuses to be made for him. At the same time, it is difficult to judge him dispassionately as a poet, because it is impossible to overlook the fact that he writes as a soldier. It is a fact, indeed, that he forces upon you, as if it were a matter of indifference to him whether you called him poet or not. We know no other writer who has shown us as effectually as Mr Sassoon the terrible pictures which lie behind the colourless phrases of the newspapers. From the thousand horrors which in their sum compose one day of warfare he selects, as if by chance, now this of the counter-attack, now that of mending the front-line wires, or this again of suicide in the trenches. 'The General' is as good an example of his method as another:

'Good-morning; good-morning!' the General said
When we met him last week on our way to the line.

Now the soldiers he smiled at are most of 'em dead,
And we're cursing his staff for incompetent swine.
'He's a cheery old card', grunted Harry to Jack
As they slogged up to Arras with rifle and pack.

*   *   *

But he did for them both by his plan of attack.

The vision of that 'hell where youth and laughter go' has been branded upon him too deeply to allow him to tolerate consolation or explanation. He can only state a little of what he has seen, a very little one guesses, and turn away with a stoical shrug as if a superficial cynicism were the best mask to wear in the face of such incredible experiences. His farewell to the dead is spoken in this fashion:

Good-bye, old lad! Remember me to God,
    And tell Him that our Politicians swear
They won't give in till Prussian Rule's been trod
    Under the heel of England. . . . Are you there?
Yes . . . and the War won't end for at least two years;
But we've got stacks of men. . . . I'm blind with tears,
    Staring into the dark. Cheero!
I wish they'd killed you in a decent show.

There is a stage of suffering, so these poems seem to show us, where any expression save the barest is intolerable; where beauty and art have something too universal about them to meet our particular case. Mr Sassoon sums up that point of view in his 'Dead Musicians'. Not Bach or Beethoven or Mozart brings back the memory of his friends, but the gramophone does it bawling out 'Another little drink won't do us any harm'. Mr Sassoon's poems are too much in the key of the gramophone at present, too fiercely suspicious of any comfort or compromise, to be read as poetry; but his contempt for palliative or subterfuge gives us the raw stuff of poetry. . . .

SOURCE: extract from 'Two Soldier-Poets', *Times Literary Supplement*, (11 July 1918), p. 323.

John Middleton Murry (1918)

It is the fact, not the poetry of Mr Sassoon that is important. When a man is in torment and cries aloud, his cry is incoherent. It has neither weight nor meaning of its own. It is inhuman, and its very inhumanity strikes to the nerve of our hearts. We long to silence the cry, whether by succour and sympathy, or by hiding ourselves from it. That it should somehow stop or be stopped, and by ceasing trouble our hearts no more, is our chief desire; for it is ugly and painful, and it rasps at the cords of nature.

Mr Sassoon's verses – they are not poetry – are such a cry. [*Counter-Attack and Other Poems* (London, 1918).] They touch not our imagination, but our sense. Reading them, we feel, not as we do with true art, which is the evidence of a man's triumph over his experience, that something has after all been saved from disaster, but that everything is irremediably and intolerably wrong. And, God knows, something is wrong – wrong with Mr Sassoon, wrong with the world which has made him the instrument of a discord so jangling. Why should one of the finest creatures of the earth be made to suffer a pain so brutal that he can give it no expression, that even this most human and mighty relief is denied him?

For these verses express nothing, save in so far as a cry expresses pain. Their effect is exhausted when the immediate impression dies away. Some of them are, by intention, realistic pictures of battle experience, and indeed one does not doubt their truth. The language is overwrought, dense and turgid, as a man's mind must be under the stress and obsession of a chaos beyond all comprehension.

> The place was rotten with dead; green clumsy legs,
> High-booted, sprawled and grovelled along the saps;
> And trunks, face downward, in the sucking mud,
> Wallowed like trodden sand-bags loosely filled;
> And naked sodden buttocks, mats of hair,
> Bulged, clotted heads slept in the plastering slime.
> And then the rain began – the jolly old rain!

That is horrible, but it does not produce the impression of horror.

It numbs, not terrifies, the mind. Each separate reality and succeeding vision is, as it were, driven upon us by a hammer, but one hammer-beat is like another. Each adds to the sum more numbness and more pain, but the separateness and particularity of each is lost.

> Bullets spat,
> And he remembered his rifle . . . rapid fire . . .
> And started blazing wildly . . . then a bang
> Crumpled and spun him sideways, knocked him out
> To grunt and wriggle: none heeded him: he choked
> And fought the flapping veils of smothering gloom,
> Lost in a blurred confusion of yells and groans.

We are given the blurred confusion, and just because this is the truth of the matter exactly rendered we cannot apprehend it any more than the soldier who endures it can. We, like him, are 'crumpled and spun sideways'.

There is a value in this direct transcription of plain, un-varnished fact; but there is another truth more valuable still. One may convey the chaos of immediate sensation by a chaotic expression, as does Mr Sassoon. But the unforgettable horror of an inhuman experience can only be rightly rendered by rendering also its relation to the harmony and calm of the soul which it shatters. In this context alone can it appear with that sudden shock to the imagination which is overwhelming. The faintest discord in a harmony has within it an infinity of disaster, which no confusion of notes, however wild and various and loud, can possibly suggest. It is on this that the wise saying that poetry is emotion recollected in tranquillity is so firmly based, for the quality of an experience can only be given by reference to the ideal condition of the human consciousness which it disturbs with pleasure or pain. But in Mr Sassoon's verses it is we who are left to create for ourselves the harmony of which he gives us only the moment of its annihilation. It is we who must be the poets and the artists if anything enduring is to be made of his work. He gives us only the data. There is, indeed, little enough harm in this; it is good that we should have the data; it is good that Mr Sassoon should have written his book, and that the world should read it. But our concern here is with Mr Sassoon the potential poet.

There is a danger that work such as his may pass current as poetry. It has the element of poetical popularity, for it produces an immediate impression. And since Mr Sassoon is a young man, he may be hypnotised by popularity into believing that his work is done, and may end by wrecking the real poetic gift which at rare intervals peeps out in a line:

> The land where all
> Is ruin, and nothing blossoms but the sky.

The last five words are beautiful because they do convey horror to the imagination, and do not bludgeon the senses. They convey horror to the imagination precisely because they contain, as it were, a full octave of emotional experience, and the compass ranges from serenity to desolation, not merely of the earth, but of the mind. The horror is in relation; it is placed, and therefore created. But in the following lines there is no trace of creation or significance:

> A yawning soldier knelt against the bank,
> Staring across the morning blear with fog;
> He wondered when the Allemands would get busy;
> And then, of course, they started with five-nines
> Traversing, sure as fate, and never a dud.

We choose these lines because they make a tolerable, if not a very distinguished, prose. Those that follow them in the piece which gives the book its name are more violent journalism. But why should such middling prose be ironed out into nominal blank verse lines, unless Mr Sassoon imagined that he was, in fact, writing poetry? What he was doing was to make a barely sufficient entry in a log-book. If the lines of the whole piece were transposed into the prose form for which they clamour, they would then, surely, appear to be the rough notes (perhaps for a novel, much less probably for a poem) which they are.

Mr Sassoon is evidently in some sense aware that an element of creation, or of art, is lacking in his work. Perhaps, on reading some of his own lines, he may have felt they were not, after all, a new kind of poetry; and he may have been sensible of some inexplicable difference between his own verses and those of Mr

Thomas Hardy, which are a new kind of poetry. For we think we can detect a certain straining after pregnant compression, due to the attempt to catch Mr Hardy's method. The overloading of epithet and verb in such a line as

He winked his prying torch with patching glare

imitates the technical accidents of a poetic method, of which the real strength and newness consists exactly in the element which as yet has found only an insignificant place in Mr Sassoon's mental composition. Against the permanence of the philosophic background in Mr Hardy's work, each delicate shade of direct emotion is conveyed with all the force that comes of complete differentiation. With Mr Sassoon there is no background, no differentiation; he has no calm, therefore he conveys no terror; he has no harmony, therefore he cannot pierce us with the anguish of discord.

The one artistic method which he employs is the irony of epigrams. On these occasions alone does he appeal to a time beyond the immediate present of sensation. There is an effort at comparison and relation, or, in other words, an effort to grapple with his own experience and comprehend it. It is true that the effort and the comprehension do not go very far, and they achieve rather a device of technique than a method of real expression; but the device is effective enough. . . . [Quotes 'The General'.] The comprehension is superficial, however. The experiences of battle, awful, inhuman and intolerable as they are, can be comprehended only by the mind which is capable of bringing their horror and their inhumanity home to the imagination of others. Without the perspective that comes from intellectual remoteness there can be no comprehension, no order and no art. Intellectual remoteness is not cold or callous; it is the condition in which a mind works as a mind, and a man is fully active as a man. Because this is wanting in Mr Sassoon we are a prey to uneasiness when confronted with his work. We have a feeling of guilt, as though we were prying into secrets which were better hid. We have read, for instance, in the pages of M. Duhamel, far more terrible things than any Mr Sassoon has to tell, but they were made terrible by the calm of the recording mind. Mr Sassoon's mind is a chaos. It is as though he had no memory, and the thing itself returned as it was. That is why the fact, or the spectacle, of Mr Sassoon is so much more impressive than his verses. That one who asked for perfect happiness so little of life as the writer of 'Break of Day' –

> Unlatch the gate
> And set Golumpus going on the grass

should be reduced to a condition in which he cannot surmount the disaster of his own experience –

> Thud, thud, thud – quite soft . . . they never cease
> Those whispering guns – O Christ! I want to go out
> And screech at them to stop – I'm going crazy,
> I'm going stark, staring mad because of the guns.

– that is awful and inhuman and intolerable. And to that it makes no difference that it is Mr Sassoon who is the martyr, and we ourselves who are the poets.

SOURCE: 'Mr Sassoon's War Verses', *Nation* (13 July 1918); reprinted in *The Evolution of an Intellectual* (London, 1920; new edition 1927), pp. 75–84.

5. ON HERBERT READ

T. S. Eliot (1919)

... Mr Read's book [*Naked Warriors*] is on a very high level of war poetry. It is the best war poetry that I can remember having seen. It is better than the rest because it is more honest; because it is neither Romance nor Reporting; because it is unpretentious; and it has emotion as well as a version of things seen. For a poet to observe that war is ugly and not on the whole glorious or improving to the soul is not a novelty any more; but Mr Read does it with a quiet and careful conviction which is not very common. His vision surpasses his ear; and he has, I guess, been impressed – how could he escape it? – by Wyndham Lewis, who is a visual and only occasionally an auditory writer. Mr Read is handicapped by his imperfection of musical sense, in the production of *tone*: the effect, that is to say, is a succession of effects of ideas and images, rather than the sharp and indefinable effect of the poem as a whole. Nevertheless, 'The Happy Warrior' and parts of 'Kneeshaw Goes to War', and particularly the prose sketch at the end, are decidedly successful. ...

SOURCE: extract from 'Reflections on Contemporary Poetry', *Egoist* (July 1919), p. 39.

6. ON WILFRED OWEN

Siegfried Sassoon (1920)

In writing an Introduction such as this it is good to be brief. The poems printed in this book need no preliminary commendations from me or anyone else. The author has left us his own fragmentary but impressive Foreword; this, and his Poems, can speak for him, backed by the authority of his experience as an infantry soldier, and sustained by nobility and originality of style. All that was strongest in Wilfred Owen survives in his poems; any superficial impressions of his personality, any records of his conversation, behaviour, or appearance, would be irrelevant and unseemly. The curiosity which demands such morsels would be incapable of appreciating the richness of his work.

The discussion of his experiments in assonance and dissonance (of which 'Strange Meeting' is the finest example) may be left to the professional critics of verse, the majority of whom will be more preoccupied with such technical details than with the profound humanity of the self-revelation manifested in such magnificent lines as those at the end of his 'Apologia pro Poemate Meo', and in that other poem which he named 'Greater Love'.

The importance of his contribution to the literature of the War cannot be decided by those who, like myself, both admired him as a poet and valued him as a friend. His conclusions about War are so entirely in accordance with my own that I cannot attempt to judge his work with any critical detachment. I can only affirm that he was a man of absolute integrity of mind. He never wrote his poems (as so many war-poets did) to make the effect of a personal gesture. He pitied others; he did not pity himself. In the last year of his life he attained a clear vision of what he needed to say, and these poems survive him as his true and splendid testament. . . .

SOURCE: extract from the Introduction to *Poems by Wilfred Owen* (London, 1920), p. v.

Edmund Blunden (1920)

Mr Sassoon, on principle, affords the reader no impressions nor records of the personality of the remarkable poet Wilfred Owen. This silence, to us, is in every way justifiable. The poems themselves enable us to realise Owen as fully and as gladly as though we had served alongside him in the line: he was that anomaly, so inexplicable to the patriots at home, the fighting man of resolution and ability who loathed the war in theory and practice. In fact, Owen was one of the few spokesmen of the ordinary fighting man. There was up to a point a certain pride in the privations and crises of active war; nor was Owen devoid of it: there were personal obligations, as from officer to man and man to officer, which together with that pride held the Line. But there could scarcely have been one mind in a hundred thousand that did not rebel. It is probable that the rebellion latent in this way would have flamed into an actual deliberate movement but for the voice which whispered, 'You can't – the battalion depends on you', or perhaps, 'Nerves – will you give way?' And so the war went on, and, bad as it was in the first stages, went from bad to worse. 1917 heard for the first time the articulate voice of rebellion; it was high time. And still somehow the voice of personal affection and responsibility made itself better heard. Thus Wilfred Owen could write in 1918: 'I came out again in order to help these boys; directly, by leading them as well as an officer can; indirectly, by watching their sufferings that I may speak of them as well as a pleader can.' In reading the twenty-three poems now collected it is almost impossible to conceive of any other point of view. The vehemence and the agony which they manifest are, and compel, conviction. None but the most sincere philosophy could express itself so. There is no other philosophy in modern war, with its monstrous attacks doomed to failure nine times out of ten, its brutalising standstills with slow mental and sudden physical butcheries. Owen's 'Apologia' is the most satisfying and the truest proportioned analysis of the man in the trenches, and why he endured as he did, yet written. 'The Show' gives the whole war, the protozoic obscenity:

. . .
On dithering feet upgathered, more and more,
Brown strings towards strings of gray, with bristling spines,
All migrants from green fields, intent on mire.
Those that were gray, of more abundant spawns,
Ramped on the rest and ate them and were eaten.

That is the whole matter. There was nothing more to it.

Or perhaps there was, but it was by way of subservient and corroborative detail; and so Wilfred Owen, having summed the war as it was and as its victims regarded it, proceeds in poems like 'The Sentry' and 'Exposure' to give, as it were, chapter and verse. Except for Mr Sassoon, no poet has so utterly grasped the terror of particular moments, although Owen has left but a few poems of this kind. He is first and foremost the witness of the war's effect on the spirit of man. In 'Strange Meeting' he is at his greatest: he thinks of the time when the reality of war will again be ignored; when

Men will go content with what we spoiled,
Or, discontent, boil bloody, and be spilled.
They will be swift with swiftness of the tigress.
None will break ranks, though nations trek from progress.

Can it be that the time is here already?

In Owen we lost a poet of rare force. We have hinted at the spirit of his verse; the letter is as masterly. The very make of his language is hard and remorseless or strange and sombre as he wills; the discovery of final assonances in place of rhyme may mark a new age in poetry.

SOURCE: 'The Real War', *Athenaeum* (10 December 1920), p. 807.

Basil de Selincourt   (1921)

. . .   The main drift of Wilfred Owen's verse is the shattering of the illusion of the glory of war, and its mood is not free from a scathing bitterness for the men who nurture this illusion. We ask ourselves in vain where among English readers these men are to be found. The suggestion is that a nation is divided into two parts, one of which talks of war and ordains it, while the other acts and suffers. We can understand how such a thought might arise, but not how it can persist and find sustenance. And does the illusion of glory still hold any one? The only glory imperishably associated with war is that of the supreme sacrifice which it entails; the trumpets and the banners are poor humanity's imperfect tribute to that sublime implication. So far as the details of military action are concerned, the horror of them has descended upon the whole world like a nightmare; and if any man is not now pacifist, it is not because he relishes the thought of battle, but only because of a paralysing apprehension that war is inexorably necessary. Above all, the idea that lack of experience explains militarism is baseless. The nation that has been most proved by the war and has most intimately felt its devastations and agonies is the nation that has the greatest difficulty in throwing off the obsession! And what shall we say finally of the strange intimation that the old men sacrifice the young? As if any father would not face death sooner than send his boys to face it for him.

Wilfred Owen's poetical gesture springs in part from an error of judgement, and we cannot appreciate his poems as they deserve without calling attention to that error. He might have been less a poet if he had not made it, for no doubt it was his sensitiveness that played him false. It was made, and it enters into and colours his whole poetical expression. His moral revolt is largely misplaced; certain wider horizons, seen for example by Whitman as a poet of war, are not revealed to him. There is one direction, however, in which he opens up and exposes to us a great range of realities: realities which, because of the horror and anguish associated with them, men do conspire to gloss over and hush up. War, in a word, involves savagery; it demands of men such cruel outrage against their human instincts that as a moral experience it is essentially unbearable. There is, consequently, a permanent division between those who have and those who have not passed through the furnace; and it has been a part of Wilfred Owen's aim to bridge the chasm and represent to the mind of peace the inconceivable, arid atrocity of the mind of war, with the suffering and death-in-life which it entails. One might have supposed that this was an impossible task for poetry; yet he has passages in which he achieves it, showing us together, by a wonderful mastery of the associations of words, both the wilderness and wreckage and the tender, trustful loveliness they have displaced:

> Red lips are not so red
>   As the stained stones kissed by the English dead.
> Kindness of wooed and wooer
> Seems shame to their love pure.
> O Love, your eyes lose lure
>   When I behold eyes blinded in my stead!

In so far then as Wilfred Owen passes a moral judgement upon imaginary non-combatants, he is beside the issue; in so far as he endeavours to evoke and perpetuate the memory of 'that execrable, wild, callous abomination called fighting' (whose accompanying virtues he also deeply understands), so as to strengthen our determination to redeem the world from it, all the strength of Truth is with him. For war is brought about not by the last decisions and the dispatch of the ultimatum, but by those innumerable, imperceptible strivings for private advantage which, taken in their bulk, place rival nations at last in positions which they find mutually intolerable; and for the prevention of catastrophe, what we need most is some motive strong enough to act through all those intervening periods of seeming calm, when the course of events is deciding whether the crisis is to come or not. If we could possess ourselves permanently of the vision of that crime in which we are tempted to connive, our egotism might be checked and our more generous motives fortified. Owen offers us such a vision, for a warning at once terrible and salutary; but he is too true a poet not to have recognised that peace is something other than the avoidance of war, and the detestation

of war is not enough to assure us of it. He gives hints and
indications of a constructive message in a poem only partially
worked out, but characterised by an ardour and compactness of
expression which suggest the tone of veritable 'prophecy':

> Let us forgo men's minds that are brute's natures,
> Let us not sup the blood which some say nurtures
> . . .
> Let us lie out and hold the open truth.
> Then when their blood hath clogged the chariot wheels,
> We will go up and wash them from deep wells.
> What though we sink from men as pitchers falling,
> Many shall raise us up to be their filling,
> *Even from wells we sunk too deep for war*
> *And filled by brows that bled where no wounds were.*[1]

Moreover, a sustaining impulse of his poetry – here, again, is a
positive feature of unimpeachable worth – is sympathy and pity.
He is pitiless with his readers, but for the sake of utter truth and
faithfulness where pity belongs. And the tenderness behind his
relentlessness gives the hard, brutal words a strange, improbable
beauty; they live, they breathe out a redemptive virtue, searing
us with an anguish which, nevertheless, they transcend:

> Happy are these who lose imagination:
> They have enough to carry with ammunition.
> Their spirit drags no pack.
> Their old wounds save with cold can not more ache.
> . . .
> Their senses in some scorching cautery of battle
> Now long since ironed,
> Can laugh among the dying, unconcerned.

Wilfred Owen's technique has one specially remarkable feature,
which readers will have already noticed in our quotations. He
invents a peculiar type of rhyme to aid him in the expression of
that prevailing emotion of disgust, of weariness of illusion, of
insistence on the bleak realities which he is determined to drive
home. To put it briefly, he substitutes for vowel identity with its
pleasing music, a consonantal identity which neither pleases nor
is intended to please, except with that remote pleasure we derive

from a recognition of a true adaptation of means to ends. The intention is to chastise our sensibilities, as it were, to shake and wake us, as has been done not infrequently through certain alliterative devices, regularly, indeed, in the old Saxon metres. But our ear being now tuned to vowel-rhyme, the poet avails himself of our disappointment to increase the biting severity of his strokes; and so, profiting not only by what he gives but also by what he withholds, he gets an effect of total desolation, as in this soliloquy of a wounded soldier:

My arms have mutinied against me – brutes!
My fingers fidget like ten idle brats,
My back's been stiff for hours, damned hours.
Death never gives his squad a Stand-at-ease.
I can't read. There: it's no use. Take your book.
A short life and a merry one, my buck!
We said we'd hate to grow dead-old. But now,
Not to live old seems awful: not to renew
My boyhood with my boys, and teach 'em hitting,
Shooting and hunting, – all the arts of hurting!

The question may possibly be canvassed whether these are rhymes at all. Should controversy arise it would be endless; for the question at issue would be either one of terminology or taste. We have here a novel device used for a purpose which it fulfils. We may wish the purpose had been different or hesitate to decide what name to give to this feature in its embodiment. But we see quite clearly what was intended and what has been accomplished; and that is all that matters. Let us add that the device is applied systematically and has a cumulative effect. Naturally, it is not every pair of lines that assaults us as does the first of those we have just quoted; but as the poem proceeds and vowel assonance is firmly refused, the sense of mournful barrenness grows heavier and heavier, and we more and more feel what an immeasurable distance divides this mud, this monotony, this slow torture, from the stuff of conventional verse, how far the 'troops who fade' are from those flowers which are 'for poets' tearful fooling'.

SOURCE: 'Wilfred Owen's Poems', *Times Literary Supplement* (6 January 1921), p. 6.

NOTE

1. These lines, from a poem apparently addressed to Sassoon by Owen in December 1917, are quoted from the 1920 edition of the poems. The reviewer's italicisation is retained here. [Ed.]

John Middleton Murry (1921)

The name and the genius of Wilfred Owen were first revealed by the publication of his finest poem, 'Strange Meeting', in the anthology *Wheels* in 1919. I vividly remember the shock of that encounter, the sudden, profound stirring by the utterance of a true poet. Since that time other fragments of Owen's work have been made known, and if none so evidently bore the impress of poetic mastery as 'Strange Meeting', they were a part of that achievement. We could be sure that when the promised volume of his poetry appeared it would be single, coherent, and unique.

And so it is. Here in thirty-three brief pages is the evidence that Wilfred Owen was the greatest poet of the war. There have been war-poets; but he was a poet of another kind. He was not a poet who seized upon the opportunity of war, but one whose being was saturated by a strange experience, who bowed himself to the horror of war until his soul was penetrated by it, and there was no mean or personal element remaining unsubdued in him. In a fragmentary preface which bears the mark of Owen's purity of purpose, he wrote 'Above all this book is not concerned with Poetry. The subject of it is War, and the Pity of War. The Poetry is in the pity.'

'The Poetry is in the pity.' Whatever the new generation of poets may think or say, Owen had the secret in those words. The source of all enduring poetry lies in an intense and overwhelming emotion. The emotion must be overwhelming, and suffered as it were to the last limit of the soul's capacity. Complete submission is an essential phase in that process of mastering the emotion with which the poet's creation begins, for the poet himself has to be changed; he plunges into the depths of his emotion to rise mysteriously renewed. Only then will the words he utters bear upon them the strange compulsion of a secret revealed; only then can he put his spell upon us and trouble our depths. For the problem of poetry is not primarily, or even largely, a conscious problem; true poetry begins with an act, a compelled and undeliberate act, of obedience to that centre of our being where all experience is reconciled.

And the further process of poetry is also an instinctive adjustment rather than a conscious seeking. The poet's being, changed by the stress of its overwhelming experience, gropes after a corresponding expression. Learning and the intellect are no better than tentative guides. The correspondence toward which the poet moves is recognised and ratified by other powers than these. And Owen's search after some garment for his new comprehension more closely fitting than the familiar rhyme arose, not from any desire to experiment for experiment's sake, but from the inward need to say the thing he had to say most exactly and finally. Consider the assonances in the opening lines of 'Strange Meeting': . . . [Quotes lines 1–24.] The reader who comes fresh to this great poem does not immediately observe the assonant endings. At first he feels only that the blank verse has a mournful, impressive, even oppressive, quality of its own; that the poem has a forged unity, a welded and inexorable massiveness. The emotion with which it is charged cannot be escaped; the meaning of the words and the beat of the sounds have the same indivisible message. The tone is single, low, muffled, sub-terranean. The reader looks again and discovers the technical secret; but if he regards it then as an amazing technical innovation, he is in danger of falsifying his own reaction to the poem. Those assonant endings are indeed the discovery of genius; but in a truer sense the poet's emotion discovered them for itself. They are a dark and natural flowering of this, and only this, emotion. You cannot imagine them used for any other purpose save Owen's, or by any other hand save his. They are the very modulation of his voice; you are in the presence of that rare achievement, a true poetic style.

Throughout the poems in this book we can watch Owen working towards this perfection of his own utterance, and at the same time working away from realistic description of the horrors of war towards an imaginative projection of emotion. The

technical refinement works parallel with the imaginative sub-
limation. But even the realistic poems are hard and controlled,
and completely free from the weakness of emotional dispersion;
while on Owen's highest plane no comparison at all between him
and the realistic poets is possible. He speaks to the imagination;
his poems evoke our reactions, not to a scene of horror played
again before our eyes, but to words spoken in silence when all
material tumult has died away; they are the expression of that
which remains in the soul when the nightmare of the senses is
over.

His poems are calm. In spite of the intense passion which is
their impulse, they have a haunting serenity. For the poet has, at
whatever cost, mastered his experience; his emotion has become
tranquil. In these poems there is no more rebellion, but only pity
and regret, and the peace of acquiescence. It is not a comfortable
peace, this joyless yet serene resignation; but it is a victory of the
human spirit. We receive from it that exalted pleasure, that sense
of being lifted above the sphere of anger and despair which the
poetic imagination alone can give. . . . [Quotes 'Anthem for
Doomed Youth'.] There the calm is unmistakable, and indeed so
evident that one might describe the sonnet as being in the
familiar sense beautiful. Beauty of this kind is not to be found in
the ghastly poem called 'The Show'; but a still deeper calm is
there. . . . [Quotes 'The Show', 1–9, 23–end.] There is horror at
its extreme point, but horror without hysteria, horror that has
been so overcome that it can be communicated direct from the
imagination to the imagination. Hence there is calm.

It is probably true, as Mr Sassoon suggests in his introduction,
that the majority of war-poets wrote for the sake of the effect of a
personal gesture, and that Owen did not. But the important
difference between Owen and the rest is a difference in the power
and quality of the imagination, which seems to arise in a
difference in the power and quality of the kindling experience. So
profound is this that we can hardly refrain from calling Owen a
great poet. He had, more surely than any other poet of his
generation, the potentiality of greatness; and he actually wrote
one great poem. 'Strange Meeting' is complete, achieved,
unfaltering, and it is not solitary, for although Owen wrote no
other poem which is wholly on this secure imaginative level, we
cannot but regard it as the culmination of poems hardly less

achieved. 'Exposure' is charged with the same sombre mystery, and the unity of technique and emotional intention is almost as close. 'Greater Love,' which seems to have been written before Owen's final period had begun, will reveal the purity of the poet's emotion to those who may be disconcerted by his later work: . . . [Quotes 'Greater Love'.]

But it is not this poem, beautiful and poignant though it is, which will vindicate the claim that Owen is the greatest poet of the war; it is 'Strange Meeting' and certain fragments of other poems which are lifted up by a poetic imagination of the highest and rarest kind – the sad serenity of the closing stanza of 'Insensibility':

> But cursed are dullards whom no cannon stuns,
> That they should be as stones.
> Wretched are they, and mean
> With paucity that never was simplicity.
> By choice they made themselves immune
> To pity and whatever mourns in man
> Before the last sea and the hapless stars;
> Whatever mourns when many leave these shores;
> Whatever shares
> The eternal reciprocity of tears.

And the magical metaphors of the last five lines of this concluding passage of 'A Terre':

> Friend, be very sure
> I shall be better off with plants that share
> More peaceably the meadow and the shower.
> Soft rains will touch me, – as they could touch once,
> And nothing but the sun shall make me ware.
> Your guns may crash around me. I'll not hear;
> Or, if I wince, I shall not know I wince.
> Don't take my soul's poor comfort for your jest.
> Soldiers may grow a soul when turned to fronds,
> But here the thing's best left at home with friends.
>
> My soul's a little grief, grappling your chest,
> To climb your throat on sobs; easily chased

On other sighs and wiped by fresher winds.
Carry my crying spirit till it's weaned
To do without what blood remained these wounds.

After all, it may be asked, even if we admit that Owen was a poet of unusual imaginative power, why is he the only poet of the war? Other poets – true poets some of them – have written of the war. Why are they less than he? For this single reason. The war was a terrible and unique experience in the history of mankind; its poetry had likewise to be unique and terrible; it had to record not the high hopes that animated English youth at the outset, but the slow destruction of that youth in the sequel; more than this, it had to record not what the war did to men's bodies and senses, but what it did to their souls. Owen's poetry is unique and terrible because it records imperishably the devastation and the victory of a soul.

There is a tragic fitness in the fact that Owen was killed in the last gasp of the expiring war, as he led his company ('The fresh-severed head of it, my head') across the Sambre Canal on November 4th, 1918. He was, beyond all other poets, dedicated to the war. By how great an effort of will he achieved his purpose we may judge from the story lately disclosed by Mr Scott Moncrieff, who was his friend. Owen was sent home in June, 1917, because his nerve had failed, and he was no longer considered fit to command soldiers in the field. Not for fourteen months was his desire to be sent out again satisfied. Almost immediately he won the Military Cross for gallantry. Possessing this story, we can see the true meaning of the words he wrote to his mother at this time, a month before his death: 'My nerves are in perfect order. I came out again in order to help these boys; directly, by leading them as well as an officer can; indirectly, by watching their sufferings that I may speak of them as well as a pleader can.' The victory of the man was a victory of the poet also.

SOURCE: 'The Poet of the War', *Nation and Athenaeum* (19 February 1921); reprinted in *The Evolution of an Intellectual* (London, 1927 edition), pp. 85–98.

Sir Henry Newbolt (1924)

. . . This week-end, ten years ago – nothing in all my life seems further away, but I can still recall the feeling of it – the splendid epic calm and tingle of every act and word. Much as I hate the idea of war and waste, and clearly as I see the obvious crash, still I imagine we are we, and if next time came we should just shoulder it again.

That's really what Sassoon said to me on Tuesday – *he* would go again, and if he then everybody. He has sent me Wilfred Owen's Poems, with an Introduction by himself. The best of them I knew already – they are terribly good, but of course limited, almost all on one note. I like better Sassoon's two-sided collection – there are more than two sides to this business of war, and a man is hardly normal any longer if he comes down to one. S.S. says that Owen pitied others but never himself: I'm afraid that isn't quite true – or at any rate quite fair. To be a man one must be willing that others as well as yourself should bear the burden that must be borne. When I looked into Douglas Haig I saw what is really great – perfect acceptance, which means perfect faith. Owen and the rest of the broken men rail at the Old Men who sent the young to die: they have suffered cruelly, but in the nerves and not the heart – they haven't the experience or the imagination to know the extreme human agony – 'Who giveth me to die for thee, Absalom my son, my son'. Paternity apart, what Englishman of fifty wouldn't far rather stop the shot himself than see the boys do it for him? I don't think these shell-shocked war poems will move our grandchildren greatly – there's nothing fundamental or final about them – at least they only put one figure into a very big equation, and that's not one of the unknown but one of the best known quantities. . . .

SOURCE: extract from letter of 2 August 1924 in Margaret Newbolt (ed.), *The Later Life and Letters of Sir Henry Newbolt* (London, 1942), pp. 314–15.

PART TWO

Opinions and Assessments
1930–1946

1. ON POETS OF THE GREAT WAR

Edmund Blunden (1930)

The Soldier Poets of 1914–1918

'Soldier Poets' – the term was a few years ago almost as familiar as a ration-card. The greatest war, breaking all records, produced the greatest number of poets (at least, in the English language) that any war has done. Moreover, on previous occasions of upheaval in Flanders or more remote fields, the poets had been fortunate enough, if not precisely

> To see what fighting there had been
> Quite clearly – on the tape-machine,

to remain in a clean, quiet, and not much distressed situation. It was one of the romantic things about Thomas Campbell that he had seen as well as sung the Battle of Hohenlinden, or at any rate people said he had seen it, which was remarkable enough. In the early days of the World War, it appeared as though the tradition of poetry might be maintained 'with due regard to decent taste', and that lyres would be struck and elegiac business carried on as usual by melodious patriots, seated at their customary tables. Some hard things have been said about these dignified performers. 'Alfred Noyes, the conventional Victorian', writes an American anthologist, 'turned from peace poems to war poems without batting an eyelash.'

It soon became evident, however, that the army (the navy does not seem to have been so vocal) did not intended to have its poetry supplied from the factory. The emotional shock that so bewildering a change of prospect meant to those who enlisted for three years or the duration of the war awoke deeper utterance than men ordinarily need or permit themselves to attempt. At first, speaking broadly, the poetry thus called into existence was concerned with the beauty of English life, made distinct by the act of separation, renunciation. The fact of war was still strange and enigmatic. Whatever war was, almost every one was, as it were, under oath not to make a song about its dreadfulness. Hardly any one could be genuinely, at that early stage, in two minds about it. The appalling destruction which it would ultimately mean, direct and indirect, was not seen; just as, had you seen a pretty Picard village one bright morning in 1916, you would not have guessed that two days later there would have been nothing but a few mounds, hundreds of large holes, and some tree stumps to represent it. So, the early war poetry is mainly insistent on chivalrous obligation, the things that matter more than death, and the affections and home pictures of the life that the soldier leaves behind him.

Conspicuous among the first poets who had gone to the wars, Rupert Brooke perfected the theme which they mostly had. He was already a man of exalted view and graceful expression. As it chanced, he did not see the war in its later unfoldings, or we might have had from him, as from C. E. Montague in prose, some noble numbers won in disenchantment. His period was that in which, undoubtedly, the romantic note was justified in any being less than an Aeschylus or a Confucius. He did not discern anything more complex in the case than sacrifice for an ideal, consolation for the sacrifice; what he discerned, that he adorned with a classical manner. Later on it became difficult to read his verse, which nevertheless resumes something of its former effect now.

Another poet who, dying, became famous, was C. H. Sorley. He, too, was denied the opportunity to witness and to condemn at length the war of attrition, and the attrition of war. He began to feel the futility of the argument, the doom of the best of men, before the battle of Loos claimed him in the autumn of 1915. He declared his largeness of spirit in a sonnet 'To Germany', which ends with true prophecy,

> When it is peace, then we may view again
> With new-won eyes each other's truer form
> And wonder. Grown more loving-kind and warm
> We'll grasp firm hands and laugh at the old pain

When it is peace. But until peace, the storm,
The darkness and the thunder and the rain.

Sorley, too, perceived how grimly it came about that the man in
the trenches was cut off by an impassable gulf from the people at
home—from himself a year younger.

When you see millions of the mouthless dead
Across your dreams in pale battalions go,
Say not 'soft things as other men have said,
That you'll remember. For you need not so.
Give them not praise. For, deaf, how should they know
It is not curses heaped on each gashed head?
Nor tears. Their blind eyes see not your tears flow. . . .

The main mystery of the Old Front Line was that it created a
kind of concord between the combatants, but a discord between
them and those who, not being there, kept up the war.

   With the multiplying of disastrous attacks, the swelling rage of
ever-stiffening masses of artillery, the extension of the ruined
areas, the tormenting of periods of rest with night-bombing, the
relentless crowding of men into the Golgotha, the cleavage
between the fighting man and the civilian, the obscuring of the
intention of Englishmen, and, simply, with the disappearance of
novelty in bullet and bayonet, the war became a recognised
error. In Mr Robert Graves's *Fairies and Fusiliers*, 1917, may be
read examples of the transition of poetry from the first en-
thusiasms to an attitude of painful questioning. On one page you
find 'A Renascence', which looks backward to the spirit of Brooke
and admires the event not only because it has made weaklings
into athletes but because

Of their travailings and groans
Poetry is born again.

On another page the poetical interest is treated personally:

Here's an end to my art!
   I must die and I know it,
With battle murder at my heart –
   Sad death for a poet!

The time was now coming when the attack on war was to be made on a large scale, without egotism or minor concern, by a poet with every qualification for his glorious and difficult crusade. Today the name of Siegfried Sassoon is perhaps associated by most readers with his finely modulated prose work, the *Memoirs of a Fox-Hunting Man*; but it was in *The Old Huntsman* of 1917 that he set out, a unique adventurer, to tell the truth about war poetically: I have called this a difficult task; by way of defining the epithet, the reader will remember that Mr Sassoon was still a soldier, that a vast amount of falsehood concerning war and Tommy's smile had been dinned into the public mind, and that the communicating of the unprecedented and solitary miseries of modern battlefields was scarcely within the bounds of hope. As for this author's qualifications, the first was a poetic nature trained in patient watchings for the significant thing and the correspondingly significant phrase; the second was a happy intimacy with peaceful life, such as had bred affectionate discernment of the beautiful in human character, in customary things, in wild nature, in the arts; the third was the long acquaintance of this philosophic lyrist with warfare, and with his friend "the average man" in the throes of warfare. *The Old Huntsman* offered portraits of the soldier seen against the dreadful horizons, or lying still on the fatal parapets; and here were outbursts of white anger against those who drowned all the cryings of truth with clamorous claptrap or vulgar excess. The humour of Mr Sassoon in his recent memoirs has delighted many; but they may see what a poet's humour can be like when just indignation commands in *The Old Huntsman*.

Mr Sassoon proceeded to write and publish in periodicals and loose sheets the fuller statement of, and against, war which appeared in the volume, *Counter-Attack*, in June, 1918. It was his triumph to be the first man who even described war fully and exactly; and had description been all that he did, the feat would have been distinguished. The face of war is one of protean changes. In order to catch those countenances, a man has to be acute in a rare degree. A fighting man, too, is busy; the whirlpool of danger, and labour, and noise which has swallowed him is not of a sort to assist him in a plain observant report. No ferocity could deflect the passion in Mr Sassoon's mind for a complete impression, such as must command the attention and understanding even of the uninitiated, of the fury. He will laugh at the figure, but he was something like one of the figures who stand their ground and draw their swords in the old battle pictures amid the thickening explosions and conflagrations. He contrived to draw a sword for a greater ideal than the colours of a regiment, by recording what war does to 'youth and laughter' in poignant epithet and striking verb, in various rhythm and in dramatic narration. He showed in many passages how life had bloomed to these men, even when they had been least analytical of their normality:

> I see them in foul dug-outs, gnawed by rats,
>   And in the ruined trenches, lashed with rain,
> Dreaming of things they did with balls and bats,
>   And mocked by hopeless longing to regain
> Bank-holidays, and picture shows, and spats,
>   And going to the office· in the train.

He showed to what extreme the failure of nations to think calmly, to consider the obvious, had withered these men; he had the power of producing in a remark or detail the scorching hopelessness in which they were imprisoned: I italicise,

> They leave their trenches, *going over the top*
> While time *ticks blank and busy* on their wrists.

There was one who had been moving in the direction of this Shelleyan revolutionary (only so, because conservative wherever the existing thing is choice and laudable) almost since the beginning of the war, but who did not discover himself very quickly. When he did, he instantly showed the power to speak with Mr Sassoon, and it was his meeting with that poet which released his energies and encouraged him to marshal his magnificent gifts with intellectual control. This young officer was Wilfred Owen, who, apparently apprehending that the war might be protracted far beyond 1918, set himself to strike a blow at it with an organised series of poems. Many of those he completed. Then, in spite of having already had much fiery experience of the shell-holes and drum-fire, he argued that he must return to the field in order not only to help his friend the fighting man as an officer, but also to equip himself with new experience for an unanswerable poetic onslaught upon the war. He was one of the last to be killed, and probably the greatest of those poets who were killed. For his poetical capacity, it is necessary to bring forward the parallel of Keats, whom he adored. He was endowed with a fruitful imagination, distilling itself into the richest cordials of phrases, and with a sense of grand music, that made him explore all known and some unknown harmonies of metre and syllabic sound. But Owen was anything but an æsthetic recluse. He was of an open, ardent, and genial sensibility, profoundly devoted to the happiness and freedom of others, yearning to see each man blessed with whatever honourable pleasure life has to give suited to individual condition. The world in which Owen came to maturity of thought was that which for four years rolled the individual into one red burial. Once he had assured himself by Mr Sassoon's example that poetry could do much to bring us back to our senses, and that the same powers which can best concentrate the beauty of things can suggest grotesque but actual horror, despair, outrage, and strange passion, he applied himself wholly to that work. What he has written will last; he has said much that may only be understood by those who were with him, but he had equally perpetuated the general wilderness, the charged atmosphere, the hardly sane constancy of the soldier, the pity which he desired above all to interpret.

I have not crowded this sketch of certain aspects of the war's poets with names; nor is it necessary to add much regarding the verse which in subsequent years has reflected and re-echoed the years of brilliance and catastrophe. Most of this literature has been in prose, and in protest; and still there is need for protest, and though *Journey's End* arouse the sympathies of millions from London to Tokyo there is need. We shall be liable to vaingloriousness if we now blame too earnestly the young soldiers of 1914 and 1915 who with their delicate and unreflecting stanzas failed to paint war as it is. They were not experienced, and, at a time when the country needed their sweetness, they gave it. Maybe in the judgement of after years it needed bitterness more; but to everything there is a season. Equally, we must not be too well satisfied that we are now making, and attending to, effectual and eager complaints against the survival of that false gross idol,

War. These have been made through the ages; and, when all had been forgotten, right out of the mephitic gulf of the bombardment, in prehistoric 1916 and 1917, arose two poets of unshakable resolution, whose protests will not be surpassed for poetic intensity and plan or for selflessness in fighting this world's battles.

SOURCE: Introduction to Frederick Brereton (ed.), *An Anthology of War Poems* (London, 1930), pp. 13–24.

W. B. Yeats (1936)

'Passive suffering is not a theme for poetry'

. . . I have a distaste for certain poems written in the midst of the great war; they are in all anthologies, but I have substituted Herbert Read's 'End of a War' written long after. The writers of these poems were invariably officers of exceptional courage and capacity, one a man constantly selected for dangerous work, all, I think, had the Military Cross; their letters are vivid and humorous, they were not without joy – for all skill is joyful – but felt bound, in the words of the best known, to plead the suffering of their men. In poems that had for a time considerable fame, written in the first person, they made that suffering their own. I have rejected these poems for the same reason that made Arnold withdraw his *Empedocles on Etna* from circulation; passive suffering is not a theme for poetry. In all the great tragedies, tragedy is a joy to the man who dies; in Greece the tragic chorus danced. When man has withdrawn into the quicksilver at the back of the mirror no great event becomes luminous in his mind; it is no longer possible to write *The Persians*, 'Agincourt', 'Chevy Chase': some blunderer has driven his car on to the wrong side of the road – that is all. . . .

SOURCE: extract from the Introduction to *The Oxford Book of Modern Verse* (1936), p. xxxiv.

2. ON WILFRED OWEN

C. Day Lewis (1934)

'A true revolutionary poet'

Gerard Manley Hopkins died young in the year 1889. His poems were not published till 1918, the year in which Wilfred Owen was killed. Hopkins would have been a poet under any circumstances: Owen, I am inclined to think, was made a poet by the war. The notes which he set down for a preface to his poems give the clue to his identity.

This book is not about heroes. English Poetry is not yet fit to speak of them.

Nor is it about deeds, or lands, nor anything about glory, honour, might, majesty, dominion, or power, except War.

Above all I am not concerned with Poetry.

My subject is War, and the pity of War.

The Poetry is in the pity.

Yet these elegies are to this generation in no sense consolatory. They may be to the next. All a poet can do today is warn. That is why the true Poets must be truthful.

If I thought the letter of this book would last, I might have used proper names; but if the spirit of it survives – survives Prussia – my ambition and those names will have achieved themselves fresher fields than Flanders. . . .

This noble, fragmentary message reached the next generation, as he hoped, and meant more to them than perhaps he ever had expected. We must be careful not to misunderstand him, though. When he says that his book 'is not concerned with Poetry', he is not simply expressing what most artists feel at times, particularly at times of great external crisis – a sense of the ineffectiveness and isolation of their own form of life. Nor does he imply that poetry can ever be concerned with itself to any advantage. He is saying,

I think, that there are times when the poet's allegiance must be divided: when his duty towards his neighbour ceases to be necessarily identical with his duty towards his god, Poetry, the former acquiring temporarily a relatively enlarged significance in his mind. In other words, circumstances may force the poet unwillingly to take up the position of prophet – 'All a poet can do today is warn.' Again when he says, 'That is why the true Poets must be truthful', he is not suggesting that there are times when true Poets are allowed to tell lies. There is poetical truth, and there is common honesty; they are very distant relations: Owen's plea was that the crisis should bring them together, that the greater – poetical truth – should temporarily put itself under the command of the lesser. Owen commends himself to post-war poets largely because they feel themselves to be in the same predicament; they feel the same lack of a stable background against which the dance of words may stand out plainly, the same distrust and horror of the unnatural forms into which life for the majority of people is being forced. They know in their hearts exactly what Owen meant when he said 'the poetry is in the pity.'

> Move him into the sun –
> Gently its touch awoke him once,
> At home, whispering of fields unsown.
> Always it woke him, even in France,
> Until this morning and this snow.
> If anything might rouse him now
> The kind old sun will know.

> Think how it wakes the seeds –
> Woke, once, the clays of a cold star.
> Are limbs, so dear-achieved, are sides
> Full-nerved – still warm – too hard to stir?
> Was it for this the clay grew tall?
> – O what made fatuous sunbeams toil
> To break earth's sleep at all?

It is difficult to call this anything but a perfect poem. Poetical truth becoming here, as in almost all his poems, the servant of common honesty – of Owen's determination to tell the factual, un-'poetical' truth, so far from being cramped and degraded, is enlarged and glorified. Owen had mastered that easy, almost conversational kind of verse at which many of the Georgian poets were aiming, in their reaction away from the laborious magni-loquence of the 'Nineties': unlike them, he never seems to lose dignity in the process; he speaks as one having authority, never condescending to language or adopting the hail-fellow-well-met tones of the poet who has a craving to be 'understood.' The first verse of the poem quoted above is an object lesson in the simplicity that never was paucity: in the second, engined with pity and indignation, the poetry leaves the ground and ascends into heaven, culminating on a line, 'Was it for this the clay grew tall?' which would stand out from the work of any but the greatest poets.

One of the traditional tests of a poet is the number of outstanding, memorable lines he has written: this test Owen passes triumphantly. The lines of his which stick most in our memory can be divided into two types. The first of these is highly 'poetical,' in the grand manner, reminding us of Keats – a poet with whom Owen had a great deal more in common than an early death. It is exemplified in such lines as –

> . . . Whatever shares
> The eternal reciprocity of tears.

> . . . Whose world is but the trembling of a flare,
> And heaven but as the highway for a shell. . . .

> . . . Mine ancient scars shall not be glorified
> Nor my titanic tears, the seas, be dried.

The second type is restrained, often witty in the seventeenth-century sense, always ironical: it works through a kind of understatement which recalls to us at once the grim and conscious irony of those who knew that 'their feet had come to the end of the world.' We find it perpetually recurring in his work. He is writing of a draft entraining for the front –

> Dull porters watched them, and a casual tramp
> Stood staring hard,
> *Sorry to miss them from the upland camp.* . . .

of a disabled soldier ('there was an artist silly for his face') helpless
in a wheeled chair –

> . . .
> Now, he is old; his back will never brace;
> *He's lost his colour very far from here,*
> Poured it down shell-holes till the veins ran dry.

Or, in his poem 'Greater Love', the lines –

> Heart, you were never hot,
>   Nor large, nor full like hearts made great with shot;

These deliberate, intense under-statements – the brave man's
only answer to a hell which no epic words could express – affect
me as being both more poignant and more rich with poetic
promise than anything else that has been done during this
century. Owen was not a technical revolutionary: his one
innovation is the constant use of the alliterative assonance as an
end rhyme – (mystery, mastery; killed, cold). But he was a true
revolutionary poet, opening up new fields of sensitiveness for his
successors. If he had lived there is no knowing what his promise
might have achieved; he would have found, active in different
guises, the cant, the oppression, the sufferings and courage which
had challenged his powers during the war. As it is, his
unsentimental pity, his savage and sacred indignation are the
best of our inheritance, and it is for his heirs to see that they are
not wasted.

Source: chapter III in *A Hope for Poetry* (Oxford, 1934), pp.
14–17.

W. B. Yeats   (1936)

'Blood, dirt & sucked sugar stick'

. . . My Anthology continues to sell & the critics get more & more angry. When I excluded Wilfred Owen, whom I consider unworthy of the poets' corner of a country newspaper, I did not know I was excluding a revered sandwich-board Man of the revolution & that some body has put his worst & most famous poem in a glass-case in the British Museum – however if I had known it I would have excluded him just the same. He is all blood, dirt & sucked sugar stick (look at the selection in Faber's Anthology – he calls poets 'bards', a girl a 'maid' & talks about 'Titanic wars'). There is every excuse for him but none for those who like him. . . .

> SOURCE: extract from letter of 21 December 1936, in *Letters on Poetry from W. B. Yeats to Dorothy Wellesley* (Oxford, 1940), p. 113.

Siegfried Sassoon   (1945)

A Reminiscence

. . . [there was] the velvety quality of his voice, which suggested the Keatsian richness of his artistry with words. It wasn't a vibrating voice. It had the fluid texture of soft consonants and murmurous music. Hearing him read poetry aloud in his modest unemphatic way, one realised at once that he had an exceptionally sensitive ear. One of his poems begins 'All sounds have been as music to my listening', and his sense of colour was correspondingly absorbent. Sounds and colours, in his verse, were mulled and modulated to a subdued magnificence of sensuous harmonies, and this was noticeable even in his everyday speaking. His temperament, as I apprehend it, was unhurrying, though never languid. Only now and then was he urgently quickened by the mysterious prompting and potency of his imagination. His manuscripts show that he seldom brought his poems to their final form without considerable recasting and revision. There was a slowness and sobriety in his method, which was, I think, monodramatic and elegiac rather than leapingly lyrical. I do not doubt that, had he lived longer, he would have produced poems of sustained grandeur and ample design. It can be observed that his work is prevalently deliberate in movement. Stately and processional, it has the rhythm of emotional depth and directness and the verbal resonance of one who felt in glowing primary colours and wrote with solemn melodies in his mind. It can be taken for granted that there were aspects of him which I never saw. To others he may have revealed much that I missed, since he had the adaptability of a beautifully sympathetic nature. But I like to believe that when with me he was at his best, and I can remember no shadow of unhappiness or misunderstanding between us. . . .

Source: extract from *Siegfried's Journey, 1916–1920* (London, 1945), p. 62.

Dylan Thomas (1946)

'Poet of all wars'

. . . Wilfred Owen was born in 1893 and killed in 1918. Twenty-five years of age, he was the greatest poet of the First Great War. Perhaps, in the future, if there are men, then, still to read – by which I mean, if there are men at all – he may be regarded as one of the great poets of all wars. But only war itself can resolve the problem of the ultimate truth of his, or of anyone else's, poetry: war, or its cessation.

And this time, when, in the words of an American critic, the audiences of the earth, witnessing what well may be the last act of their own tragedy, insist upon chief actors who are senseless enough to perform a cataclysm, the voice of the poetry of Wilfred Owen speaks to us, down the revolving stages of thirty years, with terrible new significance and strength. We had not forgotten his poetry, but perhaps we had allowed ourselves to think of it as the voice of one particular time, one place, one war. Now, at the beginning of what, in the future, may never be known to historians as the 'atomic age' – for obvious reasons: there may be no historians – we can see, re-reading Owen, that he is a poet of all times, all places, and all wars. There is only one war: that of men against men. . . .

It was impossible for him to avoid the sharing of suffering. He could not record a wound that was not his own. He had so very many deaths to die, and so very short a life within which to endure them all. It's no use trying to imagine what would have happened to Owen had he lived on. Owen, at twenty-six or so, exposed to the hysteria and exploded values of false peace. Owen alive now, at the age of fifty-three, and half the world starving. You cannot generalise about age and poetry. A man's poems, if they are good poems, are always older than himself; and sometimes they are ageless. We know that the shape and texture of his poems would always be restlessly changing, though the purpose behind them would surely remain unalterable; he would always be experimenting technically, deeper and deeper driving towards the final intensity of language: the words behind words. Poetry is, of its nature, an experiment. All poetical impulses are towards the creation of adventure. And adventure is movement. And the end of each adventure is a new impulse to move again towards creation. Owen, had he lived, would never have ceased experiment; and so powerful was the impetus behind his work, and so intricately strange his always growing mastery of words, he would never have ceased to influence the work of his contemporaries. Had he lived, English poetry would not be the same. The course of poetry is dictated by accidents. Even so, he is one of the four most profound influences upon the poets who came after him; the other three being Gerard Manley Hopkins, the later W. B. Yeats, and T. S. Eliot. . . .

To see him in his flame-lit personality, against the background, now of the poxed and cratered war-scape, shivering in the snow under the slitting wind, marooned on a frozen desert, or crying, in a little oven of mud, that his 'senses are charred', is to see a man consigned to articulate immolation. He buries his smashed head with his own singed hands, and is himself the intoning priest over the ceremony, the suicide, the sunset. He is the common touch. He is the bell of the church of the broken body. He writes love-letters home for the illiterate dead. Ignorant, uncaring, hapless as the rest of the bloody troops, he is their arguer shell-shocked into diction, though none may understand. He is content to be the unhonoured prophet in death's country; for fame, as he said, was the last infirmity he desired. . . .

SOURCE: extracts from 'Wilfred Owen', a radio talk broadcast in July 1946 and printed in *Quite Early One Morning* (London, 1954), pp. 92, 98-9, 102.

3 . ON ISAAC ROSENBERG

D. W. Harding (1935)

1 Treatment of War Experience

What most distinguishes Isaac Rosenberg from other English poets who wrote of the last war is the intense significance he saw in the kind of living effort that the war called out, and the way in which his technique enabled him to present both this and the suffering and the waste as inseparable aspects of life in war. Further, there is in his work, without the least touch of coldness, nevertheless a certain impersonality: he tried to feel in the war a significance for life as such, rather than seeing only its convulsion of the human life he knew.

   Occasionally, it is as well to say at once, he seems to simplify his experience too much, letting the suffering be swallowed up, though at his best he knows it never can be, in glory; this happens in 'The Dead Heroes', and to some extent in 'Soldier' and 'Marching'. By themselves these poems might have implied a lack of sensitiveness; actually they were in him only one side of an effort after a more complete sensitivity. He could at least as easily have written only of loss and suffering:

> Here is one not long dead.
> His dark hearing caught our far wheels,
> And the choked soul stretched weak hands
> To reach the living word the far wheels said;
> The blood-dazed intelligence beating for light,
> Crying through the suspense of the far torturing wheels
> . . .

The significance which the war held for Rosenberg might have been anticipated from his dissatisfaction with the pre-war social order (especially acute, it seems, in South Africa where he was

living when the war came). The poem he wrote on first hearing of
the war makes evident at once his deep division of feeling; on the
one hand,

> In all men's hearts it is:
> Some spirit old
> Hath turned with malign kiss
> Our lives to mould.

but also,

> O ancient crimson curse!
> Corrode, consume;
> Give back this universe
> Its pristine bloom.

His dissatisfaction with pre-war life had already shown itself in
his work, notably in the revolt against God which appears in
several passages, God being taken as someone responsible for the
condition of the world and its established order:

> Ah, this miasma of a rotting God!

And of the rotting God and his priests he exclaims:

> Who has made of the forest a park?
> Who has changed the wolf to a dog?
> And put the horse in harness?
> And man's mind in a groove?

In 'Moses', from which this passage comes, he was engrossed with
the theme of revolt against a corrupting routine; he presents
Moses at the moment of breaking free from the comfort of the
usual and politic by killing the overseer. Rosenberg never fully
defined his attitude to violence as distinct from strength, though
there is a hint in his letters that 'The Unicorn' might have
approached this question. In 'Moses' he accepts violence because
it seems a necessary aspect of any effort to bring back the power
and vigour of purpose which he felt the lack of in civilised life:

> I have a trouble in my mind for largeness.

It was because of this attitude to the pre-war world that Rosenberg, hating the war, was yet unable to set against it the possibilities of ordinary civilian life and regret those in the way, for instance, that Wilfred Owen could regret them in 'Strange Meeting'. When Rosenberg wanted to refer to an achieved culture – rather than merely human possibilities – against which to measure the work of war, he had to go back to remote and idealised Jewish history, producing 'The Burning of the Temple' and 'The Destruction of Jerusalem by the Babylonian Hordes'. More usually he opposed both to war and to the triviality of contemporary civilisation only a belief in the possibilities of life and a hope derived from its more primitive aspects:

> Here are the springs, primeval elements,
> The roots' hid secrecy, old source of race,
> Unreasoned reason of the savage instinct.

The root is the most important of the symbols which recur throughout his work, and birth, creation, and growth are his common themes.

These and related themes were to have been worked out in the unfinished play, 'The Unicorn'. But there they would have been influenced vitally by the war, and Rosenberg's account in letters of what he intends the play to be helps to reveal the significance of the war to him. The existing fragments point to his plan having changed more than once, but the letters show something of what he aimed at. The play was to have included a kind of Sabine rape by a decaying race who had no women and yearned for continuity:

> When aged flesh looks down on tender brood;
> For he knows between his thin ribs' walls
> The giant universe, the interminable
> Panorama – synods, myths and creeds,
> He knows his dust is fire and seed.

At the same time he wanted the play 'to symbolise the war and all the devastating forces let loose by an ambitious and unscrupulous will' (which might have been essentially the will of Moses seen in a slightly different light). Moreover, 'Saul and Lilith are ordinary folk into whose ordinary lives the Unicorn bursts. It is to be a play of terror – terror of hidden things and the fear of the supernatural.' It would, in fact, have been closely related to 'Daughters of War':

> We were satisfied of our lords the moon and the sun
> To take our wage of sleep and bread and warmth –
> These maidens came – these strong everliving Amazons,
> And in an easy might their wrists
> Of night's sway and noon's sway the sceptres brake,
> Clouding the wild, the soft lustres of our eyes.

The complexity of feeling here, which would probably have been still more evident in 'The Unicorn', is typical of the best of Rosenberg's war poetry. His finest passages are not concerned exclusively either with the strength called out by war or with the suffering: they spring more directly from the events and express a stage of consciousness appearing before either simple attitude has become differentiated. They express, that is, what it is tempting to call, inaccurately, a 'blending' of the two attitudes. It can be seen in this:

> None saw their spirits' shadow shake the grass,
> Or stood aside for the half used life to pass
> Out of those doomed nostrils and the doomed mouth,
> When the swift iron burning bee
> Drained the wild honey of their youth.

It is noteworthy here that Rosenberg is able and content to present contrasted aspects of the one happening without having to resort to the bitterness or irony which are the easier attitudes to such a contrast. One sign and expression of his peculiar greatness consists in his being able, in spite of his sensitiveness, to do without irony. The last two lines of the passage just quoted come from a keyed-up responsiveness to the vividness of violent death in war, but the passage possesses nothing of nationalist-militarist rapture; it is 'the half used life' that passes; and then

> Burnt black by strange decay
> Their sinister faces lie,

> The lid over each eye;
> The grass and coloured clay
> More motion have than they,
> Joined to the great sunk silences.

Rosenberg seems to have been specially impressed by the destruction of men at the moment of a simplified greatness which they could never have reached before, their destruction by the very forces that had made human strength and endurance more vividly impressive than ever. This conception of the war he tried to express through the fiction of some intention being fulfilled in the destruction:

> Earth has waited for them,
> All the time of their growth
> Fretting for their decay:
> Now she has them at last!
> In the strength of their strength
> Suspended – stopped and held.

From this it was a short inevitable step to the suggestion of some vague immortality for these lives:

> What fierce imaginings their dark souls lit?
> Earth! Have they gone into you?
> Somewhere they must have gone,
> And flung on your hard back
> Is their souls' sack,
> Emptied of God-ancestralled essences.

'Daughters of War' develops the same group of ideas. 'Earth' gives place to the more active symbol of the Blakesque Amazonian spirits who take as lovers those who have been released from Earth,

> From the doomed earth, from the doomed glee
> And hankering of hearts.

The Daughters, their voices (as Rosenberg says in a letter) 'spiritual and voluptuous at the same time', are a symbolic expression of what he felt ought to be a possible plane of living. They are an embodiment of the God-ancestralled essences, but he feels now that they can be reached only through the sacrifice of men's defective humanity, that they bring about 'the severance of all human relationship and the fading away of human love'. This was an idea that he had been feeling towards in 'Girl to Soldier on Leave'. It is only for warriors that the Daughters wait, for the simplification of living effort which Rosenberg saw in the war impressed him as a first step – a step back – towards the primitive sources of life, 'the root side of the tree of life'. Death in itself was not his concern, but only death at the moment when life was simplified and intensified; this he felt had a significance which he represents by immortality. For him it was no more than the 'immortality of the possibilities of life.'

This immortality and the value he glimpses in the living effort of war in no way mitigate his suffering at the human pain and waste. The value of what was destroyed seemed to him to have been brought into sight only by the destruction, and he had to respond to both facts without allowing either to neutralise the other. It is this which is most impressive in Rosenberg – the complexity of experience which he was strong enough to permit himself and which his technique was fine enough to reveal. Naturally there were some aspects of the war which he was not able to compass in his response: maiming and lingering death he never treats of – he thinks only in terms of death which comes quickly enough to be regarded as a single living experience. Nevertheless the complexity he did achieve constituted a large part of his importance as a poet.

To say that Rosenberg tried to understand all that the war stood for means probably that he tried to expose the whole of himself to it. In one letter he describes as an intention what he obviously achieved: 'I will not leave a corner of my consciousness covered up, but saturate myself with the strange and extraordinary new conditions of this life . . . ' This willingness – and ability – to let himself be new-born into the new situation, not subduing his experience to his established personality, is a large part, if not the whole secret of the robustness which characterises his best work. ('Robustness' is, as the fragment on Emerson indicates, his own word for something he felt to be an essential of great poetry.) It was due largely, no doubt, to his lack of conviction of the adequacy of civilian standards. In 'Troopship' and 'Louse Hunting' there is no civilian resentment at the conditions he writes of. Here as in all the war poems his suffering and discomfort are unusually *direct*; there is no secondary distress arising from the sense that these things *ought not* to be. He was given up to realising fully what *was*. He has expressed his attitude in 'The Unicorn':

> Lilith: I think there is more sorrow in the world
>   Than man can bear.
>
> Nubian: None can exceed their limit, lady:
>   You either bear or break.

It was Rosenberg's exposure of his whole personality that gave his work its quality of impersonality. Even when he imagines his brother's death he brings it into a poem which is equally concerned with the general destruction and the circumstances of life in war, and which ends with a generalisation of his personal suffering:

> What are the great sceptred dooms
> To us, caught
> In the wild wave?
> We break ourselves on them,
> My brother, our hearts and years.

The same quality is present, most finely, in 'Break of day in the trenches':

> The darkness crumbles away –
> It is the same old druid Time as ever.
> Only a live thing leaps my hand –
> A queer sardonic rat –
> As I pull the parapet's poppy
> To stick behind my ear.
> Droll rat, they would shoot you if they knew
> Your cosmopolitan sympathies
>
> .   .   .   .

It seems you inwardly grin as you pass
Strong eyes, fine limbs, haughty athletes
Less chanced than you for life,

.   .   .   .

Poppies whose roots are in man's veins
Drop, and are ever dropping;
But mine in my ear is safe,
Just a little white with the dust.

There is here a cool distribution of attention over the rat, the poppy and the men which gives them all their due, is considerate of all their values, and conveys in their precise definition something of the impersonal immensity of a war. For Rosenberg the war was not an incident of his life, to be seen from without, but, instead, one kind of life, as unquestionable as any life.

ii Handling of Language

Without attempting a systematic survey of Rosenberg's use of language, it is perhaps useful to discuss briefly one feature of his writing which must seem important even in a first approach to his work, partly because it contributes largely to his obscurity. It is that in much of his most interesting work he was only in a very special sense 'selecting words to express ideas'.

Usually when we speak of finding words to express a thought we seem to mean that we have the thought rather close to formulation and use it to measure the adequacy of any possible phrasing that occurs to us, treating words as servants of the idea. 'Clothing a thought in language', whatever it means psychologically, seems a fair metaphorical description of most speaking and writing. Of Rosenberg's work it would be misleading. He – like many poets in some degree, one supposes – brought language to bear on the incipient thought at an earlier stage of its development. Instead of the emerging idea being racked slightly so as to fit a more familiar approximation of itself, and words found for *that*, Rosenberg let it manipulate words almost from the beginning, often without insisting on the controls of logic and intelligibility. An example of what happened occurs in the prose fragment on Emerson and the parallel phrase in a letter . . . . In these he tries two ways of describing some quality that he feels in Emerson: at one time he calls it 'light dancing in light', at another, trying to be more explicit and limit further the possible meanings of the phrase, he writes 'a beaminess, impalpable and elusive only in a circle'. The elements of this idea are apparently 'lightness' and 'elusiveness' and also 'endlessness, continuity within itself' of some kind, and these elements he feels also to be inseparable and necessary to each other.

He would of course have worked further on this before considering it finished. Much of the labour he gave to writing – and he is known to have worked extremely hard – was devoted, as his letters show, to making these complex ideas intelligible without sacrificing their complexity. 'Now, when my things fail to be clear, I am sure it is because of the luckless choice of a word or the failure to introduce a word that would flash my idea plain, as it is to my own mind.' It is the creation of ideas which he takes to be his task as a poet; speaking of the cause of the faults in his poems he insists that it is not 'blindness or carelessness; it is the brain succumbing to the herculean attempt to enrich the world of ideas'. And he is reported to have worked constantly towards concentrating more and more *sense* into his poetry, disturbed at the thought of thinness or emptiness. But how remote this was from implying any respect for mere intellectual exercising in verse is evident not only from his poetry but also from his own description of what he aimed at: poetry 'where an interesting complexity of thought is kept in tone and right value to the dominating idea so that it is understandable and still ungraspable'.

It remains 'ungraspable' – incapable of formulation in slightly different terms – because Rosenberg allowed his words to emerge from the pressure of a very wide context of feeling and only a very general direction of thought. The result is that he seems to leave every idea partly embedded in the undifferentiated mass of related ideas from which it has emerged. One way in which this effect came about was his rapid skimming from one metaphor to another, each of which contributes something of its implications – one can't be sure how much – before the next appears. A clear example – though not his best as poetry – occurs in 'Moses':

  Fine! Fine!
See, in my brain
What madmen have rushed through
And like a tornado
Torn up the tight roots
Of some dead universe:
The old clay is broken
For a power to soak in and knit
It all into tougher tissues
To hold life;
Pricking my nerves till the brain might crack
It boils to my finger-tips,
Till my hands ache to grip
The hammer – the lone hammer
That breaks lives into a road
Through which my genius drives.

The compression which Rosenberg's use of language gave him is therefore totally unlike the compression of acute conversation – such for example as some of Siegfried Sassoon's verse offers – in which a highly differentiated idea is presented through the most effective *illustration* that can be found. Rosenberg rarely or never illustrated his ideas by writing; he reached them through writing.

  With this as his attitude to language it is not surprising that he should have had the habit of reworking phrases and images again and again, developing out of them meanings which were not 'the' meaning he had originally wanted to 'express' with them. Emerging, as they seem to have done, from a wide context of feeling, his more interesting images carried with them a richer or subtler meaning than Rosenberg could feel he had exhausted in one poem, and he would therefore use them again in another. This happened with 'Heights of night ringing with unseen larks', a phrase that first reports an actual incident during the war, and is then used by the Nubian in 'The Unicorn' to contrast the mystery-exploiting femininity of his own girls with the vividness of Lilith:

  Our girls have hair
Like heights of night ringing with never-seen larks,
Or blindness dim with dreams:
Here is a yellow tiger gay that blinds your night.

Moreover in the first of these poems he had said that the dropping
of the larks' song when death might as easily have dropped was

> Like a blind man's dreams on the sand
> By dangerous tides;
> Like a girl's dark hair, for she dreams no ruin lies there.
> . . .

It is this reworking of images – developing first one set of
possibilities and then another – which gives one the impression of
Rosenberg's having as it were modelled in language.

The idea of a sack for the soul is similarly reworked and
developed. It occurs twice in 'Moses': first simply, 'we give
you . . . skin sacks for souls', as a contemptuous description of
the Hebrew slaves; then the soul sack becomes the body and the
habits of ordinary life to be thrown off in Moses's spiritual
development:

> Soul-sack fall away
> And show what you hold!

And finally the emptiness and collapsedness of the sack allows it
to be used of the bodies of the dead flung on the earth:

> And flung on your hard back
> Is their souls' sack,
> Emptied of God-ancestralled essences.

'God-ancestralled essences' in turn reappears in 'The Unicorn'
where they are said to be contaminated by

> . . . . a crazed shadow from no golden body
> That poisons at the core
> What smiles may stray.

The obscurity of this is relieved if one sees that it comes from an
earlier poem beginning,

> Crazed shadows, from no golden body
> That I can see . . .

and ending,

> And poison at the core
> What smiles may stray.

That poem deals with evil abroad at night – shadows forming without any 'golden body' as source of light – and in 'The Unicorn' the ideas have been remodelled so as to suggest the humdrum middle-aged evil of Saul which is mauling Lilith's love and beauty.

All this may only amount to saying that when Rosenberg got a good phrase he tried to make the most of it, though it equally suggests what an interesting process making the most of a phrase may be. Naturally, too, it need not be supposed that Rosenberg was unique or even – among poets – very unusual in treating language in this way. What is unusual, however, is his willingness to publish several uses of the same phrase or image (and there are many more instances than I have quoted), so that what may be a fairly common process is, in Rosenberg's work, available for examination. Moreover, although the process may be familiar in the writing of poetry, it is by no means usual in ordinary language, and there can be no doubt that it has special significance as a means of exploring and ordering the affective sources from which we draw our more manageable mental life.

SOURCE: 'Aspects of the Poetry of Isaac Rosenberg', *Scrutiny*, III, 4 (1935); reprinted in *Experience into Words* (London, 1963), pp. 91–103.

Siegfried Sassoon   (1937)

'A strenuous effort for impassioned expression'

It has been considered appropriate that I should say something about the poems of Isaac Rosenberg. I can only hope that what I say, inadequate though it may be, will help to gain for him the full recognition of his genius which has hitherto been delayed. In reading and re-reading these poems I have been strongly impressed by their depth and integrity. I have found a sensitive and vigorous mind energetically interested in experimenting with language, and I have recognised in Rosenberg a fruitful fusion between English and Hebrew culture. Behind all his poetry there is a racial quality – biblical and prophetic. Scriptural and sculptural are the epithets I would apply to him. His experiments were a strenuous effort for impassioned expression; his imagination had a sinewy and muscular aliveness; often he saw things in terms of sculpture, but he did not carve or chisel; he *modelled* words with fierce energy and aspiration, finding ecstasy in form, dreaming in grandeurs of superb light and deep shadow; his poetic visions are mostly in sombre colours and looming sculptural masses, molten and amply wrought. Watching him working with words, I find him a poet of movement; words which express movement are often used by him and are essential to his natural utterance.

  Rosenberg was not consciously a 'war poet'. But the war destroyed him, and his few but impressive 'Trench Poems' are a central point in this book. They have the controlled directness of a man finding his true voice and achieving mastery of his material; words and images obey him, instead of leading him into over-elaboration. They are all of them fine poems, but 'Break of Day in the Trenches' has for me a poignant and nostalgic quality which eliminates critical analysis. Sensuous front-line existence is there, hateful and repellent, unforgettable and inescapable. And beyond this poem I see the poems he might have written after the war, and the life he might have lived when life began again beyond and behind those trenches which were the limbo of all sane humanity and world-improving imagination. For the spirit of poetry looks beyond life's trench-lines. And Isaac Rosenberg was naturally empowered with something of the divine spirit which touches our human clay to sublimity of expression.

Here, in this book, we have his immaturity and achievement. Both are wonderful and manifold in richness. Having said what I can, I lay this reverent wreath upon his tomb.

SOURCE: Foreword to Gordon Bottomley and Denys Harding (eds), *The Collected Works of Isaac Rosenberg* (London, 1937), pp. vii–viii.

PART THREE

Recent Studies

1. ON THE WAR POETS IN LITERATURE

Philip Hobsbaum   The Road Not Taken
(1961)

Modernism in English poetry is beginning to seem something of an American imposition. Forty years after its publication it is not hard to see that *The Waste Land*, whatever its merits, has prompted some of the worst writing in English. At the moment, critics appear to be in search of a tradition of English verse which could adapt itself to modern needs. Some of the critics who attack modernism have turned to the Georgians instead.

They feel, I suppose, that the Georgians preserved the English tradition in the face of modernist incursion. And there is enough truth in this to make it a dangerous heresy. I would certainly agree that Eliot and Pound attacked a moribund Victorian tradition and substituted for it what was very much an American one. But if the Georgians preserved the tradition at all they did so only in so far as they mummified it. The very best of them – Masefield, say, or Sassoon – do seem to be handling modern experience, but with rather a late-Victorian technique.

Because of this, it seems that neither English Georgianism nor American Modernism had much to offer the rising generation. That such a choice should have arisen was really a historical accident, and of the grimmest kind: I mean the first world war. At least three poets died who, if they had survived, would surely have constituted a big challenge to the prevailing standards in poetry: as big a challenge, perhaps, as in their own time was presented by the Romantics. I am thinking of Edward Thomas, Wilfred Owen and Isaac Rosenberg.

Only a superficial classification would relate Edward Thomas to the Georgians. His poems certainly relate to an English tradition. But it was one that had been much misunderstood, as was shown by the cool reception of Hardy's *Wessex Poems* in 1898. This tradition was as much one of prose as of verse: the tradition of Cobbett and Jefferies – on whom, as a critic, Thomas had written most eloquently. Indeed, it was Thomas's own prose that led his friend, Robert Frost, to suggest that he should try his hand at poetry. Thomas never actually followed Frost's advice to write up his nature studies into free verse. But there is no doubt that much of Thomas's strength is that he has no time for the merely 'poetic'. His poetry really is 'a valley of this restless mind'. He objectifies his inner emotions in terms of landscape, or even fiction. That is to say, Thomas will often act out his feelings in terms of story, scene and character, rather than state it in his own person. And this brings him close to the writings of the Romantics – Wordsworth, for example, whose best work is in narrative form, and is akin to the great nineteenth-century novelists, themselves the heirs of Shakespeare. This inclination towards fiction rather than autobiography or lyric is character-istic of much good English poetry.

Palgrave's attempt to exclude all but lyric from the canon of English verse gave us a singularly denuded *Golden Treasury*. Hardy, who had grown up in the age of Palgrave, was concerned to point out rather deprecatingly – in his introduction to *Wessex Poems* – the fictional element in his own verse. And perhaps it was this element of fiction in Thomas's work, as well, that disturbed the Georgians. It is notable that the lyric 'Adlestrop', rather a conventional production, was for years Thomas's prime an-thology piece, as 'The Darkling Thrush' was Hardy's. There is nothing so decisively great in Thomas's output as Hardy's cycle *Veteris vestigia flammae*. But no more than for Hardy does the countryside represent for Thomas an escape. Thomas has been much admired for his powers of observation and presentation of particulars. And they are remarkable. But more remarkable still is Thomas's placing of war as a senseless evil against the life-giving rhythms of the countryside. This can be seen in his poem entitled 'As the Team's Head-brass'. Here, the certainty of the ploughman's coming and going is contrasted with the delays and uncertainties of the war. The lovers going into the wood, the ploughman harrowing the clods, are an assertion of life against maiming and death. And the war's encroachment on these rhythms is symbolised by the fallen tree that, if the ploughman's mate had returned from France, would have been moved long ago. The relationship with Hardy's war poems is clear enough. One thinks most immediately of 'In Time of "The Breaking of Nations"'—where there is also a pair of lovers and a ploughman.

The difference between Thomas and even the better Georgians is that his work is an advance on that of the poetry of a previous generation. His is a genuinely modern sensibility. His view of life has none of the heroics easily assumed by those who never saw action, or who joined the army in a spirit of public-school patriotism. But Thomas had little chance to write trench poetry. His best work was written before going to France, while training as an officer. He had time to contrast the English countryside he was leaving with the Front—known only by hearsay and implication—he was going to. And he was killed soon after reaching it.

There were Georgians who saw more action than Thomas; most notably Sassoon. And Sassoon's poems certainly include much first-hand reaction to experience. But I am not so sure that his technique is equal to his sensibility. In 'Break of Day' he presents an escape from battle into the memory of a happy day's hunting. Here we have the detailed realism for which Sassoon was to become famous. No doubt this is a strong poem if compared with the early, and now suppressed, war poems of Graves. Graves is prone to smother his action in whimsy and allusion. But, if we think of Edward Thomas, Sassoon's tone seems overinsistent; and perhaps the most telling comparison is with Wilfred Owen.

It cannot be too often stressed that Owen's technique is not just a matter of half-rhyme. Half-rhyme had been used before in English; though not, it is true, so systematically. Owen's genius can be localised in the actual function of the play of the vowels. They mute those over-confident metres which Owen, in common with other war poets, inherited from the previous, more peaceful, generation. He makes them as exploratory and tentative as his feelings about war. In comparison, Sassoon's verse seems too assured for its content. It is impossible to feel that 'Strange Meeting', for example, will ever date.

Owen's verse, like Thomas's, is akin to fiction rather than lyric. He will use himself, as in 'Strange Meeting', as an interlocutor; or he will don the mask of narration or of dramatic monologue.

Even when he seems to be speaking more directly, as in his poem 'Exposure', he will use the first person plural rather than singular. So that he seems to be speaking for all the soldiers of the war, not just himself. His details are never merely descriptive. In 'Exposure', they are selected to create an atmosphere and a human attitude – the cold, and the soldiers waiting. It is rather too simple to regard Owen as the poet who hated war. His verse has a distinctively modern ambivalence. In 'Exposure' as well as a grim endurance on the part of the troops, there is a desire for action – a desire which is mocked by the way in which the weather is presented in this poem through a metaphor of war: dawn massing in the east her melancholy army.

Owen recognises with startling modernity that death can be as certain out of battle as in it, and dispiritingly inglorious. His poems are the defeat of lyric; anything but a subjective cry of pain. We are not asked to take an interest in something just because it was happening to Wilfred Owen. A point is made, through the evocation of a war, about war itself. Owen's landscape has all the conviction of Sassoon's with an impersonality which Sassoon never achieved. Not one death is expressed in Owen's work, but many.

> Tonight, His frost will fasten on this mud and us,
> Shrivelling many hands, puckering foreheads crisp.
> The burying-party, picks and shovels in their shaking grasp,
> Pause over half-known faces. All their eyes are ice,
>   But nothing happens.

Like Owen, Isaac Rosenberg characteristically uses the plural first person. But he appears to use words (as Professor Harding has remarked) without any of the usual couplings – as though the poetry were formed at a subconscious pre-verbal level. Although as authentic as Owen's stretcher-party, that of Rosenberg is alarmingly unexpected.

> A man's brains splattered on
> A stretcher-bearer's face;
> His shook shoulders slipped their load,
> But when they bent to look again
> The drowning soul was sunk too deep
> For human tenderness.

One can see why Gordon Bottomley, Rosenberg's first editor, was so hesitant about publishing this poetry. And why, even when it was published, it took so long to make its way. Even the iambic metres have been abandoned in this plasm of verse.

Rosenberg's technical innovations cannot be so readily discussed in terms of a past norm as those of his fellows. One can see in the lines of Owen's 'Strange Meeting' the rhythms of the induction to 'The Fall of Hyperion'; but muted down, made tentative by the half-rhyme. The poem gains much of its strength through an application of familiar material to an utterly new situation. Keats's goddesses occur, too, in Rosenberg's 'Daughters of War'. But that is as far as resemblance goes. The myth is created in strikingly personal terms – a kind of sprung verse, for example, developed quite independently of Hopkins. To find Rosenberg's antecedents, one has to look at the juvenilia, as one does with Hopkins's surprisingly Keats-like fragments. The mature poems resemble nothing but themselves – though there are signs that gifted young poets of our own time, such as Ted Hughes and Peter Redgrove, have learned from them. It would be absurd, then, to call Rosenberg a traditionalist, except in the sense that he is in the tradition of Keats and Shakespeare. His sprung verse, use of myth, are wholly unlike anything produced by the 'traditional' Georgians. It is as though an overmastering experience had blasted out a new form.

> The old bark burnt with iron wars
> They blow to a live flame
> To char the young green days
> And reach the occult soul; they have no softer lure –
> No softer lure than the savage ways of death.

Nobody could call this traditional in manner or content. Yet it is certainly not modernist, if by modernist one thinks of a play of images, a montage in free verse. If Rosenberg's verse has affinities, it is not with Eliot or Pound but with the apocalyptic prose of Lawrence. Not, indeed, with Lawrence's verse, which seems to go more diffuse as it gets further from Hardy and nearer to Whitman. Rosenberg, unlike the modernists, does not go in for phanopoeia or free association. His poems exist through images, but never for them. And the poems are not autobiographical, though they may be a projection of his inner feelings, in terms of myth. Rosenberg projects outwards. As in 'Daughters of War', he creates a fiction in which feelings are acted out. Like Thomas and Owen, he conveys his emotion through poems about something other than himself.

These poets used forms and, at the same time, changed them. Thomas used Wordsworthian blank verse that had also learned from the nineteenth-century novelists, and so could absorb narrative and symbolic properties. Owen muted the rhythms of the romantics by the use of pararhyme, and applied the romantic sensuousness to a new and grimmer end. Rosenberg manipulated events even more resourcefully than the others, and revitalised dramatic blank verse into a sprung rhythm that has not been fully exploited even now. They all marked an advance not only in technique but in sensibility. The world of 1911 must have seemed very remote in 1915. A glance at the newspapers of the time would establish the difference in terms of an increased sense of strain, a wedge driven between the generations, criticism of hitherto accepted values by the young. But it was only the exceptional writers who could get much of this into their verse. In the last analysis, the success of Thomas, Owen and Rosenberg as poets could be attributed to their recognition of the need to adapt the old forms to express new experience.

This should differentiate them on the one hand from the modernists, who broke forms down, and, on the other, from the Georgians, who relied on them even when they proved inapplicable to modern experience. But Thomas, Owen and Rosenberg died young. And, after the war, two rival schools of poetry contended for attention in the anthologies *Georgian Poetry* and *Wheels*. The debate was irrelevant to the facts, as J. M. Murry pointed out at the time, in a review of the two volumes. He said that the only distinction he himself would be prepared to recognise was one of quality. And such quality he found in the one good poem which appeared in either of the anthologies: it was 'Strange Meeting'.

The younger progressive critics, such as Leavis and Roberts, got rather taken in, it seems to me, not by Eliot's poetry but by his position vis-á-vis tradition. They commended Eliot's example to the rising generation; a generation which, it is now acknowledged, went dangerously off the rails. Certainly it never fulfilled its promise. One remembers the pylon poetry and the hopeful pastiches that used to be made of Ezra Pound. And there is all that vague intimation of impending revolution that dissipated so promptly after Spain. The similarities between the so-called social realists of the nineteen-thirties and the romantics who followed hard upon their heels are very evident. They most of them misapplied the stream-of-consciousness technique and used free verse of extraordinary obscurity. Common to most of them, also, was the free association of autobiographical symbols. In the nineteen-forties it became the fashion for writers, even those of undeniable talent, to switch off their intellect before they started composing.

Poets of Auden's generation could have saved themselves by learning less from Eliot and Pound and more from Thomas, Owen and, perhaps especially, Rosenberg. But history was against them. My main thesis, I suppose, is that English poetry in the twentieth century has had four atrocious strokes of luck. They are worth enumerating. First of all, that the wrong emphasis should have been placed on the work of the one great Victorian who could have had a useful influence – I mean Hardy. Secondly, that the Georgians, for the most part, should have chosen to regard tradition as a resting-place rather than a spring-board. Third, that three of the poets who *were* developing an essentially English modernity should have been killed in the war – their publication, too, was a delayed and incomplete one. And, lastly, that Eliot and Pound should have chosen to start an essentially American revolution in verse technique over here rather than in the United States, and so filled the gap which the death of the war poets left with an alien product whose influence has been a bad one.

Of these points, the third is undoubtedly the most important. If Thomas, Owen and Rosenberg had lived, there would have been no question of having to choose between revolution . and reaction – a choice which has never particularly appealed to the English temperament. What is best in English poetry generally is what we find in the uncompleted work of these three poets: what Thom Gunn called 'vigour within the discipline of shape'. Freedom won, that is, not through breaking down a form but through reshaping it. These poets represent the central line of English poetry through the Romantics back to Shakespeare, and

I cannot see much good work being done far away from it. But, like any tradition, it is only alive as long as it can be recreated. Nevertheless I do not think I am being too hopeful when I say that it seems to be in process of recreation, after a long quiescence, at the present time.

SOURCE: Third Programme talk, published in *The Listener*, 23 November 1961, pp. 860, 863; another version of this study appears as chapter 11 in *Tradition and Experiment in English Poetry* (London, 1979).

Donald Davie   In the Pity (1964)

When Yeats in 1936 excluded Wilfred Owen from the *Oxford Book of Modern Verse*, there was a storm of protest. Now when a professor from West Virginia painstakingly and at length endorses Yeats's verdict, no one complains.[1] I find this depressing. 'The poetry is in the pity', said Owen. And Yeats was right: that is not the place for poetry to be, or not so exclusively. Owen was too categorical, and British poetry since has suffered for it. It has been, and it is still, too humanitarian to be altogether human. But failure on these terms is almost more honourable than success; it was certainly more honourable for Owen, writing as and when he did. Professor Johnston's sub-title, 'A Study in the Evolution of Lyric and Narrative Form', from this point of view seems comically irrelevant, even to those of us who are professional students of literature, at least if we are British. There were war-poets writing in German, in French, in Italian, in Russian; and it would have done no harm for Professor Johnston to remind himself of this. And there are Canadian and American poets in Brian Gardner's new anthology,[2] as well as Yeats himself, with 'An Irish Airman Foresees his Death'. But among English-speakers the experience of the Flanders trenches was overwhelmingly a British experience, and was felt to be so at the time. In fact, the poems themselves characteristically appeal to 'England' and 'the English', and it's not clear in every case that England means Britain, and English British. At any rate, this writing which Johnston deals with as a case in the evolution of *genre* can be seen, and I think must be seen by the British reader, as documenting a crisis in the life of his nation. The British imagination, it may be, has never to this day recovered from the shock of Passchendaele; and the damage done to it there puts the British writer out of step with the Americans, not just Graves out of step with Eliot, but at the present day Larkin and Hughes out of step with Charles Olson and William Stafford.

Yeats the Irishman did not think like this, nor does the American Johnston. Johnston would have to deny the thesis in any case, because he believes there is one work in which a British imagination comprehended and mastered the Flanders experience, and this is David Jones's *In Parenthesis*, written in 1937, which draws on the precedent of *The Waste Land* and so heals the breach between British and American. It was high time that such claims were made for *In Parenthesis*, but even so Jones's book may still be the exception which proves the rule – the rule that since 1917 the British imagination has been as it were cauterised, numbed to large sectors of experience.

These are the sectors which Johnston would label epic and tragic. For his argument is that trench-warfare demanded, if it was to be comprehended in poetry, some form other than lyric, though lyric was all that the poets of the trenches could command. This means that Johnston is not after all of one mind with Yeats. For Yeats's objection to Owen was quite bluntly that Owen wrote badly. He said he considered him 'unworthy of the poets' corner of a country newspaper'. And he exhorted Dorothy Wellesley to 'look at the selection in Faber's Anthology – he calls poets "bards", a girl a "maid" and talks about "Titanic wars." ' – Yeats is simple-minded here, because there are surely contexts in which 'bard' for 'poet', and 'maid' for 'girl', are perfectly acceptable expressions and in fact better than any others. One of the best things in Johnston's book is the persuasive case he makes for the war-poems of Blunden, whose diction is characteristically very choice and elaborate and 'poetical'. This doesn't help Owen, however. Blunden maintains decorum, and is consistent within his often stilted conventions, as Owen is not. Owen *does* write badly, he just is not skilful nor resourceful enough to do justice to his own conceptions:

> Kindness of wooed and wooer
> Seems shame to their love pure.
> O love, your eyes lose lure
>   When I behold eyes blinded in my stead!

That sequence of rhymes – *wooer, pyuer, luer* – is excruciating. And if this is true of Owen, what shall we say of Rosenberg? Even Johnston, who seldom stoops to notice these niceties and nastinesses of wording, is worried about whether Rosenberg's 'Dead Man's Dump' is not just a sheet of memoranda for a poem that never got written.

But even if Yeats is thus proved right, what follows? That 'Dead Man's Dump', and Owen's 'Greater Love', ought to be forgotten? They will not be. If we are moved when we read them, far more moved (this is certainly my own case) than by Yeats's 'Irish Airman', ought we to be ashamed? Certainly as a poem in any strict sense 'Dead Man's Dump' is indefensible. But the truth is surely that for the British reader these pieces by Rosenberg and Owen are not poems at all, but something less than that and more; they are first-hand and faithful witnesses to a moment in the national destiny. Or if that sounds chauvinistic, think of them as high-water marks in the national psychology. In Owen's 'Anthem for Doomed Youth' an Englishman is brought to the point where, like Ivan Karamazov, he 'returns God the ticket'. The nightmare perspectives of Dostoievskyan psychology, which in 1880 had seemed outside the range of British experience, by 1917 are being verified in that experience. And these gulfs and vistas are experienced not vicariously, not in the imagination of a novelist, but directly: it is as if the poems were written by Ivan Karamazov, and no wonder if Karamazov is not so good a novelist as Dostoievsky. It is part of the pathos and the meaning of Owen and Rosenberg that they should be amateurs – amateur soldiers but amateur poets too, and amateurs not as Robert Gregory was ('our Sidney and our perfect man,' said Yeats of that Irish airman), but in a sense that has everything to do with the amateurish. So too with Sassoon:

The House is crammed: tier beyond tier they grin
And cackle at the Show, while prancing ranks
Of harlots shrill the chorus, drunk with din;
'We're sure the Kaiser loves our dear old Tanks!'

I'd like to see a Tank come down the stalls,
Lurching to rag-time tunes, or 'Home, sweet Home',
And there'd be no more jokes in Music-halls
To mock the riddled corpses round Bapaume.

Any beginner can see that calling chorus-girls 'harlots' loses all
the actuality of them as girls and gets nothing in return except the
scandalised huffing and puffing of some Mrs Grundy Alderman;
and he can see that having the line-break between 'grin' and
'cackle' only shows up how little 'cackle' has to add. But for
heaven's sake, what does it matter? Sassoon's eight lines are
amateurish writing – who ever thought otherwise? The value of
the eight lines, for a British reader, has really nothing to do with
their very dubious status as poetic art.

The professional of that generation was Blunden. Earlier it had
been Brooke. And if Brooke had not existed, it would have been
necessary to invent him. For without Rupert Brooke as their foil,
both Owen and Sassoon would shrink; to the poetry of the
trenches considered as recording a moment in the national
destiny, Brooke's 'If I should die' weighs equal with 'Strange
Meeting'. Grenfell's 'Into Battle' will not do instead of Brooke's
sonnet, nor will Sorley's 'All the hills and vales along', which
alone among the poems of the early years can bear up under our
hindsight. For Grenfell and Sorley are both amateurish beside
Brooke; and just as Sassoon and Owen need to be amateurish if
they are to keep their legendary pathos, so Brooke on the other
hand has to be, in every corrupted suavity of style as well as in all
we know of his biography, the professional master of language,
the expensively schooled rhetorician equipped as it must have
seemed completely against all eventualities that Edwardian
England could conceive of.

The myth must be symmetrical. It must be a golden boy who
fails. So it is as wide of the mark to see Brooke as a bad, a hollow
and dishonest and heartless poet, as it is to pretend that Owen,
because he rhymed badly and knew it and took the sensible
precaution of allowing himself half-rhyme, was by that token an

artistic innovator who transformed and renewed the medium for himself and others. 'Above all', said Owen, 'I am not concerned with Poetry.' And Johnston does not convince me that the poetry which Owen here disowned was 'the thoughtless pursuit of beauty', or else that Brookean poetry which he had begun by writing himself. Owen means, surely, that if he is to be set up against Rupert Brooke, it is not as one kind of poet against another kind (as it might be, the clumsily honest against the brilliantly hollow), but as the English soldier of 1917 against his own still illusioned self, the English soldier of 1914. It is a quarrel with history, or with God; but it is a very private quarrel, having to do with one generation in one nation at one very precisely specified time.

Johnston does not see the trenches poets in this way, and there is no reason why he should. For us as British readers it is salutary to be made to realise what a specially insular and self-regarding attitude we have to these poets, and how impossible it is for others to share our assumptions. In particular we need to have it brought home to us how, so long as the poetry is in the pity, it cannot be tragic poetry. But in fact Professor Johnston has rather little to say of tragedy: what he misses in the trenches poets is less the tragic note than the note of epic. *The Battle of Maldon* is his example of what he means by an epic poem. And it is just as well that we have this example, otherwise we might be thinking rather of something like *Sohrab and Rustum*. For there is a distinctly high-Victorian ring, an inflection of Arnold or Pater, about the terms in which the epic is commended to us: its breadth and harmony, its proportion and reposefulness or at least its composure – these are the qualities which Johnston looks for in vain until he gets to David Jones.

In Parenthesis, he suggests, is modern epic; and therefore necessarily superior to the poems written between 1914 and 1918, all lyrics of various kinds. The trouble is that we get no definition of modern epic. It seems that it will be narrative; and yet one of the few modern poems which explicitly offers itself as epic, Pound's *Cantos*, is not narrative at all. Nor is *Y Gododdin*, the ancient Welsh poem which stands behind *In Parenthesis*. Johnston concedes that *Y Gododdin* 'may not be epic poetry in the formal sense' (what other sense can the word have?) 'but it communicates the heroic spirit nearly as well as any epic narrative'.

It is that 'heroic spirit' that gives the game away. The truth is that Professor Johnston just wants to like war and warfare more than Owen and Sassoon will permit. There is nothing more subtle than that at stake when he deplores in them the lack of the heroic spirit. There could be no better testimony to the continuing sharpness and relevance of these poems, Sassoon's in particular, than the signs of how they have needled one reader into 350 pages of muffled expostulation, so as to argue himself out of accepting what they incontrovertibly assert.

SOURCE: article in *New Statesman*, 28 August 1964, pp. 282–3.

NOTES

1. John H. Johnston, *English Poetry of the First World War* (Princeton, N. J., 1964). [An extract from this book is given below – Ed.]
2. B. Gardner (ed.), *Up the Line to Death: War Poets 1914–18* (London, 1964; new edn 1976).
3. The relevant passage from Yeats's letter is given in Part Two above [Ed.].

Paul Fussell   Roses and Poppies (1975)

As Rupert Brooke asserts in 'The Soldier', one of England's main attractions is that she provides 'flowers to love'. As Brooke and his friends knew, a standard way of writing the Georgian poem was to get as many flowers into it as possible. Edward Thomas could make virtually a whole poem by naming flora, as he does in 'October'. In the same tradition is Brooke's 'The Old Vicarage: Grantchester', written in 'exile' in Germany before the war. The garden Brooke imagines there is 'English' both in the careless variety of its species and in the freedom in which they flourish:

> Just now the lilac is in bloom,
> All before my little room;

> And in my flower-beds, I think,
> Smile the carnation and the pink;
> And down the borders, well I know,
> The poppy and the pansy blow.

The trouble with Germany is that everything is orderly and forced and obedient:

> Here tulips bloom as they are told.

It is different in England, where

> Unkempt about those hedges blows
> An English unofficial rose.

Brooke wrote this poem two years before the war, but already the Georgian focus was appearing to narrow down to the red flowers, especially roses and poppies, whose blood-colours would become an indispensable part of the symbolism of the war. Stephen Graham's gardener-soldiers instinctively grasped the principle when . . . they massed 'the crimson of many blossoms . . . to give a suggestion of passion and loyalty and suffering'.[1] The troops who used *rose-coloured* as a jocular periphrasis for *bloody* perhaps understood, in their way, the same principle. An ancient tradition associates battle scars with roses, perhaps because a newly healed wound often does look like a red or pink rose. In *The Tribune's Visitation* David Jones's Roman officer explains this association in his pep talk:

. . . within this sacred college we can speak *sub rosa* and the rose that seals our confidence is that red scar that shines on the limbs of each of us who have the contact with the fire of Caesar's enemies, and if on some of us that sear burns, then on all, on you tiros no less than on these *veterani*. . . .[2]

The time-honoured image wound/rose has found its way into Wallace Stevens's 'Esthétique du Mal':

> How red the rose that is the soldier's wound,
> The wounds of many soldiers, the wounds of all
> The soldiers that have fallen, red in blood,
> The soldier of time grown deathless in great size.

Redness: when the news of a soldier's death is brought to his parents' house in Hardy's 'Before Marching and After', written in September 1915,

>   the fuchsia-bells, hot in the sun,
> Hung red by the door.

In 'Bombardment', Lawrence conceives of a town being bombed as

>   a flat red lily with a million petals

The person who waited outside Buckingham Palace on 3 August 1914, hoping to catch a sight of the King, and who testified later to noticing that 'the red geraniums . . . looked redder than they had ever looked before', was deepening their red in retrospect.[3]

Roses were indispensable to the work of the imagination during and after the Great War, not because Belgium and France were full of them, but because English poetry was, and because since the Middle Ages they had connoted 'England' and 'loyalty' and 'sacrifice'. As Frye says:

In the West the rose has a traditional priority among apocalyptic flowers; the use of the rose as a communion symbol in the *Paradiso* comes readily to mind, and in the first book of *The Faerie Queene* the emblem of St George, a red cross on a white ground, is connected not only with the risen body of Christ and the sacramental symbolism which accompanies it, but with the union of the red and white roses in the Tudor dynasty.[4]

A typical use of the rose during the war was to make it virtually equal to the idea of England. Even though France has her roses, they are somehow not hers but England's. 'Life was good out of the line that September', writes Philip Gibbs of the year 1915. 'It was good to go into the garden of a French château and pluck a rose and smell its sweetness, and think back to England, where other roses were blooming. England!'[5] For David Jones, the rose means more than England: it means England-in-the-spring. The dog-rose, he says, 'moves something in the Englishman at a deeper level than the Union Flag' because English poetry, 'drawing upon the intrinsic qualities of the familiar and common June rose, has . . . managed to recall and evoke, for the English, a June-England association.'[6] For ordinary people roses connoted loyalty to England, service to it, and sacrifice for it. When after Loos Liddell Hart was carried wounded through Charing Cross station, he found roses cast on to his stretcher by the crowd. And 'this happened again the following year', he says, 'when I was brought back from the battle of the Somme.'[7] The 'bar' to the Military Cross indicating a second award is not a bar at all: the device added to the ribbon is a little silver rose.

The rose is indispensable to popular sentimental texts of the war, from the song 'Roses of Picardy' to

> The roses round the door
> Makes me love mother more,

'the favourite song of the men', as Owen reports from France in January, 1917; 'they sing this everlastingly'.[8] 'Crimson roses' symbolising sacrificial love are at the centre of one of Stephen Graham's most sentimental anecdotes. A Sergeant Oliver of the Sixth Black Watch was shot, Graham tells us, when he went forward in violation of orders to fraternise with the enemy on Christmas Day, 1915. (Sentries on both sides had been ordered to kill anyone trying to re-enact the famous Christmas truce of the year before.) This sergeant, Graham found, is buried in 'a little old cemetery by the side of the road a mile or so from Laventie'. From his grave is growing – this is English literature, we realise – 'a tall rose tree with crimson roses blooming even in autumn'. It is especially noticeable because 'beside him lies one who was both captain and knight, with only a dock rising from his feet'. Indeed, 'On all graves are weeds except on that of the man who gave his life to shake hands on Christmas Day.'[9] And because crimson roses are thus associated with sacrificial love, they have been made a conspicuous feature of the British military cemeteries in France.

In a brilliant essay Erwin Panofsky has discovered that ever since the eighteenth century the English have had an instinct not shared by Continentals for making a special kind of sense out of the classical tag *Et in Arcadia ego*. Far from taking it as 'And I have dwelt in Arcadia too', they take it to mean (correctly) 'Even in Arcadia I, Death, hold sway'. As Panofsky says, this meaning, 'while long forgotten on the Continent, remained familiar' in England, and ultimately 'became part of what may be termed a specifically English or "insular" tradition – a tradition which tended to retain the idea of a *memento mori*'. Skulls juxtaposed with roses could be conventionally employed as an emblem of the omnipotence of Death, whose power is not finally to be excluded even from the sequestered, 'safe' world of pastoral. 'In . . . Waugh's *Brideshead Revisited*', Panofsky points out, 'the narrator, while a sophisticated undergraduate at Oxford, adorns his rooms at college with a "human skull lately purchased from the School of Medicine which, resting on a bowl of roses, formed at the moment the chief decoration of my table. It bore the motto *Et in Arcadia ego* inscribed on its forehead." ' [10] This 'specifically English or "insular" tradition' added a special resonance of melancholy to wartime pastoral in general and to the invocation of roses in particular. 'Rose Trench', says Sassoon, 'Orchard Alley, Apple Alley, and Willow Avenue, were among the first objectives in our sector [of the Somme attack], and my mind very properly insisted on their gentler associations. Nevertheless, this topographical Arcadia was to be seized, cleared, and occupied. . . .' [11] Speaking of the rude violation by facts of the troops' early illusions, C. E. Montague puts it in this very English, indeed Blakean, way: 'At the heart of the magical rose was seated an earwig.' Those finally saw the earwig who saw 'trenches full of gassed men, and the queue of their friends at the brothel-door in Béthune.' [12] The English understanding of *Et in Arcadia ego* is enacted when Cloete's Jim Hilton, wandering amidst the rubble at Ypres, comes upon 'a little courtyard garden'. There, 'a rose was in flower. He picked it. . . . There were dead buried in the rubble. You could smell them – sickly, sweet, putrid – an odour that mixed with that of the red rose in his hand.' [13] It is like the smell of the aging Billy Pilgrim's breath when late in nights after drinking he decides to telephone his old Army friends all over the country: on those occasions his breath smells 'like mustard gas and roses'. [14]

The case of the other red flower inseparable from writings about the Great War, the poppy, is even more complicated and interesting. Properly speaking, the Flanders poppy – it is called that now – is *Papaver rhœas*, to be distinguished from the kind generally known in the United States, the California poppy, or *Platystemon californicus*. The main difference is that the California poppy is orange or yellow, the Flanders poppy bright scarlet. The familiarity of the California poppy to Americans has always created some impediment to their accurate interpretation of the rich and precise literary symbolism of Great War writing. If one imagines poppies as orange or yellow, those that blow between the crosses, row on row, will seem a detail more decorative than symbolic. One will be likely to miss their crucial relation (the coincidence of McCrae's* and Milton's rhyme-sound will suggest it) to that 'sanguine flower inscrib'd with woe' of *Lycidas* and with the 'red or purple flower', as Frye reminds us, 'that turns up everywhere in pastoral elegy'.[15] Flanders fields are actually as dramatically profuse in bright blue cornflowers as in scarlet poppies. But blue cornflowers have no connection with English pastoral elegiac tradition, and won't do. The same principle determines that of all the birds visible and audible in France, only larks and nightingales shall be selected to be remembered and 'used'. One notices and remembers what one has been 'coded' – usually by literature or its popular equivalent – to notice and remember. It would be a mistake to imagine that the poppies in Great War writings get there just because they are actually there in the French and Belgian fields. In his sentimental, elegiac *The Challenge of the Dead* (1921), Stephen Graham produces a book of 176 pages without once noticing a poppy, although he chooses to notice plenty of other indigenous flowers, including roses and cornflowers. We can guess that he omits poppies because their tradition is not one he wants to evoke in his book, the point of which is that survivors should now imitate the sacrifice of the soldiers, who in turn were imitating the sacrifice of Christ. There is something about poppies that is too pagan, ironic, and hedonistic for his purposes. The same principle of literary selection – as opposed to 'documentary' or photography – is visible in a poem of the Second War by Herbert Corby. In 'Poem' he is projecting a contrast between pastoral serenity and its sinister opposite, the emblems of which are the flowers near his aerodrome and his own metallic airplane. The flowers he selects for this purpose are not any old flowers; they are specifically the two species already freighted with meaning from the earlier war:

> The pale wild roses star the banks of green
> and poignant poppies startle their fields with red, . . .

* In his 'In Flanders Fields', discussed below–Ed.

> I go to the plane among the peaceful clover,
> but climbing in the Hampden, shut myself in war.

By the time the troops arrived in France and Belgium, poppies had accumulated a ripe traditional symbolism in English writing, where they had been a staple since Chaucer. Their conventional connotation was the blessing of sleep and oblivion (that is, of a mock-death, greatly to be desired), as in Francis Thompson's 'The Poppy' or Tennyson's 'The Lotos-Eaters' (both in the *Oxford Book*). But during the last quarter of the nineteenth century the poppy began to take on additional connotations, some of which are discreetly glanced at by W. S. Gilbert in *Patience* (1881). There the aesthete Bunthorne, an exponent of 'sentimental passion', is made to sing.

> . . . if you walk down Picadilly with a poppy or a lily in
>   your medieval hand,
> . . . everyone will say,
> As you walk your flowery way,
> . . . what a most particularly pure young man this pure
>   young man must be!

Bunthorne's poppy is *Papaver orientale*, the floppy, scarlet kind. For late Victorians and Edwardians, it was associated specifically with homoerotic passion. In Lord Alfred Douglas's 'Two Loves', the allegorical figure who declares that he is 'the love that dare not speak its name' is a pale youth whose lips are 'red like poppies'. For half a century before the fortuitous publicity attained by the poppies of Flanders, this association with homoerotic love had been conventional, in works by Wilde, Douglas, the Victorian painter Simeon Solomon, John Addington Symonds, and countless others. No 'poppy' poem or reference emerging from the Great War could wholly shake off that association. When Sassoon notes that 'the usual symbolic scarlet poppies lolled over the sides of the communication trench',[16] he is aware, as we must be, that they symbolise something more than shed blood and oblivion.

One of the neatest 'turns' in popular symbolism is that by which the paper poppies sold for the benefit of the British Legion on November 11 can be conceived as emblems at once of oblivion and remembrance: a traditional happy oblivion of their agony by the dead, and at the same time an unprecedented mass remembrance of their painful loss by the living. These little paper simulacra come from pastoral elegy (Milton's Arcadian valleys 'purple all the ground with vernal flowers'), pass through Victorian male sentimental poetry, flesh themselves out in the actual blossoms of Flanders, and come back to be worn in buttonholes on Remembrance Day. In his 'A Short Poem for Armistice Day' Herbert Read is struck by the paper poppy's ironic inability to multiply as well as by its ironic resistance to 'fading' and dying. When he sees it as a sad antithesis to something like Milton's unfading amaranthus of *Lycidas*, we are reminded of the war's tradition of ironic wonder that the metal 'bramble thicket' is, as R. H. Sauter finds it in his poem 'Barbed Wire', 'unflowering'. Read's poem on the paper poppy enacts the inverse consolation appropriate to an inverse elegy involving inverse flowers.

The most popular poem of the war was John McCrae's 'In Flanders Fields', which appeared anonymously in *Punch* on December 6, 1915. Its poppies are one reason the British Legion chose that symbol of forgetfulness-remembrance, and indeed it could be said that the rigorously regular metre with which the poem introduces the poppies makes them seem already fabricated of wire and paper. It is an interesting poem because it manages to accumulate the maximum number of well-known motifs and images, which it gathers under the aegis of a mellow, if automatic, pastoralism. In its first nine lines it provides such familiar triggers of emotion as these: the red flowers of pastoral elegy; the 'crosses' suggestive of calvaries and thus of sacrifice; the sky, especially noticeable from the confines of a trench; the larks bravely singing in apparent criticism of man's folly; the binary opposition between the song of the larks and the noise of the guns; the special awareness of dawn and sunset at morning and evening stand-to's; the conception of soldiers as lovers; and the focus on the ironic antithesis between beds and the graves where 'now we lie'. Not least interesting is the poem's appropriation of the voice-from-the-grave device from such poems of Hardy's as 'Channel Firing' and 'Ah, Are You Digging on My Grave?' and its transformation of that device from a mechanism of irony to one of sentiment:

In Flanders fields the poppies blow
Between the crosses, row on row,
   That mark our place; and in the sky
   The larks, still bravely singing, fly
Scarce heard amid the guns below.

We are the Dead. Short days ago
We lived, felt dawn, saw sunset glow,
   Loved and were loved, and now we lie
   In Flanders fields.

So far, so pretty good. But things fall apart two-thirds of the way through as the vulgarities of 'Stand Up! Stand Up and Play the Game!' begin to make inroads into the pastoral, and we suddenly have a recruiting-poster rhetoric apparently applicable to any war:

Take up our quarrel with the foe:
To you from failing hands we throw
   The torch; be yours to hold it high.

(The reader who has responded to the poppies and crosses and larks and stand-to's, knowing that they point toward some trench referents, will wonder what that 'torch' is supposed to correspond to in trench life. It suggests only Emma Lazarus.)

If ye break faith with us who die
We shall not sleep, though poppies grow
   In Flanders fields.

We finally see – and with a shock – what the last six lines really are. They are a propaganda argument – words like *vicious* and *stupid* would not seem to go too far – against a negotiated peace; and it could be said that for the purpose, the rhetoric of Sir Henry Newbolt or Horatio Bottomley or the Little Mother is, alas, the appropriate one. But it is grievously out of contact with the symbolism of the first part, which the final image of poppies as sleep-inducers fatally recalls.

   I have not broken this butterfly upon the wheel for no reason. I have it to suggest the context and to try to specify the distinction of another 'poppy' poem, Isaac Rosenberg's 'Break of Day in the

Trenches', written seven months after McCrae's poem. I think it
superior even to Rosenberg's 'Dead Man's Dump', which would
make it, in my view, the greatest poem of the war. It is less
obvious and literal than 'Dead Man's Dump': everything is done
through indirection and the quiet, subtle exploitation of conventions of English pastoral poetry, especially pastoral elegy. It is
partly a great poem because it is a great traditional poem. But
while looking back on literary history in this way, it also acutely
looks forward, in its loose but accurate emotional cadences and in
the informality and leisurely insouciance of its gently ironic
idiom, which is, as Rosenberg indicated to Edward Marsh, 'as
simple as ordinary talk'.

>BREAK OF DAY IN THE TRENCHES
>The darkness crumbles away –
>It is the same old druid Time as ever.
>Only a live thing leaps my hand –
>A queer sardonic rat –
>As I pull the parapet's poppy
>To stick behind my ear.
>Droll rat, they would shoot you if they knew
>Your cosmopolitan sympathies.
>Now you have touched this English hand
>You will do the same to a German –
>Soon, no doubt, if it be your pleasure
>To cross the sleeping green between.
>It seems you inwardly grin as you pass
>Strong eyes, fine limbs, haughty athletes
>Less chanced than you for life,
>Bonds to the whims of murder,
>Sprawled in the bowels of the earth,
>The torn fields of France.
>What do you see in our eyes
>At the shrieking iron and flame
>Hurled through still heavens?
>What quaver – what heart aghast?
>Poppies whose roots are in man's veins
>Drop, and are ever dropping;
>But mine in my ear is safe,
>Just a little white with the dust.

The filaments reaching back to precedent poetry are numerous and richly evocative:

   The darkness crumbles away

inverts Nashe's

   Brightness falls from the air,

just as the literal trench *dust* of the last line translates Nashe's

   Dust hath closed Helen's eye

and invokes as well all the familiar *dusts* of Renaissance lyric-elegy which fall at the ends of lines:

   Leave me, O Love, which reacheth but to dust. (Sidney)

   Golden lads and girls all must,
   Like chimney-sweepers, come to dust. (Shakespeare)

   Only the actions of the just
   Smell sweet and blossom in their dust. (Shirley)

The *only* with which the third line begins recalls the opening dynamics of another poem which begins by finding a scene looking 'normal' only to discover that there is something disturbing in it that will require some unusual thought, feeling, or action. I am thinking of 'Dover Beach':

   The sea is calm tonight . . .
   Only . . .

So Rosenberg begins:

   The darkness crumbles away –
   It is the same old druid Time as ever.
    Only a live thing leaps my hand –

'You might object to the second line as vague', he wrote Marsh,

'but that was the best way I could express the sense of dawn.'
Despite the odd way the darkness dissipates in tiny pieces (like
the edge of the trench crumbling away), the dawn is the same as
in any time or place: gray, silent, mysterious. 'Only' on this
occasion there's something odd: as the speaker reaches up for the
poppy, a rat touches his hand and scutters away. If in Frye's
terms the sheep is a symbol belonging to the model – that is,
pastoral or apocalyptic – world, the rat is the creature most
appropriate to the demonic. But this rat surprises us by being less
noisome than charming and well-travelled and sophisticated,
perfectly aware of the irony in the transposition of human and
animal roles that the trench scene has brought about. Normally
men live longer than animals and wonder at their timorousness:
why do rabbits tremble? why do mice hide? Here the roles are
reversed, with the rat imagined to be wondering at the unnatural
terror of men:

> What do you see in our eyes . . .
> What quaver – what heart aghast?

The morning which has begun in something close to the normal
pastoral mode is now enclosing images of terror – the opposite of
pastoral emotions. It is the job of the end of the poem to get us
back into the pastoral world, but with a difference wrought by
the understanding that the sympathetic identification with the
rat's viewpoint has achieved.

All the speaker's imagining has been proceeding while he has
worn – preposterously, ludicrously, with a loving levity and a
trace of eroticism – the poppy behind his ear. It is in roughly the
place where the bullet would enter if he should stick his head up
above the parapet, where the rat has scampered safely. He is
aware that the poppies grow because nourished on the blood of
the dead: their blood colour tells him this. The poppies will
finally fall just like the 'athletes', whose haughtiness, strength,
and fineness are of no avail. But the poppy he wears is safe for the
moment – so long as he keeps his head below the parapet, hiding
in a hole the way a rat is supposed to. The poppy is

> Just a little white with the dust,

the literal dust of the hot summer of 1916. It is also just a little bit
purified and distinguished by having been chosen as the vehicle
that has prompted the whole meditative action. But in being
chosen it has been 'pulled', and its death is already in train. Its
apparent 'safety' is as delusive as that currently enjoyed by the
speaker. (Rosenberg was killed on 1 April 1918.) If it is now just a
little bit white, it is already destined to be very white as its blood
runs out of it. If it is now lightly whitened by the dust, it is already
fated to turn wholly to 'dust'. The speaker has killed it by pulling
it from the parapet. The most ironic word in the poem is the *safe*
of the penultimate line.

As I have tried to suggest, the poem resonates as it does because
its details point to the traditions of pastoral and of general elegy.
As in all elegies written out of sympathy for the deaths of others,
the act of speaking makes the speaker highly conscious of his own
frail mortality and the brevity of his time. Even if we do not hear
as clearly as Jon Silkin the words 'Just a little while' behind 'Just
a little white', we perceive that the whole poem is saying 'Just a
little while'. We will certainly want to agree with Silkin's
conclusions about the poem's relation to tradition. The poem
pivots on what Silkin calls 'the common fantasy' about poppies,
that they are red because they are fed by the blood of the soldiers
buried beneath them. 'It is one thing to invent', says Silkin; it is
'quite another to submit one's imagination to another's, or to the
collective imagination, and extend it, adding something new and
harmonious.' [See extract from Silkin's *Out of Battle*, below–Ed.]
'Extend' is just what Keith Douglas does twenty-seven years later
in North Africa. He writes 'Desert Flowers', aware that

> . . . the body can fill
> the hungry flowers. . . .

'But that is not new.' As he knows,

> Rosenberg I only repeat what you were saying.

Pastoral has always been a favoured mode for elegy, whether
general or personal, because pastoral contains perennial flowers,
and perennials betoken immortality. Especially flowers that are
red or purple, the colours of arterial and venous blood. Here is a

pastoral elegy by Ivor Gurney associating homoerotic emotion
with a literal pastoral setting and bringing into poignant (but still
very literary) relation the redness of appropriate memorial
flowers and the redness of blood nobly and sacrificially shed. Not
the least of its merits is the complex play on the idea of
'remembrance' undertaken by the last stanza:

TO HIS LOVE

He's gone, and all our plans
   Are useless indeed.
We'll walk no more on Cotswold
   Where the sheep feed
    Quietly and take no heed.

His body that was so quick
   Is not as you
Knew it, on Severn river
Under the blue
   Driving our small boat through.

You would not know him now . . .
   But still he died
Nobly, so cover him over
   With violets of pride
   Purple from Severn side.

Cover him, cover him soon!
   And with thick-set
Masses of memoried flowers –
   Hide that red wet
   Thing I must somehow forget.

('Cover him over / With violets of pride / Purple from Severn
side': one can't help observing that the beauty of those lines
might seem to go some small way toward redeeming the
ghastliness of the misbegotten events that prompted them. *O felix
culpa!*)

Given the tradition, one can write a pastoral elegy in prose, as
Cecil Lewis does in *Sagittarius Rising*. For a change he is not flying
over the Somme battlefield but walking over it a bit back from

the line, observing its desolated, riven trees, its debris and rubble and ravaged cemeteries, its overlapping filthy craters for scores of miles. 'It was diseased, pocked, rancid, stinking of death in the morning sun':

Yet (Oh, the catch at the heart!), among the devastated cottages, the tumbled, twisted trees, the desecrated cemeteries, opening, candid, to the blue heaven, the poppies were growing! Clumps of crimson poppies, thrusting out from the lip of craters, straggling in drifts between the hummocks, undaunted by the desolation, heedless of human fury and stupidity, Flanders poppies, basking in the sun.

And suddenly 'a lark rose up from among them and mounted, shrilling over the diapason of the guns. . . .'

SOURCE: extract from *The Great War and Modern Memory* (Oxford, 1975), pp. 243–54.

NOTES

1. Stephen Graham, *A Private in the Guards* (London and New York, 1919), pp. 166–7.

2. David Jones, *The Sleeping Lord and Other Fragments* (London, 1974), p. 57.

3. C. S. Peel, *How We Lived Then, 1914–1918* (London, 1929), p. 16.

4. Northrop Frye, *Anatomy of Criticism* (Princeton, N.J., 1957), p. 144.

5. Philip Gibbs, *Now It Can Be Told* (London and New York, 1920), p. 131.

6. David Jones, *The Anathémata* (London, 1952), p. 22.

7. Liddell Hart, *Memoirs* (London, 1965, 2 vols), I, p. 16.

8. H. Owen and J. Bell (eds), *Wilfred Owen: Collected Letters* (Oxford, 1968), p. 423.

9. Stephen Graham, *The Challenge of the Dead* (London, 1921), pp. 80–1.

10. Erwin Panofsky, in *Philosophy and History: Essays Presented to Ernest Cassirer* (London, 1936), pp. 295–320.

11. Siegfried Sassoon, *Memoirs of an Infantry Officer* (London, 1930), p. 60.

12. C. E. Montague, *Disenchantment* (London, 1922), p. 162.

13. Stuart Cloete, *How Young They Died* (London, 1969), p. 103.
14. Kurt Vonnegut, *Slaughterhouse Five* (New York, 1971), p. 4.
15. Northrop Frye, *Fables of Identity* (New York, 1963), p. 25.
16. Sassoon, . . . *Infantry Officer*, op. cit., p. 61.

2. ON EDMUND BLUNDEN

Paul Fussell   'Pastoral Oases' (1975)

. . . There is an addendum [to *Undertones of War*] of thirty-one
poems (thirty-two in the 1956 edition, which adds 'Return of the
Native'), titled, in Blunden's old-fashioned, retrogressive way, 'A
Supplement of Poetical Interpretations and Variations'. Almost
a fourth of these poems establish pastoral oases as an ironic gauge
of what things are like further on up. A literal pastoral oasis is
imagined in 'The Guard's Mistake'. The battalion has left the
line and marched back to rest at a miraculously undamaged
town, so untouched by the war that even nature has not forgotten
that she is supposed to be friendly to man:

> The cherry-clusters beckoned every arm,
> The brook ran wrinkling by with playful foam.
>> And when the guard was at the main gate set,
>> Surrounding pastoral urged them to forget.

So benign and homelike is the setting that one sentry, a former
keeper of cows, forgets himself – or remembers himself – and
replaces his rifle with a country cudgel:

> . . . Out upon the road, gamekeeper-like,
> The cowman now turned warrior measured out
> His up-and-down *sans* fierce 'bundook and spike',
> Under his arm a cudgel brown and stout;
>> With pace of comfort and kind ownership,
>> And philosophic smile upon his lip.

It is too good to last. A minute later

> . . . a flagged car came ill-omened there;
> The crimson-mottled monarch, shocked and shrill,
>> Sent our poor sentry scampering for his gun,
>> Made him once more 'the terror of the Hun'.

A constant element in the poems is the equivalent of the staff officer's reimposition of 'the war' on the pastoral sentry: namely, the insistent ravaging of innocent, unpretentious rural houses and trees. 'A House at Festubert', apostrophised as 'Sad soul', is nothing now but 'one wound'; 'La Quinque Rue' is lined with 'trees bitterly bare or snapped in two'. There is a free transfer between feelings evoked by torn-up farmhouses and trees and those evoked by torn-up human bodies. In someone else this might suggest some lack of interest in misery that is specifically human. But not in Blunden: his vision of nature ravaged always in human terms and images indicates what his gentle heart has been attentive to all the while.

SOURCE: extract from *The Great War and Modern Memory* (Oxford, 1975), pp. 267–8.

3. ON RUPERT BROOKE

Timothy Rogers   'War Poet' (1971)

. . . In a way inseparable from the 'beautiful young poet' myth, and yet requiring separate notice, is the aura which clings to Brooke as a 'war poet'. The '1914' sonnets first appeared in December 1914 in the fourth (and last) instalment of the quarterly, *New Numbers*. On Easter Sunday 1915, 'The Soldier' was quoted in St Paul's by Dean Inge; *The Times* reported the sermon, and gave the sonnet in full. *The Cambridge Magazine* (ironically, one day after Brooke's death) included a précis of Dean Inge's comment:

The enthusiasm of a pure and elevated patriotism, free from hate, bitterness and fear, had never found a nobler expression. And yet it fell somewhat short of Isaiah's vision and still more of the Christian hope. It was a worthy thought that the dust out of which the happy warrior's body was once compacted was consecrated for ever by the cause for which he died. Yet was there not a tinge of materialism in such an idea?

Brooke received a cutting from *The Times*, and his last recorded remark was a regret that the Dean hadn't thought him as good as Isaiah.

The first tentative jottings of four of the '1914' sonnets were made in a small field-notebook. Interspersed among them are notes from military lectures – 'Every officer should be easily found', 'German explosive shells carry further back than forward', 'Keep *strict* discipline' – and personal memoranda – 'Thompson, Officer's Mess, doesn't make his bed up', 'Wanted: 1 curtain . . . table . . . chairs'. It is well that the beginnings of these idealistic sonnets should be thus preserved among tokens of a more practical concern. At the same time they are poems, not of war, but of preparation for war (Brooke's first title for 'The Soldier' was 'The Recruit'). The attitude to war expressed in them recalls Lord Reading's picture of him in August 1914 at a parade in Regent's Park:

> . . . clad in civilian clothes but equipped with rifle and haversack, and he had crowned this hybrid 'turnout' with a rakish, challenging, wide-brimmed black felt hat, worn with the air of an ancient Greek turned modern Mexican, which was the Poet's latest gesture of freedom before capitulating to the uniform drab.

The late Professor J. B. Trend suggested that contemporary leaders in *The Morning Post* might have prompted Brooke's attitude in the sonnets and been the source of some of the expressions in them. We may not accept this suggestion as it stands; Brooke was always capable of thinking for himself, nor at the height of his enthusiasm would he have succumbed to and reiterated the naïve sentiments expressed in that newspaper. But the articles do show that many of his ideas were 'in the air' at the time. Expressions that 'manly animosities of war' are preferable to the sloth, selfishness and cowardice of 'a shameful peace' ('. . . war is not altogether an evil: it cleans and purifies: it invigorates . . .'), that 'the soul of England is the soul of the sum of Englishmen living and dead', and that all people are 'parts of a great whole, whose destiny and interest are of infinitely higher importance than their own' – all these are exactly reflected in the sonnets.

They are reflected, too, in the writings of other poets at this time, in none more than in the jubilant John Freeman's:

> A common beating is in the air –
> The heart of England throbbing everywhere.
> And all her roads are nerves of noble thought,
> And all her people's brain is but her brain;
> Now all her history
> Is part of her requickened consciousness –
> Her courage rises clean again.

It is well to remember, too, that the feeling of those two poets who, more vividly than any, were express to the later mood of disillusion, were very different in the early months. Wilfred Owen at the outset felt a sense of 'new crusade and modern knightliness'. In the summer of 1915, shortly after Brooke's death, Siegfried Sassoon could write in 'Absolution':

> The anguish of the earth absolves our eyes
> Till beauty shines in all that we can see.
> War is our scourge; yet war has made us wise,
> And, fighting for our freedom, we are free.
>
> Horror of wounds and anger at the foe,
> And loss of things desired; all these must pass.
> We are the happy legion, for we know
> Time's but a golden wind that shakes the grass.

Brooke, like Tennyson in 'Blow, Bugle, blow' and Henley in 'England, my England', called on bugles to maffick the 'rich dead'; Owen was later to ask, 'What passing bells for these who die as cattle?' But Brooke's only glimpse of war had been at Antwerp, where the long sad columns of Belgian refugees had greatly moved him. After Antwerp he wrote: 'it's a bloody thing, half the youth of Europe, blown through pain to nothingness' – a phrase which anticipates Owen (cf. 'The Parable of the Old Man and the Young'). In another letter he writes to Cathleen Nesbitt: 'All those people at the front who are fighting – muddledly enough – for some idea called England – it's some faint shadowing of the things you can give that they have in their heart to die for' ('Whatever hope is yours was my life also'). His friend and fellow officer, Patrick Shaw-Stewart, wrote a month after Brooke's death: 'There was another heap of dead in front of the trench, and at dawn a lark got up from there and started singing – a queer contrast. Rupert Brooke could have written a poem on that, rather his subject.' The young Isaac Rosenberg was to do almost that in 'Returning, we hear the larks'.

The truth is, surely, that no one could have written more bitterly, more ironically, more truly of war than Rupert Brooke. There is small doubt that he would have done so, had he lived: he was acutely sensitive to the sorrows and the beastliness of war; his early 'realistic' vein was always near the surface. It could be that in later disillusionment he might have regretted those early poems. Some of his friends believed he would. Edward Dent wrote a fortnight after Brooke's death:

It was grotesquely tragic – what a characteristic satire he would have written on it himself! – that he should have died (at Lemnos, too!) just after a sudden and rather factitious celebrity had been obtained by a few poems which, beautiful as they are in technique and expression, represented him in a phase that could only have been temporary.

D. H. Lawrence repudiated the sonnets for himself but re-cognised that they were true for Brooke: 'It is terrible to think that there are opposing truths – but so it is.' Brooke's view of the truth would, no doubt, have changed, but he could have looked back on the sonnets as the faithful expression of a then prevailing mood. He captured the thoughts and feelings of the moment, and gave eloquent expression to them. 'Rupert expressed us *all*', said Henry James, 'at the highest tide of our actuality.' But the moment was to pass; the simple rhetoric became outmoded, the attitude of mind suspect. . . .

SOURCE: extract from the Introduction to *Rupert Brooke: A Reappraisal and Selection* (London, 1971), pp. 7–10.

4. ON WILFRED OWEN

Dennis Welland   Elegies to This Generation (1960)

To see some of the ways in which Owen makes poetry out of the quarrel with himself we may conveniently start with 'Inspection' which, by its very structure, immediately illustrates the dilemma of a poet who is 'not concerned with poetry'. The first eight lines are dramatically factual in a convincingly colloquial manner; the second half uses a heightened poetic idiom (in something of the way in which, in 'S.I.W.', 'The Poem' is separated from 'The Action') for commentary and as a vehicle for the coherent expression of ideas which the character could not, in actuality, have formulated nearly so articulately. Yet the poem's unity is maintained not only by its continuity of dramatic scene as well as its theme but also by the skilful placing of a literary allusion which eases the transition and strikes the keynote of the poem. The young soldier, who has been punished for being dirty on parade,

> told me, afterwards, the damned spot
> Was blood, his own. 'Well, blood is dirt', I said.

'The damned spot' deliberately recalls the occasion of Lady Macbeth's sleepwalking, when blood was indeed dirt – the irremovable dirt of guilt – and the association is sustained a few lines later by the reference to the washing out of stains, but the same image also carries a sacrificial overtone ('Are you washed in the Blood of the Lamb?') which anticipates the grim irony of the final lines:

> But when we're duly white-washed, being dead,
> The race will bear Field-Marshal God's inspection.

This reversion to the vernacular contributes to the unity of the poem, but equally important is its sardonic suggestion of the military ritual that survives even in war-time of 'white-washing' a camp before a GOC's inspection, a process so familiar to the soldier that he has his own terse but expressive synonym for it. What the inspecting officer sees – and is presumably gratified to see – is not the living reality of the camp but the camp in an artificial state of, to use Milton's phrase, 'excremental whiteness' from which the vitality has been drained off in the interest of outward show and dull conformity. This is a poem about guilt, but not the guilt of the young soldier so much as of a hypocritical world that is trying vicariously to expiate its own sins by the sacrifice of its youth ('Young blood's its great objection'). The process, however, is not purgative but negative, for the washing out of stains washes out the life as well. Another 'Parable of the Old Men and the Young', 'Inspection' becomes less of an overt quarrel with others than the 'Parable' by the irony of its situation which makes the young soldier the odd man out. Not only does the inspecting Deity this time want the sacrifice which in the other poem he rejected, but here Owen, in his primary dramatic role of an officer carrying out his duty, tacitly assumes a share in this universal guilt which, in his secondary role as poet, he is exposing.

The divided responsibility dramatised here causes the quarrel with himself out of which he makes poetry, as the dualism of the blood imagery here and elsewhere conveniently illustrates. Blood is a symbol of guilt, so that, for his 'Mental Cases', oppressed by the guilt of the 'multitudinous murders they once witnessed', blood has become obsessive:

> Sunlight seems a blood-smear; night comes blood-black;
> Dawn breaks open like a wound that bleeds afresh.

The dramatic emphasis of this poem, as of 'Inspection' and 'The Show', is on the incrimination of others, of the readers and of the poet who are mercilessly indicted in its closing lines, for the blood of these men is on their hands. Throughout his poetry blood is painful not merely because of its association with pain and suffering but painful in the vividness of its representation. In

'Insensibility' he half envies those 'who lose imagination', because

> Having seen all things red
> Their eyes are rid
> Of the hurt of the colour of blood for ever

but he has no intention of allowing his readers the luxury of this insensibility. The ubiquity of blood in the 'crimson slaughter' of war is insisted upon time and again in pictorial imagery of striking intensity, but seldom in an exclusively sensational way. The shell-shocked soldiers of 'Mental Cases' see all nature in terms of blood, but it is more usual for his poetry to present blood in terms of nature. Thus, in 'Asleep',

> And soon the slow, stray blood came creeping
> From the intrusive lead, like ants on track;

in 'Spring Offensive',

> earth set sudden cups
> In thousands for their blood

and in 'The Kind Ghosts',

> Not marvelling why her roses never fall
> Nor what red mouths were torn to make their blooms.

A pointer to the significance of this may again be found in 'Inspection' where to the young soldier the association of blood and dirt takes his thought

> Far off to where his wound had bled
> And almost merged for ever into clay.

To complain, as Yeats did, that Owen is 'all blood and dirt' is not only to ignore the prominence of those elements in the world of which Owen wrote but also to underestimate the genius with which his poetry fuses them symbolically and invests them with a life-giving significance.

Blood merging with clay or, as he puts it in 'Disabled', being poured 'down shell-holes till the veins ran dry', had become so familiar to the serving soldier that Owen allows his crippled spokesman in 'A Terre' to dilate upon it with philosophic humour:

> 'I shall be one with nature, herb, and stone',
> Shelley would tell me. Shelley would be stunned:
> The dullest Tommy hugs that fancy now.
> 'Pushing up daisies' is their creed, you know.

Nothing was more characteristic of the vast battlefield of the Western Front than the atmosphere of decay that hung over it. No honest writer of memoirs could ignore it: Barbusse described it graphically in *Le Feu*, Arthur Græme West tried to capture it in poetry, and time and again reference is made to it by soldiers in their private correspondence. Battle conditions often made it impossible to bury the dead in a fiercely contested area sometimes for weeks on end and the troops were obliged to live in close proximity to them. Many who were buried suffered an untimely and grisly resurrection through a bursting shell, a land subsidence or a digging party, and many became visibly assimilated into the squelching mud. There was no escaping the sight or smell of this putrescence. Owen defines it elsewhere:

> . . . when bones and the dead are smelt
> Under the mud where long ago they fell
> Mixed with the sour sharp odour of the shell.

And yet, in that Aceldama, cut off from all the more congenial aspects of civilisation and living in what the modern soldier aptly designates 'foxholes', many felt themselves in singularly close touch with nature, and nature, despite all man's savagery, seemed thriving. Indomitably, whenever the absence of shell-fire permitted it, trees grew, grass came up and birds sang. On earlier battlefields crops flourished; in forward areas the size of the rats became well-nigh phenomenal, and everywhere the poppies of Flanders nodded their blood-coloured heads. It was impossible to resist the natural inference. Hamlet might let 'imagination trace the noble dust of Alexander, till he find it stopping a bung-hole', but then Hamlet had never shared a mess-tin with Alexander.

Many must have echoed his thought: 'To what base uses we may return, Horatio!' but for the sake of sanity this speculation was not to be pushed too far when 'we' included one's friends, the men beside whom one fought, marched, and did fatigues, and when the least repulsive of the 'base uses' was acting in this fertilising capacity. In short, faced with this contrast between decaying man and flourishing nature, what more natural solution for a sensitive man than the euphemising of this process into a belief that man after death does become part of the universal spirit and does, spiritually as well as physically, become 'one with nature, herb and stone'? At least it provided a grain of consolation and that was too precious to waste. A psychologist might contend that it 'satisfies the counter movement of feeling towards the surrender of personal claims and the merging of the ego within a greater power – the "community consciousness" ', which is what Miss Maud Bodkin sees as one of the functions of the tragic hero's death, but whether one uses those or simpler terms one is bound to recognise a unificatory and regenerative value dominating the guilt-association of Owen's blood-imagery.

That Owen derived this in part from his religious upbringing, as well as from his reading of Romantic poetry, is clearly established in 'Strange Meeting':

> I would have poured my spirit without stint
> But not through wounds; not on the cess of war.
> Foreheads of men have bled where no wounds were.

The implied reference to Christ's 'agony and bloody sweat' is inescapable, illuminating, and wholly successful, but I wish to defer consideration of the Christian element in Owen's work and to turn first to one final value that he gives to this sacrificial aspect of the blood-image. In 'Apologia pro Poemate Meo' it becomes a symbol of the fellowship by which the soldier and his comrades are held together, 'bound with the bandage of the arm that drips'. There is a directly parallel passage in Robert Graves's 'Two Fusiliers':

> Show me the two so closely bound
> As we, by the wet bond of blood,
> By friendship blossoming from mud,
> By Death.

The parallelism is increased by the earlier line 'By wire and wood and stake we're bound', (Owen, also in the 'Apologia', has friendship 'wound with war's hard wire whose stakes are strong'), so that one wonders whether Owen, writing the 'Apologia' at Craiglockhart in 1917, had seen Graves's poem (sent perhaps to Sassoon to whom it would appear to be addressed) and whether that accounts for the 'too' in his opening line: 'I, too, saw God through mud'. Owen was forced by circumstances of war to join the

> wise, who with a thought besmirch
> Blood over all our soul

but the wisdom which those lines from 'Insensibility' attribute to the imaginative apprehension of the many values of 'the wet bond of blood' is richly exemplified throughout his poetry.

One of the last comments on his own poetry that Owen ever made to Siegfried Sassoon is contained in a letter of 22 September 1918: 'I don't want to write anything to which a soldier would say *No compris!*' By his echoing of the current army slang as much as by the statement itself Owen indicates the solidarity that he had come to feel with the men under his command. On his first arrival in Flanders his immediate reaction was to identify them with the popular cartoons: 'The men are just as Bairnsfather has them – expressionless lumps. We feel the weight of them hanging on us.' This on 4 January 1917; in November of the same year he wrote his 'Apologia', having shared 'With them in hell the sorrowful dark of hell' and come to recognise that 'These men are worth/ Your tears'. Though there may be some idealisation of the relationship in that poem, there is no idealisation of the men themselves, who curse, scowl, and murder, and whose 'foulness' is redeemed only temporarily by their 'passion of oblation'.

A small group of Owen's poems might be called poems of dramatic description, and in all of them the men are presented with this same honesty of vision. Such a poem as 'The Chances' makes it clear that if the soldier's reply in 'Inspection' is lacking in verisimilitude this is not because of any inability on Owen's part to handle ordinary speech in poetry. Where in Kipling, for example, one is conscious at times that the poet is affecting a dialect, in Owen the usage is so much more naturally idiomatic as to be taken for granted, especially in its command of army slang. 'The Chances' relies on slang for its atmosphere of knowingness, half-amused resignation, easy banter, and sardonic understatement until in the last four lines a new, more emotive communication is achieved by the tacit abandoning of slang so that the solitary epithet in the last line receives added weight and intensifies the protest:

> But poor young Jim, 'e's livin' an' 'e's not;
> 'E reckoned 'e'd five chances, an' 'e 'ad;
> 'E's wounded, killed, and pris'ner, all the lot,
> The bloody lot all rolled in one. Jim's mad.

That this is intentional is illustrated by the progressive strengthening of the manuscript versions of that line: 'The old, old lot' gives way to 'the 'ole damn lot', then 'the ruddy lot' and finally 'the bloody lot', although until 1931 'ruddy' had always been printed.

An unpublished poem similar to this is 'The Letter' in which a soldier's letter to his wife is interspersed with verbal asides to his companions. The poem culminates in a surprise bombardment in which the letter-writer is mortally wounded and leaves to his friend the completion of the letter. Although there is some confusion between the spoken and written idiom, there is as in 'The Chances' a keen ear for the soldier's general blasphemy of utterance, his tendency to hyperbolical abuse, and the exasperated pettinesses of which he is capable, but these are effectively contrasted with the cheerful mendacity by which he tries to convince his wife of his complete safety; his rough expressions of consolatory tenderness and his solicitude for her financial position are convincingly expressed in the semi-articulate phraseology of the unpractised letter-writer. The total dramatic effect is corroborative of the view of the men embodied in such poems as 'Insensibility' and 'Apologia', a view that is realistic, wide in its scope, sympathetic and essentially human.

It is these same qualities, derived from the same sources of experience and first-hand observation, that characterise Owen's attitude to death in these poems, and to that attitude in particular no soldier 'would say *No compris!*'. The brevity with which 'The Chances' disposes of the man who 'got the knock-out, blown to chops' is, in the apparent brutality of its vernacular bluntness, symptomatic: the clean-cut finality of death occasions no anxiety, especially when it is, as in this case, instantaneous, or when, as in 'Asleep',

> in the happy no-time of his sleeping
> Death took him by the heart.

In some circumstances death is even welcome, and thus of the suicide in 'S.I.W.' it can 'truthfully' and unemotionally be recorded that 'Tim died smiling'. Certainly death is preferable to the physical mutilation described in 'Disabled' and 'A Terre', the gas poisoning of 'Dulce et Decorum Est', the blinding of 'The Sentry', and the terrible agony of 'Mental Cases'; these to the soldier are the causes of fear more potent than death. Although to the present-day reader after two world wars this may appear self-evident to the point of obviousness, it was not so widely realised in 1917, nor was it a familiar element in poetry. Robert Graves's war poetry in expressing what he himself called 'a frank fear of physical death' had struck a new note of faithfulness to fact but his poetry, like much of Blunden's, is particularly memorable for its capturing of the soldier's perennial ability to derive a consolatory amusement and protection from the trivial, the unexpected or the inconsequential occurrence. Fear is held at bay as long as possible by a sense of humour or a sense of 'friendship, blossoming from mud'. In Sassoon fear is sometimes frankly recognised and vividly presented (as in 'Attack' or 'The Rear-Guard'), sometimes transmuted into satiric anger. A comparison of 'Does it matter?' with 'Disabled' will show how Sassoon's indignation at civilian callousness withdraws the emphasis from the psychological effect of mutilation that Owen so fearlessly and feelingly explores:

> Now he will never feel again how slim
> Girls' waists are, or how warm their subtle hands;
> All of them touch him like some queer disease.

It is against this background that the buoyancy of 'The Next War' must be understood. Its confident assertion that 'Death was never enemy of ours' has its basis in actuality but it must not obscure the recognition in the closing lines that in another and more important sense death is still the last enemy. The 'greater war' of which Owen speaks in those lines –

> when each proud fighter brags
> He wars on Death – for Life; not men – for flags

– is the war with which Owen's finest poetry is vitally concerned, and it is in this war that the pity for suffering humanity which he had learnt in the war in Flanders was to become so important a weapon.

In 'Futility', an elegy for one soldier, unnamed and not individualised, becomes more even than a requiem for the war-dead. It opens on a subdued note of saddened but not extinguished faith:

> Move him into the sun –
> Gently its touch awoke him once,
> At home, whispering of fields unsown.
> Always it woke him, even in France,
> Until this morning and this snow.

From this, by a natural and easy transition, it moves towards the weary resentment of

> O what made fatuous sunbeams toil
> To break earth's sleep at all?

The wealth of scorn implicit in 'fatuous' – an epithet that Hardy might well have chosen in a similar context – and the bitterness of the whole couplet seem close to the Sophoclean 'Not to have been born at all were best', but that is not the point of this poem. Sophocles, having reached a conclusion, makes a statement where Owen asks – and leaves unanswered – a question. The lines that precede it are a reassertion of the value of life:

> Are limbs, so dear-achieved, are sides,
> Full-nerved – still warm – too hard to stir?

True pity implies a code of values: you can only pity a person when you can visualise better conditions that have been denied him. Sophocles pities the living for not being dead: Owen pities the dead for not being alive. The very means by which he expresses that in 'Futility', the controlled sensuousness of his emphasis on physical life – limbs, sides, sinews, and warmth – are evidence of a positive belief. We are deliberately invited to 'Think, how it wakes the seeds', to think, in other words, of the process of organic development at which he hints in the imagery of 'Wild with all regrets':

> Spring air would find its own way to my lung,
> And grow me legs as quick as lilac-shoots.

Imagery of spring and natural growth is prominent in Owen's poetry because spring itself is also engaged in a war 'on Death – for Life', and much of Owen's most memorable work is in those poems where this natural parallel is most imaginatively exploited. In the early poem 'The Seed' he tries to see the war as itself part of this regenerative process:

> But now the exigent winter, and the need
> Of sowings for new spring, and flesh for seed.

Blunden's comment that this 'was his reading of the War as an abstract subject' is confirmed by the more mature and strikingly different use he makes of similar imagery in 'Futility', 'A Terre', and 'Spring Offensive'.

His poems of dramatic description have an historic and documentary significance in the vividness of their presentation of the actuality of trench warfare and the suffering it caused; his poems of personal response (such as 'The Calls', 'Apologia' and 'Greater Love') are deeply moving in the eloquent directness of their sincerity of feeling and honesty of expression; but his poems of imaginative description are in many ways more far-reaching in their implications and more satisfactory as poetry. These poems do not attempt the direct, generalised philosophical summing up that is represented by the personal poems, but the incident or scene is here subjected to a more extensive modification by the poetic imagination than in the poems of dramatic description. They do not seek to present an illusion of actuality by means of realistic speech: there is no dialogue in them at all. They do not put forward one clearly defined episode and leave us to decide how far that is representative of war. 'Exposure' is not localised except in its application to trench warfare: it could be a record of the thoughts of any soldiers on the Western Front, on either side of No Man's Land, at almost any period of the war. 'Spring Offensive' suggests no one particular attack but many, and 'The Send-Off,' though it too may be based on experience, is similarly universalised:

> So secretly, like wrongs hushed-up, they went.
> They were not ours:
> We never heard to which front these were sent.

A good example of this process is the composition of 'Asleep'. An unpublished letter to his cousin, with whom he had spent a day's leave on 14 November 1917 near Winchester, describes how, as he walks back to Winchester alone across the downs in the dusk, his imagination unexpectedly visualises the trenches with such vividness that he can 'almost see the dead lying about in the hollows of the downs'. This poem is an imaginative concentration on one of these figures, a man killed in his sleep, and is clearly a recollection in tranquillity of the emotion Owen must have experienced on some occasion in France, but what matters is not the mere interval in time between the experience and the poem. Some of the poems of dramatic description are just as distanced in time and space from the events they describe – 'The Sentry', on which he was working in September 1918 is clearly based on an incident outlined in a letter of 16 January 1917 – but these poems seek to maintain an illusion of contemporaneity with the event to which such poems as 'Asleep' do not pretend. The vision on the downs indicates how the poetic imagination has, by the Coleridgean process of dissolving, diffusing, and dissipating, re-created the original experience. The externals are briefly indicated in the first nine lines; no localising background is given, no attempt made to individualise the sleeper: like the dead soldier in 'Futility' he is the prototype of the Unknown Warrior:

> Under his helmet, up against his pack,
> After the many days of work and waking,
> Sleep took him by the brow and laid him back.

In the imaginative process of re-creation the individual and the episode become universalised. Consideration of the dead soldier gives way to speculation about death, but such speculation is constantly and carefully related to its source. Not only does the grammatical structure of the poem's second paragraph ensure a return to the dead soldier, but the grandiloquent vision of heaven,

>   the shaking
> Of great wings, and the thoughts that hung the stars,
> High pillowed on calm pillows of God's making
> Above these clouds, these rains,

is immediately checked by the ambivalent image 'these sheets of lead' (a leaden-coloured sleety day, or the 'hail' of lead bullets) which prepares us for the unmistakably warlike image of the wind's scimitars. (Compare, in 'Exposure', 'the merciless east winds that knive us'). So too in the next four lines Owen contrives at once to underpin metaphysical speculation with inescapable physical fact:

> – Or whether yet his thin and sodden head
> Confuses more and more with the low mould,
> His hair being one with the grey grass
> And finished fields of autumns that are old. . . .

In the insistence here on bleak desolation, dampness, and decomposition (intensified by the verb 'confuses') Owen is rejecting the consolation of the 'Tommy's creed' of 'pushing up daisies' in order to emphasise his main theme of death. The feigned indifference with which speculation is broken off – 'Who knows? Who hopes? Who troubles? Let it pass' – indicates by its telling sequence of verbs the emotional gradations and the ironic, preparing us for the ambivalence of the last two lines which have the appearance of purely factual statement: 'He sleeps'; but which by their reiteration and expansion of the statement bring us back to life:

> He sleeps less tremulous, less cold,
> Than we who must awake, and waking, say Alas!

What is so sadly wrong is not that we must awake but that we must awake to such grief. The poem, far from being morbidly obsessed with the dead, is ultimately much more disturbed about the living: the state of the dead needs less pity than that of the living but the terms in which it is presented effectively preclude our feeling that death is in any absolute sense desirable, however tempting it may appear for the moment. Though death may be seen as befriending this particular soldier, Owen leaves us in no doubt that death is the poet's enemy on whom the poet has to war – 'for Life'.

A less successful instance of a similar creative process at work is to be found in the sonnet 'Hospital Barge at Cérisy'. The octave presents us with the objectified description of the scene, the sestet relates the scene to the onlooker and tries to universalise it imaginatively by linking it with the passing of Arthur, but the two parts are inadequately integrated, and it is Fancy rather than Imagination that is at work. In the first part the barge is portrayed with rather too much detail (a mistake he does not make in 'Asleep'):

> Softly her engines down the current screwed
> And chuckled in her . . .
> The lock-gate took her bulging amplitude.
> Gently into the gurgling lock she swum.

The one phrase intended presumably to act as a precursor of the changed note of the sestet, 'fairy tinklings', is too much at variance with the realistic note of the rest of the description. This realism also makes the inaccuracy of 'her *funnel* screamed' more discordant, and the final transition to Arthur, euphonious as it is, a little self-conscious. Its literariness seems artificial and over-wrought by comparison with the spontaneity and intensity of first-hand emotion that informs most of his work, but its method is, with this exception, the same as in the other poems of imaginative description.

There are two fundamental antitheses common to most of these poems, the contrast between two states of being (the present and the past, as in 'Exposure' and 'Hospital Barge'; the present and the problematical future, as in the artillery sonnet and 'The Send-off'), and the contrast between life and death (as in 'Asleep, 'Futility', and 'Spring Offensive'). Coupled with this and related to it is a greater preoccupation with eternity than Owen has displayed in either of the other two groups. Here he is enlarging his work to enable it to cope with the great poetic verities that he had tentatively sought after in his juvenilia. What attracts him in these poems is death, not simply as death, not merely as an end of life, but as a state of transition between two existences.

It is this that the poem which Blunden entitles 'Fragment: A Farewell' records, and again it is pregnant with much more meaning than might at first appear. This description of death is at first sight more ornate than Owen usually allows himself to be, but it is a much more disciplined poem than any of his juvenilia. The sensuousness of the opening is relaxed in a way unusual in Owen when writing of blood:

> I saw his round mouth's crimson deepen as it fell,
>   Like a Sun, in his last deep hour.
>   •

This, the only hint of war, in the poem, contrasts so markedly with his description of wounds elsewhere that we are instantly prepared for something different. The imagery, too, which in so many of his poems is belittling and calculated to shock, is here expansive, Romantic. Elsewhere nature is compared to man and the works of man, as in the lines of 'Exposure':

> Dawn, massing in the east her melancholy army,
> Attacks once more in ranks on shivering ranks of gray

with their magnificent dual suggestion of dawn breaking and of a German dawn attack; and nature and death are linked only in ugliness, as they are in this fragment:

> Cramped in that funnelled hole, they watched the dawn
> Open a jagged rim around; a yawn

Of death's jaws, which had all but swallowed them
Stuck in the bottom of his throat of phlegm.

In 'A Farewell', however, the process is reversed; it achieves its
unity by its consistently cosmic imagery. The dying man is
pictured in terms of the universe: 'like a Sun', 'clouding', 'the
heavens of his cheek', 'cold stars' and 'skies'; and yet paradoxi-
cally this magnification of the individual does not produce any
sense of exaltation. The first five lines maintain an equilibrium –
they are indeed 'half gleam, half glower' – but in the last three
the image, being more fully developed, takes charge and the
occasion of the image, the eyes, is dwarfed by the stern grandeur
of the last two lines:

The cold stars lighting, very old and bleak
    In different skies.

The emotion has been transferred from the subject to the image:
it is not a man that is dying, but a universe, and language that
might have been used to make this microcosm's death sublime
has instead been employed to conjure up a chilling vision of a
doomed world. There is added force in the suggestion that the
last line carries of 'indifferent skies': the play on words may be as
grimly deliberate as the near-pun on curse and corpses at the
beginning of 'The Sentry'. This is no more hopeful, no more
Christian, a poem than 'The End' which it recalls, but its
compactness and technique, its masterly control of language and
movement, make it much superior to 'The End'. In its brevity
there is a self-contained unity and an evocative power to which
Blunden's title 'Fragment' does less than justice. The very doubt
that it is intended to communicate preordains a sense of
incompleteness, but its organic coherence, as well as its manuscript (an untitled fair copy with only one small amendment),
contradict the idea of fragmentariness.

   The best of these poems that seem on the brink of two worlds is
'Spring Offensive'. It sustains the distinction made in 'Insensibility' between those who, having lost imagination, can sleep
carelessly in the shade of 'a last hill', and the others more sensitive
who

stood still
To face the stark, blank sky beyond the ridge,
Knowing their feet had come to the end of the world.

The stark blankness of this sky may strengthen the interpretation
of indifferent skies in the final line of the poem just discussed, for
like that poem, 'Spring Offensive' rests on a number of antitheses
of which this is one. Another is the contrast between the
unnaturalness of what these men are doing and the natural
background against which they are doing it. Contrasted with
some of the attempts by other poets . . . at a similar evocation of
natural beauty, these lines provide an excellent example of how,
by deliberately stripping it of personal associations and allusions,
Owen avoids sentimentalising the theme. This can and does pass
as a reflection of the mood of soldiers before an attack, but it is
also a clear instance of how the poetic imagination has transmuted the experience of others, giving it at once universality and
yet the quality of an intensely personal vision. The inversion
'Marvelling they stood' throws into immediate prominence the
keynote of beauty-inspired wonder. The generalised picture of

the long grass swirled
By the May breeze, murmurous with wasp and midge

is evocative but not limiting – each reader can relate it to a scene
he knows and his confidence is increased by the almost Pre-
Raphaelite selection of significant detail. Only then does Owen's
imagination take charge, unobtrusively, but for the alert reader
unmistakably:

For though the summer oozed into their veins
Like an injected drug for their bodies' pains . . .

The modern, clinical image, arresting and yet perfectly appropriate, gives individuality to a belief in 'the healing power of
Nature' and helps to remove any objection to it as an automatic
literary convention. Here again is the blood symbol and Owen's
sense of the oneness of all created life, the indestructible unity
between man and nature: 'Summer *oozed into their veins*' (and the
simile that follows heightens the literalness of this), 'Sharp *on their*

souls hung the imminent line of grass', 'the *warm* field', the brambles 'clutched and clung to them *like sorrowing hands*', 'They breathe *like trees* unstirred'.

In this poem, with its packed wealth of suggestion, Owen's technique is at its most mature. The tense, apprehensive mood of the soldiers is well indicated by their geographical position, the 'blank sky beyond the ridge' contrasted with the certainty of 'the far valley behind', and the powerful suggestion of 'the imminent line of grass', while their reluctance to leave this comfortable, known, natural world is hinted at merely in 'their *slow* boots coming up'. The tempo, too, is skilfully varied from the meditative slowness of the opening three stanzas, working up through the tension of the fourth to the exhilarating action of

> So, soon they topped the hill, and raced together
> Over an open stretch of herb and heather
> Exposed.

The heavy caesura after 'Exposed' heralds the dramatic abruptness with which the counter-fire bursts on attackers and readers alike:

> And instantly the whole sky burned
> With fury against them; earth set sudden cups
> In thousands for their blood; and the green slope
> Chasmed and steepened sheer to infinite space.

A row of dots then preludes the return to the meditative note for the conclusion. Admirable too is the way in which the actual attack is presented in terms of the scene already described. The blankness of the sky gives way to positive hatred – 'the whole sky burned /With fury against them' – but earth is still friendly, and the buttercups, their blessing unavailing, are recalled in grimmer context in the allusion to the shell-holes: 'earth set sudden cups/ In thousands for their blood'; and the hill ridge has become the brink of consciousness:

> and the green slope
> Chasmed and steepened sheer to infinite space.

More perhaps than any of his other poems, 'Spring Offensive' in its alternation between life and death does convey imaginatively the nervous tension of the soldier in moments of crisis. Other poets have described an attack, seeing it as exhilarating or terrifying according to their temperaments; it is characteristic of Owen that he should concern himself also with the lasting effects of such an attack on the survivors. The spring to which they come 'crawling slowly back' still arouses wonder in them, but it is not the same spring nor the same wonder as those of the earlier stanzas. They have their own secret, their reluctance, even inability, to speak of 'comrades that went under', and if Owen offers no reason for this it is because he has already answered his own question in the sonnet 'Happiness'. The survivors, having besmirched 'blood over all their souls', can no longer see their world as it was: the buttercups have become receptacles for blood, not givers of benisons:

> The sun may cleanse
> And time, and starlight . . .
> But the old Happiness is unreturning.

In an unpublished letter of 27 November 1917 he drew Sassoon's attention to an image in a poem by his cousin and identified it as his own; it is a felicitous reference to young bracken:

> Like carven croziers are the curled shoots growing
> To bless me as I pass.

The recurrence of this idea in the buttercup image in 'Spring Offensive' is paralleled by another echo: in 'The Unreturning' 'the indefinite, unshapen dawn' had led the poet to a dread of 'a heaven with doors so chained', and in 'Spring Offensive' 'the stark, blank sky' is markedly contrasted with the rich organic unity of man and nature. The hostile menace of the dawn in 'Exposure' and 'Mental Cases' is directly related to conditions of war, but the line, 'Fearfully flashed the sky's mysterious glass', is closer to the dawn of 'The Unreturning' in its suggestion of a supernatural hostility symbolised by the sky itself. The antithesis between the unsympathetic impenetrability of the sky and the

luminous warmth of the sun is inescapable in the reference to the
waiting soldiers:

> . . . eyes that faced
> The sun, like a friend with whom their love is done.
> O larger shone that smile against the sun,
> Mightier than his whose bounty these have spurned.

As in 'Futility' the sun is a life force, a creative principle from
which the soldier is cut off, but this time it is by an act of
deliberate rejection. The insistence, in the final stanzas of 'Spring
Offensive', on imagery of hell and damnation, as well as the
calculated doubt and hesitancy of '*Some say* God caught them',
introduces an ethical note not present in 'Futility'. The sense of
alienation in 'Spring Offensive' is the more terrible because it is
the result of active choice, not passive suffering, and because it
reflects so keenly the schism in Owen's own soul.

SOURCE: chapter 4 of *Wilfred Owen: A Critical Study* (London,
1960, revised edn 1978), pp. 62–83.

John Bayley   But for Beaumont Hamel . . . (1963)

'I sought a theme and sought for it in vain' . . . the opening line
of Yeats's poem is the candid cry of the professional bard, and it
contains the real reason for Yeats's antipathy to Wilfred Owen.
Owen's theme was thrust upon him by the war, which he could
not absorb or surround with the hard pearly shell of poetic
egotism. 'Tennyson was a great child', he wrote, 'so should I have
been but for Beaumont Hamel.' It is unjust, but its injustice
reveals a basic antagonism which – between poets as between
other human beings – divides beyond the reach of sympathy and
understanding. This division, between Us who have had the
experience and You who have not, was deeply and terribly

apprehended in the First War, overriding all national feelings, and its comparative absence in Hitler's war perhaps accounts for the absence there of the kind of war poetry to which Yeats so strongly objected. It also accounts for the alienation in the inter-war period between the young poets, spellbound by Owen, and an audience who resented being told that the poetry they loved was not fit to speak and that they themselves were not fit to hear.

For Yeats has a shrewd point. Hieratic manipulator of his own experience as he is, that experience still remains unexclusive and available: he does not cut himself off from us. Terrible and unimaginable as it was, the war trauma that cut off its victims from us also produced its discharge of cant, hysteria and self-pity – the 'blood, dirt and sucked sugar-stick' that repelled Yeats. He had not the generosity to sympathise on the human level with what repelled him aesthetically; he could not see that that dangerous phrase, 'the poetry is in the pity', which would be cant in most poets, is miraculously true in Owen. The most remarkable thing in all Owen's great range of poetic weight and fulfilment is his ability to make permanently sublime sentiments which in any other poet would become localised, dated, shrill.

> Nevertheless, except you share
>> With them in hell the sorrowful dark of hell,
> Whose world is but the trembling of a flare,
>> And heaven but as the highway for a shell,
>
> You shall not hear their mirth.
> . . .
>
> Heart, you were never hot
>> Nor large, nor full like hearts made great with shot.
> . . .
>> Weep, you may weep, for you may touch them not.

Amazing how it works, for nothing is more tiresome than to be told that one is utterly deficient in feeling for and understanding of something which one was not there to understand. Yet there is no element here of the historically curious, of the powerful localised satire of Sassoon:

> I'd like to see a tank come down the stalls
> Lurching to rag-time tunes or Home Sweet Home,
> And there'd be no more jokes in music halls
> To mock the riddled corpses round Bapaume.

nor of Owen, the rather priggish young officer, who wrote to his brother, 'I deliberately tell you all this to educate you to the actualities of war', and who proclaimed: 'All a poet can do today is warn.' Many bad poets after him – and a few good ones – were to be obediently, but not very effectively, minatory.

'Hearts made great with shot' – that is the clue to the great and permanent stature of Owen. Like Tolstoy and Shakespeare, he celebrates with majestic understanding that enlargement of the human spirit which makes (or has made) even out of war a value, like the value of love. And like them he is able to do this only because he came to a full comprehension of its misery, and of the misery of the human situation which made such injustices possible. 'Miners' is as moving as any of the war poems; and one of the most haunting of all, 'The Send-Off', seems both to contain and transcend all the muted terrors to which this century has since accustomed us – trains of deportees, hidden outrage, guilt, the desire not to know.

> So secretly, like wrongs hushed-up, they went.
> They were not ours:
> We never heard to which front these were sent.

But in transcending it cannot but lay a kind of benediction. Owen knew this. 'These elegies are to this generation in no sense consolatory. They may be to the next.' It is the truest and most perceptive comment in his preface. The effect of distancing is remarkable. . . . 'It seemed that out of battle I escaped.' ('Strange Meeting', however, is by no means Owen's best poem: too much a Georgian frontal assault and lacking the oblique compressed originality of 'The Send-Off' or

> Men remember alien ardours
> As the dusk unearths old mournful odours.
> In the garden unborn child souls wail
> And the dead scribble on walls.

But his sublime effects are sometimes weirdly simple, as in the very immature poem 'Storm':

> Glorious will shine the opening of my heart;
> The land shall freshen that was under gloom.

His effects of diction are extremely personal and don't depend on the vocabulary of a war-poet – stick-bombs, five-nines and so forth. Significantly he says of a poem that does: 'I wrote something in Sassoon's style' (he worshipped Sassoon) and he was anxious that the ordinary soldier should not think him arty ('Above all I am not concerned with poetry'), but in fact he is as dependent as Keats on an idiom worked out of literature. Continually we find him revising out the emphases of war. The marvellous line, 'And finished fields of autumns that are old' originally ended with 'of wire-scrags rusty-old'.

Cecil Day Lewis's Collected Edition of the poems, with variants and revisions, enables us to pick out this kind of thing, and also contains all the surviving juvenilia. It is an immense advance on the Blunden edition and it also contains as a postscript Blunden's excellent memoir. Mr Day Lewis's own introduction is full of the illumination that one would expect from a poet who followed Owen. He seems to have discovered in a letter of 1916 Owen's first use of assonance: 'I was isolated scouting – felt like scooting.' This suggests to me that the device was not so much technical as a part of the natural movement of Owen's mind, facetiousness turning under the pressure of feeling into effects of pathos and calm, lopsided horror. It is this verbal personality, sometimes clumsy –

> They will be swift with swiftness of the tigress.
> None will break ranks, though nations trek from progress.

– sometimes what used to be called 'mawkish', but always intensely and disconcertingly characteristic, which most connects Owen with his admired Keats. Keats, too, has a verbal odour which many (I suspect Yeats was one) find a bit repellent, too close to the real and shapeless yearning and tears of living; but it is surely this aspect of Keats, rather than his more obviously romantic side, which is most fulfilled in Owen. Assonance is alive in him, not one of the artifices of eternity. The Keats who writes of 'close bosom-friend of the maturing sun' and of lips 'warm with dew at ooze from living blood' is very close to Owen, though Owen's sexual admirations were obviously different: consider his relation to the 'strange friend' in 'Strange Meeting', a poem like 'Three rompers run together . . .', or the very remarkable 'Maundy Thursday', written before the war and I think published here for the first time. In it Owen describes with astonishing skill the ways in which a congregation kiss the silver crucifix 'between the brown hands of a server-lad':

> Above the crucifix I bent my head:
> The Christ was thin, and cold, and very dead:
> And yet I bowed, yea, kissed – my lips did cling
> (I kissed the warm live hand that held the thing).

It is a poem full of gentleness and humour as well as, I suppose, sex, and it certainly does not reject Christianity: we see from the war poems how much the figure of Christ (as opposed to God) meant to Owen. All this in him may seem muddled and disasteful, but the point is that in Keats and Owen sex is important – as in Owen war is supremely important – as the focus to generalise and reverberate human sympathy. Keats and Owen are much more appealing figures than D. H. Lawrence, but it would not be absurd to see the three of them as representing something unique and admirable in English life, decent, unclassed, intelligent-hearted and refusing (almost unwittingly in Keats's and Owen's case) to endorse the current forms and decorums of war, love and language. . . .

SOURCE: article in *The Spectator* (4 October 1963), p. 419.

John H. Johnston   'Pity Was Not Enough'
(1964)

. . . Despite Owen's extraordinary sensitivity and his efforts to reconcile that sensitivity to the demands of formal poetic art, his achievement does not measure up to the vast tragic potentialities of his material. His sense of personal involvement in the war resembled Rupert Brooke's in that it was a motive as well as a source of poetry. Although he moves far beyond the Georgian attitude with his vision of pity, that vision was not enough. His compassion and his concept of the 'greater love' grew out of his perhaps too exclusive concern with the aspects of suffering and sacrifice; these aspects do not assume their place or proportion in the total reality. Unlike Blunden, whose poetic interests range less intensely but more widely over the field of war, Owen cannot shift his eyes from particulars that represent merely a part of an enormous complex of opposed human energies comprehensible only on the historic or tragic scale. Although he attempts to give these particulars a universal significance, his vision of pity frequently obscures rather than illuminates the whole; we are likely to lose sight of the historical reality as well as the underlying tragic values that inspire the pity. In Owen's case the pity produces the poetry; only in a partial and sporadic fashion does the poetry produce pity as an effect of tragic events. Furthermore, if it is true that an enlightened compassion was apparently the only poetically fruitful point of view permitted by the nature of modern warfare, is it not also true, as Stephen Spender suggests in his essay on Owen, that 'poetry inspired by pity is dependent on that repeated stimulus for its inspiration'?[1] The best of Owen's lyrics are necessarily developed in terms of a single emotion – an emotion that cannot be maintained or repeated without psychological strain or aesthetic loss. How many successful poems can be written in the tenor of 'Disabled'? The very intensity of the author's compassion tends to exhaust both the emotion and the force of its stimulus. Unless pity is generated and objectified within a large tragic context, it cannot of itself support a tragic vision; as a motive for lyric poetry, it tends to become sentimental or obsessive regardless of the eloquence with which it is developed. When the compassionate attitude is apparently the only attitude with which war can be truthfully described, the possibilities of poetry are severely restricted: only passive suffering and death can provide its materials.

William Butler Yeats excluded Owen's poetry from his *Oxford Book of Modern Verse* on the basis of his judgement that 'passive suffering is not a theme for poetry'. A 'pleader' for the sufferings of others necessarily makes those sufferings his own; 'withdrawn

into the quicksilver at the back of the mirror', he loses his
objectivity and his sense of proportion: 'no great event becomes
luminous in his mind.' [See extract in Part Two, above.] The
function of the epic narrative, of course, was to communicate that
luminous effect; the epic poet, dealing with and illuminating
great events, interpreted his tale in the light of heroic values.
These values affected the form as well as the materials of the
narrative; the epic vision determined the attitude and technique
of the poet as well as the motivations and actions of his characters.
In Owen's poetry we have the physical background of war, the
sense of hazard and duress, the pathos of suffering, and even a
perception of tragic extremity. But these, at best, are but
fragmentary aspects of the whole. They appear not as products of
a unified and comprehensive poetic vision but as effects of a lyric
sensibility vainly attempting to find order and significance on a
level of experience where these values could not exist – where, in
fact, they had been destroyed. Owen and his contemporaries
inherited a sensibility deprived of vision and value; their
experiences – so alien to anything dealt with by the romantic
tradition – required an intellectual and imaginative discipline far
beyond that provided by the vision of pity, which was itself a
product of tortured sensibility. Unlike Sassoon, Owen recovered
from an early experiential bias; this bias, he discovered, was as
poetically unproductive as the Georgian 'retrenchment' from
which it was an abrupt and sensational reaction. His ironic use of
romantic terms and concepts indicates the conflict between a
sensibility long devoted to 'Poetry' and experiences that demanded the truth. Lacking a positive and comprehensive lyric
vision, Owen drew his poetry from this inner conflict while
attempting to find his bearings in a period of rapid historical and
artistic transition. 'Strange Meeting' is his final word on the
social responsibilities of the 'true Poet', but even in this
statement, where the 'truth untold' is seen as the pity – 'the pity
war distilled', Owen can present no further justification of the
poet's new role than his sensitivity to suffering.

   The omission of Owen's poems from the *Oxford Book of Modern
Verse* provoked much censure from critics and reviewers. In a
letter to Lady Dorothy Wellesley (21 December 1936), Yeats
somewhat irascibly defended his action . . . [See extract in Part
Two, above.] The private nature of these remarks undoubtedly

encouraged a measure of willful or careless exaggeration. Yeats's main and more justifiable thrust is against those who for doctrinaire political reasons had exalted the 'prophetic' elements of Owen's work. Yet his case against Owen's verse strikes shrewdly – if unkindly – into the critical problem. Owen's sensibilities had indeed developed along the line Yeats indicates; 'Poetry' – the 'sucked sugar stick' element – was prominent in his work, although he was gradually eliminating it or making it the source of ironic reference. The 'blood and dirt' or experiential element, Yeats implies, could hardly be combined in a poetically palatable manner with the sucked sugar stick of 'Poetry'. Yet if we drop the metaphor and its distracting associations, we may see that Owen's combination of the two is a significant aspect of his achievement and one which illustrates both his keen awareness of transition and his ability to incorporate its meaning into the substance of his poetry. For those who are also conscious of that transition, one of the most poignant effects in the poetry of World War I is created by his use of the romantic idiom to suggest, by contrast or default, what it could no longer express.

Owen's influence on the postwar poets has been summarised by C. Day Lewis, who nominates Hopkins, Owen, and Eliot as the 'immediate ancestors' of the Auden group. Owen's contribution, however, was less technical than inspirational. Auden, Day Lewis, and Louis MacNeice employed Owen's notable innovation – half-rhyme – for a variety of effects, but with the exception of Day Lewis they did not seriously explore the musical possibilities of this device, which does not lend itself to every poetic purpose. It is rather as a prophet that Owen earns Day Lewis' designation as 'a true revolutionary poet'. Owen's protest against the evils of war has been rather unwarrantably extended to the social and economic evils of modern life; he 'commends himself to post-war poets largely because they feel themselves to be in the same predicament; they feel the same lack of a stable background against which the dance of words may stand out plainly, the same distrust and horror of the unnatural forms into which life for the majority of people is being forced'. [See Day Lewis's study in Part Two, above.] Owen is actually a symbol rather than a prophet; his youth, his small but eloquent body of verse, his intense dedication to the truth, his untimely and unnecessary death – all of these factors combined to make him an irresistible figure to the succeeding generation, whose 'stable background' of traditional forms and values had, like Owen's, been destroyed by the war. He is a 'revolutionary poet' not in the sense that he deliberately undertook any radical reformation of his art but in the sense that his work embodies, more dramatically than that of any other poet, the changing values of the time.

SOURCE: extract from *English Poetry of the First World War* (Princeton, N.J., 1964), pp. 205–9.

NOTE

1. Stephen Spender, *The Destructive Element* (London, 1935), p. 219.

David Perkins   'Owen's Romanticism' (1976)

. . . If Owen at his best wrote more powerfully than the other war poets . . . , it is not through a greater realism but through an ampler gift in traditional and 'Romantic' qualities of style and imagination, which unite with the realism and qualify it. His earlier poems show the influence not only of contemporaries and immediate predecessors but also . . . of Shelley and especially Keats. When he sought later to make readers feel the war as he felt it, he did not lose these earlier sources nor did he cease to be interested in technique. 'I am a poet's poet', he wrote in a letter of 1917. One finds in his greater poetry a combination of qualities that often appear only in separation: traditional Romanticism with realism, moral and political passion and purpose with technical elaboration and control. Though there is only one theme ('My subject is War, and the pity of War') there is a great variety of treatment – parable and vision, narrative, subjective lyric, dramatic monologue, case history – and a wide range of feeling.

The realism appears most nakedly in such poems as 'The Sentry' (based on an actual experience) or 'Dulce Et Decorum Est':

Bent double, like old beggars under sacks,
Knock-kneed, coughing like hags, we cursed through sludge,
Till on the haunting flares we turned our backs
And towards our distant rest began to trudge.
Men marched asleep. Many had lost their boots
But limped on, blood-shod. All went lame; all blind;
Drunk with fatigue; deaf even to the hoots
Of tired, outstripped Five-Nines that dropped behind.

Gas! Gas! Quick, boys! – An ecstasy of fumbling,
Fitting the clumsy helmets just in time;
But someone still was yelling out and stumbling
And flound'ring like a man in fire or lime . . .
Dim, through the misty panes and thick green light,
As under a green sea, I saw him drowning.

In all my dreams, before my helpless sight,
He plunges at me, guttering, choking, drowning.

The effect of reality is achieved primarily through the action itself, the shock and terror of a gas attack. It is sustained through unpoetic, observed detail ('Bent double', 'Knock-kneed', 'Many had lost their boots') and through Owen's care to find the word that accurately corresponds to the sensation, as in the 'hoots' of the shells, or the 'misty panes' of the gas mask, or the 'thick green' of the gas. It further determines the deliberately disagreeable metaphors out of Synge or Yeats ('old beggars under sacks'), and the diction of brutal, unqualifying directness ('hags', 'cursed', 'sludge', 'yelling out') and colloquial casualness ('turned our backs', 'just in time'). There is also the rhythm, manipulated through many caesuras to break poetic swing and emphasise or dramatise the action. With its realism and horror, bitterness and irony, force and directness, the poem seems far from the traditionally 'poetic', but there is, even here, something of a 'Romantic' heightening. It appears in the phrases 'All went lame; all blind', where the repeated 'all' lends something sublime

and visionary to the scene. It appears also in the controlled use of
assonance and alliteration to bind the lines together, so that even
in a poem that seems an immediate report of actual experience,
one finds the complex pattern of 'l' and 'b' alliteration in,

> But limped on, blood-shod. All went lame; all blind.

This use of vowel and consonant pattern Owen had caught from
Keats. It is as obvious an example as could be found of Owen's
combination of romantic tradition with realism. The start of
'Strange Meeting', for example, goes:

> It seemed that out of battle I escaped
> Down some profound dull tunnel, long since scooped
> Through granite which titanic wars had groined;

or there are the echoing 'w's', 'r's', and 's's' in,

> But wound with war's hard wire whose stakes are strong,

or the 'I's', 'd's', and short 'u's' of,

> Treading blood from lungs that had loved laughter.

This lingering Romanticism is often mentioned reproachfully, as
though it were a survival of earlier bad habits from which Owen,
dying young, had not yet freed himself. It may be so, but I view it
more as a strength in the poetry. Because Owen's style was more
traditional, it was more accessible than most of the modern
poetry that commands the respect of critics. Poem after poem
illustrates the transition from the romantic tradition to the
realistic – for example, the often-quoted 'Anthem for Doomed
Youth':

> What passing-bells for these who die as cattle?
>   Only the monstrous anger of the guns.
>   Only the stuttering rifles' rapid rattle
> Can patter out their hasty orisons.
> No mockeries now for them; no prayers nor bells,
>   Nor any voice of mourning save the choirs, –

> The shrill, demented choirs of wailing shells;
> And bugles calling for them from sad shires.

The last line is a fine instance of Romantic suggestion, and doubtless many readers are also haunted by literary reminiscence in the two previous lines. But if one remembers Keats's ode 'To Autumn',

> Then in a *wailful choir* the small gnats *mourn*,

the lines become a striking example of literary transplantation, or rather transformation. Despite the bitterness in which it begins, the sonnet gives the kind of pleasure to which readers of poetry were accustomed. Only from a doctrinaire Modernist point of view, now itself outdated, could it be condemned for this reason.

Owen's diction has also been attacked for its Romantic elements. Yeats, having never been able to exclude such items from his own poetry, excluded Owen from his *Oxford Book of Modern Verse* on the ground that 'He is all blood, dirt, and sucked sugar stick . . . he calls poets "bards", a girl a "maid" & talks about "Titanic wars". 'Titanic wars' comes from Owen's 'Strange Meeting', which also has such phrases as 'made moan', 'grieves richlier', and the Yeatsian 'hunting wild / After the wildest beauty of the world'. The poem also contains Romantic props such as 'sullen hall', 'tigress', 'citadels', and 'chariot wheels'. Whether these are appropriate to the context may be argued, but what seems more important is that the poem, which Sassoon calls Owen's 'passport to immortality', achieves a greater aesthetic distance, and with this a more complex resonance, through the Romantic mode of visionary poetry. This is a further contribution of the more traditional and Romantic elements in Owen's style – a certain distance from the subject.

The Romanticism of Owen's temperament also reveals itself in an intense and emotional idealisation of the common soldier, and this gives his attitudes toward the war a greater complexity. He once described himself as a 'conscientious objector with a very seared conscience'. With a moral loathing of the war and a huge anger at the civilians who tolerated, supported, or profited from it, he thought of himself as a voice through which the sufferings of the soldiers could be pleaded. And he believed that only if he shared their sufferings had he the right to speak for them. He also felt guilty about the soldiers whom he, as an officer, was leading like cattle to the slaughterhouse. Something of this conflict appears in a letter of 1918:

> For 14 hours yesterday I was at work – teaching Christ to lift his cross by numbers, and how to adjust his crown; and not to imagine he thirst till after the last halt. I attended his Supper to see that there were not complaints; and inspected his feet that they should be worthy of the nails. I see to it that he is dumb, and stands to attention before his accusers. With a piece of silver I buy him every day, and with maps I make him familiar with the topography of Golgotha.

To see the soldiers as Christ implied that they were innocent and crucified; but Owen also felt their suffering released or created in them a spiritual worth. Among his better-known poems, 'Apologia Pro Poemate Meo' and 'Greater Love' are built on the paradox of the spiritual emerging out of the foulness of war:

> I, too, saw God through mud –
>   The mud that cracked on cheeks when wretches smiled.
> . . .
> And witnessed exultation –
>   Faces that used to curse me, scowl for scowl,
>   Shine and lift up with passion of oblation,
> . . .
> I have perceived much beauty
>   In the hoarse oaths that kept our courage straight;
>   Heard music in the silentness of duty;

and,

> Red lips are not so red
>   As the stained stones kissed by the English dead.
> Kindness of wooed and wooer
> Seems shame to their love pure.
> O Love, your eyes lose lure
>   When I behold eyes blinded in my stead!

In these verses the invidious comparison of the lesser love, faith,

and sacrifice of the civilian is plain; it is underlined at the end of
'Apologia Pro Poemate Meo'.

> These men are worth
> Your tears. You are not worth their merriment.

A word should also be said about his important technical
innovation: consonant-rhyme (escaped/scooped; groined/groan-
ed). Owen used this in a rather strict way, preserving the
same consonants with a different vowel. Later poets employed
the device more loosely (winter/ladder). It was not unknown in
English and Welsh poetry before Owen, or he may have picked it
up from French sources, but it is equally or more probable that he
developed it on his own. Later poets learned it from him. He
adopted it in about a third of his mature poems.

Only four of Owen's poems were published in his lifetime. In
1919 Edith Sitwell published some of his poems in *Wheels*, and in
1920 she and Siegfried Sassoon brought out a volume of poems
from manuscripts. This was reprinted in 1921 and there was no
further printing until the edition of Edmund Blunden in 1931.
Then, however, Owen had his impact on the younger English
poets, notably Auden, Spender, MacNeice, and Day Lewis.
Leftist or Communist in sympathy at that time, they were
attracted to his use of poetry for a political purpose, his
idealisation and celebration of common men, and his wrathful
indignation against those who were exploiting them. They also
picked up some features of his style, especially his consonant
rhyme. In 1935 Spender remarked that Owen was 'the most
useful influence in modern verse'. Most of these poets gave
similar testimonials, but what they could not learn were Owen's
personal qualities of emotional intensity, directness, boldness,
and imaginative grandeur. Lines such as

> Heart, you were never hot
> Nor large, nor full like hearts made great with shot,

or, in prophecy of the postwar world,

> None will break ranks, though nations trek from progress,

or

Was it for this the clay grew tall?

show how much that might have been magnificent was lost
through his death.

SOURCE: extract from *A History of Modern Poetry* (Cambridge,
Mass., 1976), pp. 279–85.

5. ON ISAAC ROSENBERG

Jon Silkin   'Break of Day in the Trenches'
and 'Dead Man's Dump' (1972)

. . . Rosenberg's experience of the war seems not to have made a poet of him in the way that it forced on Owen a rapid development. Not that Owen was 'made' by the war, but his development was spectacular by comparison with Rosenberg's.

Of course, as Sassoon asserted, one should never speak of the war as having done anything for anybody, except the armaments industry; and those who see Owen's development as even the merest justification for war are vulgarly insulting not merely the other twenty-one millions killed in it,* but Owen's own moral indignation and pity. Thus even the celebration of a 'war poet' creates unease. What appeals to us is the expression of outrage at the irony and the waste. This is as it should be, and yet it is not, if we expend our watchfulness in the easing of our guilt, our outrage. Once these are spent society is vulnerable to further wars. There are other grounds for unease. What happens to the war poet is that the sacrifice becomes pictorialised. Owen's death is made to dramatise and illustrate the irony and tragedy of which he was unwillingly a part. He did not return to the front to get killed, but to share as best he could the others' suffering, as a pleader. Yet what the image pictorialises is not so much Owen's judgements as the brilliant revelation which his death uncovers.

Rosenberg's death, on the other hand, does not as easily satisfy any such categories. It is true he was young – twenty-eight – when he died, but the circumstances of his death were uncertain.

---

* '21 million people died in the Great War; some $8\frac{1}{2}$ million men fell in action, and $12\frac{1}{2}$ million civilians died as a result of military action, through massacre, starvation and disease.' Patric Bridgwater, 'German Poetry and the First World War', *European Studies*, I, no. 2 (1971).

It is thought that he went out with a wiring party, and it is certain that whatever he did go out to do, he did not return, although we lack witnesses even for this. It is uncertain how much Rosenberg's working-class origins and Jewishness contributed to his comparative oblivion between the two wars, but it is not a factor to be dismissed. What nationalistic country can be expected to honour one who was in many ways so alien to the culture? Disraeli of course was a Jew, yet not only was he converted to Christianity but with piratic expertise expanded the empire, and in this sense was a man of his own country as much as of any nineteenth-century European state. Rosenberg, like Owen, hated war, but he joined up without any convictions, and from poverty as one reason. This made him an unwilling mercenary, and perhaps he felt that there was nothing else he could have done; but he maintained his unwillingness. He lacked patriotic belief, though he had cosmopolitan and Tolstoyan ones.

Owen has seemed to be more a 'war poet' than Rosenberg. Apart from his poems concerning war little remains of value. This is not the case with Rosenberg, although I believe that he wrote some of the most interesting poems concerned with the War. Owen's achievement centres on his poems of hatred, irony, and pity; Rosenberg's on struggle and change, of which the war was a part but not a culmination. There is no sense of the war climaxing his ideas. Not belonging to either conveniently classifiable context, but making each context a part of his work, Rosenberg will fit no category. I believe that Owen would have continued to develop as a poet had he survived the war, but his work does, in an illusory way probably, convey a sense of completeness, which death contrived. But because Rosenberg developed before the war, and moulded war into his thinking, he ought not to be the less regarded. It is all the more ironic that his achievement is so often casually spoken of as fragmentary.

His 'war poems' are nearly all contained in his so-called 'Trench Poems' (1916–18), if, that is, we exclude the versions of 'The Unicorn'. These do not alter the direction of the work, but sometimes ramify the ideas, and more often concentrate certain aspects of them. Yet these poems necessarily introduce elements of experienced struggle which his work had lacked before.

'On Receiving News of the War', written in 1914 when he was

still in Cape Town, expresses two attitudes. The first is the
corrosive effect of war:

> Some spirit old
> Hath turned with malign kiss
> Our lives to mould.

Noticeable is the word 'kiss', which qualifies, with frightening
complexity – or is it romanticism, merely? – the malignity of war.
It does not seem to be used to emphasise the differences between
love and war, although the implicit paradox depends on such a
distinction being made. It conveys the sense of something
insidiously and deliberately harmful being done (as if by
Rosenberg's female deities); yet, also implicit is the sense of it
being beneficial, ultimately through purgation, which of course
is Rosenberg's intended meaning. The word has, too, the
properties of euphemistic romanticism, but even if Rosenberg is
using 'kiss' in this way it does not smother the poem. The war/kiss
moulds our lives into temporary evil but finally purges us of our
sickness:

> O! ancient crimson curse!
> Corrode, consume.
> Give back this universe
> Its pristine bloom.

There are striking similarities of meaning between this poem
and parts of *Maud*. Rosenberg hoped war would restore man's
first innocence, but the stylisation prevents us from taking the
idea with absolute literalness. That he swiftly changed his belief
all his 'Trench Poems' show. And however much he hoped war
might cleanse, neither in the poems nor in his letters was he in any
doubt that war was an affliction. No such recognition is deeply
present in *Maud*, or, for that matter, in Brooke's '1914'. I
deliberately cite Brooke again because his defenders sometimes
suggest that, as with Owen, he would have adopted, had he lived,
as scrupulous an anti-war position as Owen did. This seems to me
to devalue Owen considerably, but it also seems fair to point out
that, Rosenberg's (and Sorley's) initial reaction to the war
notwithstanding, neither of them had seen any more of conflict

than Brooke had. Contrast Brooke's perception of war in 'The Dead' – 'they gave, their immortality' – with Rosenberg's 'Red fangs have torn His face'. Rosenberg's poem was written shortly after the declaration of war; Brooke's sequence was published in *New Numbers*, November-December 1914.

Rosenberg's strength as a 'war poet' arises partly from his ability to particularise powerful physical horror and take it, without losing its presence, to a further stage of consciousness. Owen's particularities sometimes get *absorbed* into his universals . . . . Rosenberg admitted most of his experience in a conscious attempt to form his poetry from it:

I will not leave a corner of my consciousness covered up. . . . I have thoughts of a play round our Jewish hero, Judas Maccabeus. I have much real material here, and also there is some parallel in the savagery of the invaders then to this war. I am not decided whether truth of period is a good quality or a negative one.

The thoughtfulness of the final comment bears an interesting relation to Sassoon's realism, although there is no evidence that Rosenberg ever read his work.

A version of 'Break of Day in the Trenches' was probably completed by the end of July 1916, if this is the poem he refers to in his letter to Marsh of 6 August: 'I am enclosing a poem I wrote in the trenches, which is surely as simple as ordinary talk. You might object to the second line as vague, but that was the best way I could express the sense of dawn.' If this is 'Break of Day', it would seem that he wrote it after one month's experience of the trenches. This is an astonishingly swift development of insight into the horror *and* absurdity of war, although, given the depth of insight already revealed in 'Moses', we ought not to be surprised.

> Only a live thing leaps my hand –
> A queer sardonic rat –
> As I pull the parapet's poppy
> To stick behind my ear.
> Droll rat, they would shoot you if they knew
> Your cosmopolitan sympathies.

Since rats haunted the trenches, it is not surprising to find them represented in poetry which has any pretence to realism; both the rat and the poppy (another familiar war creature) occur in Herbert Asquith's 'After the Salvo',[1] for instance. Superficially, in fact, the poems are curiously similar, but whereas in Asquith's poem the rat's purpose is to emphasise, photographically, the general dereliction created by shellfire, Rosenberg's creature appears without such graphic intention.[2] The rat commutes freely between the two enemies' trenches. By bringing in the idea of cosmopolitanism – the expression of which (except between allies, and then in moderation) was a political offence – Rosenberg indicates the absurdity of the situation by permitting the rat, a supposedly lesser creature, to do what men dare not.

In 'God Made Blind' and 'God', man may be in rebellion against God but he occupies a rational position, in that if God is envious and cruel it is rational to resist His demands, by guile in the former case, force in the latter. Rosenberg emphasises this rationality in man by giving God the supposedly irrational rat-soul ('God'). And as with his image of the root, he here creates relationships between his poems and ideas by using an image of the same referent but giving it a differing meaning through a different context. By the time he had come to write 'Break of Day', man and God had exchanged attributes, or, at least, man had acquired those which he had previously and only attributed to God. Man may rule the earth, but war is a man-made irrational activity which brings with it absurd, irrational restrictions – national boundaries demarcated with hatred and death. Man absurdly incarcerates himself in the battlefield for an unknown number of years, but the rat freely traverses these demarcations:

> Now you have touched this English hand
> You will do the same to a German –
> Soon, no doubt, if it be your pleasure
> To cross the sleeping green between.
> It seems you inwardly grin as you pass
> Strong eyes, fine limbs, haughty athletes
> Less chanced than you for life. . . .

As the rat commutes, he mocks the absurd plight of the

supposedly superior creatures – 'It seems you inwardly grin' – an attitude that rationally we are forced to endorse, however painful and offensive we may find it. The harshness of this judgement does not impair the tenderness with which the poem ends, as the harshness does not impair the tenderness in 'Dead Man's Dump'.

Because Rosenberg has elsewhere given God a rat-soul we may associate the complexity and draw some of the meaning there into this poem. Thus the normal[3] attitude in the context of war would be to envisage a benign God sorrowfully regarding the agony of His supreme creation – a perhaps presumptuous assumption for man to have. In 'Break of Day' God is noticeably absent. The implication may be drawn that, since man can do no better than murder his own kind, he deserves no better witness to his suffering, and no better comforter, than the rat (rat-God) who in this poem usurps the rational position man has abandoned. Whatever the original rights were, in the poem conflict has obliterated them. There remains the tragic and absurd destruction of living creatures. The rat's mocking is rational but heartless; but then so here is the position of man, and it is this that the animal mirrors, while at the same time profitably sharing those conditions unprofitable to man. This mockery is the judgement man receives for his conduct. It is not a destructive retribution such as nature provides for man in Owen's 'Exposure', it might be noted, although the judgement in Rosenberg's poem is more explicitly harsh and disheartening. No further punishment needs to be given. It is both judgement and evaluation.

The lesser creature sees its condition as fortunate by comparison with the 'strong athletes'. It 'grins' at a perceived absurdity, but also perhaps in revenge for man's oppression. It is as much an answer to the oppressor, as is the mice's rejoicing in 'Exposure'. The rat's grinning is an image at the core of Rosenberg's achievement, an image complex, vital, and informed by a tragic apprehension. For, in abandoning God and any religious mode, man no longer has a scapegoat on which he can disburden blame for his actions; he is forced into a position of responsibility. Only he can terminate the activities he has set in train. In holding up to us the rat-image, Rosenberg holds up a partial complement to man's self. To recognise the rat is to recognise our absurdity; but if we can recognise our absurdity, we may arrest those activities which otherwise threaten to destroy us. In recognising that he has lost God, man gains himself; but if he recognises and still refuses responsibility, he is entirely lost, without the more traditional assistance of religion, and without the power to act on his own behalf. He is his own burden but not his own action, and the tragic implications are that, so burdened, he may perish. The relationship between the rat and the men is a hierarchical one, but it is also a mirror that answers much more than reflecting merely what is presented to it. The grin is the answer, the point at which man has almost lost the capacity to save himself, and tragedy must issue from such loss of potentiality. This is what the rat's grin recognises and conveys. The point of offence at which men feel judged by a rat has been passed, for more is now at stake than man's rather pitiful pride ('haughty athletes') – pitiful also in that man judges himself as superior to the rat but cannot act as freely. From this point in the poem, Rosenberg develops the tragic extent to which man is mutilating himself, and everything else in nature within the area of conflict.

   This mutilation is implied in the phrase 'the torn fields of France'. Rosenberg manages to envisage a landscape but synchronises the image of it with the image of something smaller. 'Torn' would normally be applied to paper, an object or substance in scale with human beings (made by, and thus in scale with, them). 'Torn' implies a relationship between the object and the person, and the scale adjusted between the two. Also, the verb *tear* has a deliberate, human sense to the action. Landscape, on the other hand, cannot be torn, at least not by human hands and in the way paper is. By making the landscape 'torn', by merging the two scales, the poet suggests that the ground is torn with as much ease as hands tear paper, a suggestion that indicates the power in the implements of war and the vulnerability of man and nature. At this point (line 15) the poem becomes more violent, but one feels that Rosenberg has earned the right at this stage of the poem's development to release his sense of war's violence:

> What do you see in our eyes
> At the shrieking iron and flame
> Hurled through still heavens?

The poem ends tenderly:

> Poppies whose roots are in man's veins
> Drop, and are ever dropping;
> But mine in my ear is safe,
> Just a little white with the dust.

The poppies, of course, represent the dead, their violently shed blood, and in using the image Rosenberg is employing a familiar emblem. The poppy in his fantasy (and everyone else's, one imagines) is nourished by blood that has soaked into the earth and turned the petals red. Rosenberg took this common fantasy a stage further. In return for nourishing the flower and the plant as a whole, the poppy gives man the ambiguous gift of mortality. Its 'roots are in man's veins'; or rather, though this is circular, the poppies feed off man but they feed off his *mortality*, and therefore emphasise it. They too 'Drop, and are ever dropping'. The extension of meaning that Rosenberg has given to the original fantasy is organic to it; the graft seems entirely natural, as primitive and folk-like as the original he has extended. Such achievement attests the strength and tact of his imagination; for it is one thing to invent, quite another to submit one's imagination to another's, or to the collective imagination, and extend it, adding something new and harmonious.

Yet even here Rosenberg has linked this poem with 'Daughters of War', for the same kind of logic operates in both poems. Death is nourished by mortal life; the Daughters lust for soldiers who must however be killed (for them) in their prime. There is also an echo in this of 'God Made Blind', for the female deities are envious of the male human activity – 'envy of the days of flesh' – as much as God was of the human lovers.

The last two lines of 'Break of Day in the Trenches' quietly emphasise the perception of death that is not due to age. 'Just a little white' may evoke 'just a little while', a phrase of everyday speech 'as simple as ordinary talk', which in its turn suggests not only the comparatively brief span of a man's life, and a flower's, but the likelihood of the soldier's life being foreshortened. The device subtly underlines the transience of life in war.

'Break of Day in the Trenches' is a fine poem, and its metrical and rhythmical composition is integral to its meaning.[4] The line

length is controlled by stress and rhythm rather than by a
specified counted number of syllables operating in a single
metrical frame. In the main there are three or four stresses per
line, but the number of syllables may vary, just as the kind of unit
itself may; the line is neither basically iambic nor trochaic.
Rosenberg moves his rhythm to originate his meaning:

> Thĕ dárknĕšs crúmblĕš ăwáy –
> Ĭt iś thĕ samĕ olď dŕuiď Timĕ ăs évĕr. . . .
>
> Nów yoŭ havĕ toúched thĭs Eńglĭsh hánd
> Yoŭ wĭll dó thĕ sámĕ tŏ ă Gérmañ –

One notices how, in the second set of lines, the shift of stress and
the alteration in pace (between the two lines) not only emphasises the opposition between the English and the German hand,
but also initiates a sense of the rat moving from one set of trenches
to another; each line initiates a location on the battlefield.

Rosenberg's longest war poem, 'Dead Man's Dump', contains
most of what he had to say about the war. In a letter to Marsh
dated 8 May 1917, he wrote, 'I've written some lines suggested by
going out wiring, or rather carrying wire up the line on limbers
and running over dead bodies lying about.' The poem may at
first seem picaresque, but what Rosenberg does is to present a
number of complex responses to combat, and then unify them
into a single realisation of how war entails one damaging,
continuous impact on the body and the mind. The poem opens
with what may seem a biased complaint of the enemy's brutality:

> . . . the flood of *brutish* men
> Upon our brothers dear.   [my italics]

This may seem like gratuitous half-honesty: honest only in that
war is brutish, and therefore the enemy behaves brutishly, but
only half honest because we behave by the same token as
brutishly. It seems unlikely, however, that a man of Rosenberg's
intelligence, in one of his central poems and with his professed
attitudes to war, should see, or profess, only half the situation. He
might of course have changed in his attitude towards the
Germans, but nothing in his letters indicates this. External

evidence is ambiguous, although his letters are usually corroborative of the attitudes and ideas in the poems. So that in the absence of any expressed belief that the Germans are more brutish than the English, and taking into account the cosmopolitanism of 'Break of Day in the Trenches', it might be reasonable to try another explanation. Rosenberg is saying perhaps that when you are fighting, the enemy will always seem brutish, and that you will not notice your own behaviour. If this seems viable then the poet is re-creating, not immediate judgements, but the *responses* which he felt he and others made to the enemy's attack. And surely it is a correct one, as correct as what the Germans would similarly feel when the British attacked. Again, if this is correct, it shows, as Harding indicates, how Rosenberg managed to remain, as he said he wished to, open to 'the strange and extraordinary new conditions. . . . I will not leave a corner of my consciousness covered up'. Now he is not pre-judging the issue with ready-made ideas, but responding to the situation, and making his judgement on it when he has responded as fully and finally as possible.

The second stanza contains the 'limber' passage referred to above:

> The wheels lurched over sprawled dead
> But pained them not, though their bones crunched,
> Their shut mouths made no moan.

'Lurched' is the painful, exact word. Limbers (carriages for ammunition and equipment) running over bodies will lurch. The word also seems to use Rosenberg's device of transposition, for 'lurch' may also refer to the feelings of the person as he empathetically 'feels' the limbers running over the bodies. Rosenberg presumably felt this enough for him to have remarked on it to Marsh. What is painful in this passage is the sense that the limbers' weight will damage the body as much as if it were alive. The watcher *feels* that if he can see the body he cannot feel that it is dead; the corpses are still perhaps too nearly human. The 'crunched' bones emphasise this, and emphasise too how close to the dead the living were drawn by the shared experience of conflict in which chance decimates some and not others. Finally the reader, like the watcher, identifies himself with the crushed corpses. The seemingly unnecessary 'But pained them not' confirms this sense of the dead not being so, by telling you something you know, but cannot fully feel, partly because the identification is so strong. The conscious intelligence and the emotional responses suffer dissociation. The passage moves into a recognition of how all suffer in war, and surely contradicts any possible partiality in the first stanza. 'Friend and foeman' lie together 'And shells go crying over them'. Here again Rosenberg makes 'crying' have two agents. The shells cry out, as do the humans mutilated by fragments of exploding shells. The same kind of device is used in 'Break of Day in the Trenches':

> What do you see in our eyes
> At the shrieking iron and flame . . . ?

The third stanza brings in a theme expressed by most of the war poets (the non-combatant ones also, as F. S. Flint in 'Lament'):

> Earth has waited for them,
> All the time of their growth
> Fretting for their decay:
> Now she has them at last!
> In the strength of their strength
> Suspended – stopped and held.

This stanza, which as Dennis Silk observed is often omitted or truncated in anthologies,[5] is an important one, being in many ways a fuller version of a passage in 'Daughters of War':

> I heard the mighty daughters' giant sighs
> In sleepless passion for the sons of valour, . . .

Both passages assert that the earth/daughters desire 'the sons of valour' at the peak of their virility (as art, in Keats's 'Ode on a Grecian Urn', arrests and fixes youth at its most graceful and passionate). In 'Dead Man's Dump' such suspending of the youthful lives is shown to be more evil than in 'Daughters of War'; Rosenberg keeps the question open until the end of the latter poem, since to have done otherwise would be to have made redundant the accumulating of dramatic responses and ideas which structure the poem. In 'Dead Man's Dump' he is not working for one compact movement towards a final accumulation of response and meaning, but towards a series of different but cohering responses.

To return to the stanza itself, 'stopped and held' is powerful in that each participle corroborates and seems to contradict the other: 'held' suggests a tenacious holding on, as the soldier would hold on to his life; but 'held' is also consonant with 'stopped', because it is the earth that does the holding of their lives, which are obtained at their peak. But where, in Keats's poem, art fixes the youthful lives in such a way that both the lives and the image interact on each other and produce a sense of immortality, in Rosenberg's it is death which does this; and, as Harding indicates, shows up even more the value of what is being destroyed. As Owen perceived in 'Strange Meeting', it is 'the truth untold' (pity), and the value lost sight of, one might add, that are so often casualties in war.

Stanza four begins to question the immortality habitually attributed to the soldier dying in battle. Where do the dead go, and what becomes of them?

> Earth! Have they gone into you?
> Somewhere they must have gone,
> And flung on your hard back
> Is their soul's sack
> Emptied of God-ancestralled essences.

The question is exclamatory and in part deliberately tautological, since it is clear to Rosenberg that their journey is no further than into the earth. They have no other immortality, except of a metaphysical kind. Life is brutally foreshortened and its value, if we are lucky, fully realised at that moment of death. The real question is placed at the end of the stanza: 'Who hurled them out? Who hurled?' We may realise that man has done the expulsion, but the question that answer raises is, for what reason and to what end?

Stanza six expresses not only the *illusion* of safety, created by survival, but also the feeling of immortality which youth lends to the one illusioned, 'ichor', the food of the immortals, is only seemingly fed 'as' to the soldiers, and 'lucky limbs' stresses the fiction of such immortality:

> Or stood aside for the half used life to pass
> Out of those doomed nostrils and the doomed mouth,
> When the swift iron burning bee
> Drained the wild honey of their youth.

The terms are Keatsian, with 'wild' recalling a similar debt in Owen's 'Strange Meeting': 'I went hunting wild/After the wildest beauty'. In Rosenberg's poem the wildness of the shells is made to qualify the wildness of youth, but without reducing that wildness. 'Half used', in fact, shows Rosenberg not so much concerned with the soldiers' being dead, as with the instant of their death, and with that fraction of their lives so far lived. The moment of their death is ever-present, and it is a way of enforcing the value of what has been lost. Rosenberg's Keatsian moment differs in emphasis, however, from Owen's in 'Strange Meeting', in that he makes his moment of understanding synchronise with the actuality of the battlefield. Thinking about the event is not separated from its happening. In this sense, at least, Rosenberg's apprehensions are more intimate because more immediately connected with the event itself. There is less evident distancing than there is in Owen's poem, but then the problem of distancing is a less necessary or mechanical problem than *we* have perhaps, with Eliot's help, supposed it to be. It is not the distance that matters so much as the quality of the relationship between the poet's ego and what he is writing of; and to speak of distance and recollection, in Owen for instance, as demonstrating a superior human response or a better poetic one is, to say the least, not proved. It would be just, I think, to say that Owen's responses are more retrospective, in his poems, than Rosenberg's are. Compare almost any passage in 'Dead Man's Dump' with, say:

> If anything might rouse him now
> The kind old sun will know.

In stanza seven of 'Dead Man's Dump' Rosenberg still concentrates on the specific response:

> In bleeding pangs
> Some borne on stretchers dreamed of home,
> Dear things, war-blotted from their hearts.

Event for event, some comparison with this might be made with Owen's 'Dulce et Decorum Est':

> If in some smothering dreams you too could pace
> Behind the wagon that we flung him in,
> And watch the white eyes writhing in his face; . . .

Owen's lines are vivid, precise, terrible; but the difference between the two, apart from Owen's more dramatic rendering, is the energy of 'war-blotted' and the way in which the mass of the noun 'war' is converted into descriptively verbal force. The effect of Rosenberg's energy here is to bring the scene upon the reader with extra insistence, although it might be said that 'Dulce et Decorum Est' presents the event in such a way as to make the reader re-enact it. Nevertheless, the comparison between the one poet's immediacy and the other's recollectedness will in general hold. The didactic nature finds it easier to manipulate the event if it is recollected rather than immediately experienced, and this accounts I think for the shift in Owen's poem from the re-enactment of the gas-attack to the subsequent recollection of some man thrilling the 'children' with tales of danger.

Stanza eight of Rosenberg's poem shows man as his own destroyer:

> What dead are born when you kiss each soundless soul
> With lightning and thunder from your mined heart,
> Which man's self dug, and his blind fingers loosed?

'Blind' of course suggests unheeding; incapable of heeding by how much man has lost the capacity to recognise what he is doing to himself. The admonition implicit in the line extends through the next stanza in an overt expression of tenderness:

> A man's brains splattered on
> A stretcher-bearer's face;
> His shook shoulders slipped their load,

But when they bent to look again
The drowning soul was sunk too deep
For human tenderness.

The violence of the first three lines emphasises the tenderness of
the three following; but one gets no sense of manipulation
because Rosenberg's direct and immediate expression does not
permit one to think the variation a dramatic device operating
separately from his feelings. The tenderness gets emphasis
because it is of no practical value to the wounded – and then
dead – man. The poet's registration does not heartlessly include
him as one more item in his rehearsal of war's brutalities, and it
disdains this precisely in that his tenderness is of no practical use
to the man. Rosenberg, that is, was not a propagandist, in the bad
meaning of that word. On the contrary, precisely because the
man is included, we feel the value of the poet's tenderness and
thus, ultimately, of his judgement of war's destruction. The
'uselessness' of his tenderness, a precursory echo of the poem's
ending, turns out to be another fully experienced instance of
futility in war; and the single death becomes representative.

I speak of tenderness rather than pity, because I would make a
distinction between Rosenberg's and Owen's response to war's
brutalities. Owen's compassion may be unhesitating in its
generosity, as I am certain it is, but it moves over war's victims as
they are recollected. The pity is universal. His tendency (not with
his anger and satire) is to move from specificity to an inclusive
ethic that will cover all war's victims. He represents all men. The
whole stands for each part assembled together. With Rosenberg
it is otherwise, and the difference lies between Owen's compassion and Rosenberg's tenderness. Compassion is sacred, and
distanced. Rosenberg's tenderness is that of a man intimately
speaking of one death. It does not try to include the others. This
specific tenderness for a particular man makes the man representative without losing his specificity.

Even in the next stanza, Rosenberg does not lose sight of the
particular death:

They left this dead with the older dead,
Stretched at the cross roads.

In the second line an emblematic and more generalised implication emerges; the cross-roads may represent the dilemma of
man's future. The dead accumulating at this 'juncture' are both
admonitory and accusing. But even these, in stanza ten, are
identified, although negatively, by their loss of human identity:

> Burnt black by strange decay
> Their sinister faces lie,
> The lid over each eye,
> The grass and coloured clay
> More motion have than they,
> Joined to the great sunk silences.

'Strange' in the sense of alien, not now belonging to the human
tissue, the bodies will soon be a part of grass and clay, which have
more life now. 'Sunk silences' suggests the silence of the earth, but
also the silence and space of the air which they filled when alive.
It suggests, moreover, the tomb-like spaces which they now fill
with their death. Silence. A silence of speculation left for the
living; a void where nothing is known except that the dead are
inert to us. The question of an afterlife is raised, but answered
only with silence. It is raised earlier in the poem with the
platonist image 'soul's sack', but in this second instance, more
tentatively. Even in the first case, no sense of the platonist's belief
in the soul returning to its spiritual and collective home after the
death of the body is permitted:

> And flung on your hard back
> Is their soul's sack . . .

– all that is rejected. If the body is treated thus, can there really be
a soul, which is any better treated? The spiritual part of man dies
with his body. The body is parted from life, not from a soul.

The last two stanzas move from this question, for, in the poem's
terms, even if man has a soul, its existence seems incapable of
affecting the way in which we treat each other – as the 'soul's
sack' is treated. The poem returns after one line of scene-setting
('Here is one not long dead') to the expectations of a dying man,
who is waiting for help that, in this instance, would seem to be of
no use. He is expecting it from a party of men who know nothing

of his need until it is too late. Rosenberg makes a distinction between actively wishing for death and passively accepting it:

> Swift for the end to break
> Or the wheels to break, . . .

When they reach him, he is dead, and at the end he had even wanted them to arrive:

> 'Will they come? Will they ever come?'
> . . .
> So we crashed round the bend,
> We heard his weak scream,
> We heard his very last sound,
> And our wheels grazed his dead face.

The man's death is particular and representative. The failure to reach him in time represents the war's process of inevitable erosion. The tenderness, on the other hand, without destroying the representative quality, holds our attention upon this man and his death. The tenderness and the barbarity in the situation modify each other, and will continue to do so, even perhaps as one man kills another. And perhaps the tenderness will itself become hardened. This is also a cost of war; to elicit the tenderness which itself is consumed. . . .

Source: extract from *Out of Battle* (Oxford, 1972), pp. 273–89.

NOTES

1. See Brian Gardner (ed.), *Up the Line to Death* (London, 1964), p. 81.

2. Creatures in malign relationship to man appear forcefully in several of Rosenberg's poems. The 'rotting God' image appears in 'God' and 'Moses' (*Works*, p. 51) and so does the wolf (ibid.); a toad 'shifting his belly' in 'Moses' (*Works*, p. 59); the worm in 'A Worm Fed on the Heart of Corinth' (*Works*, p. 74), one of the few Greek references in his work; lice appear in both 'The Immortals' and 'Louse Hunting' (*Works*,

pp. 78, 79). Like Owen, Rosenberg sees nature as sometimes in malign relationship to man, but it is not so much a transformation caused by war (man's making) as the emphasis of perception caused by the man's unpleasant or fearful context. Partial exceptions to this exist, as, for example, 'the swift iron burning bee' in 'Dead Man's Dump' (*Works*, p. 82).

3. Normal: a word with many users, and uses. Newbolt regarded Owen's disgust at the war as 'hardly normal'. [See the extract from Newbolt's letter in Part One, above. – Ed.]

4. 'Regular rhythms I do not like much, but of course it depends where the stress and accent are laid' (*Works*, p. 317).

5. Dennis Silk, 'Isaac Rosenberg, 1890–1918'. *Judaism*, XIV, 4 (Autumn, 1965) p. 466.

6. ON SIEGFRIED SASSOON

Jon Silkin   'Brilliant Juxtaposition'
(1960)

. . . We are inclined to forget the ferocity of attack in the war poems of Sassoon. Of course, we are familiar, or think we are, with his attitude towards war. We know he felt, because he recorded, a sense of betrayal – a betrayal brought about by a government that was, he asserted, needlessly prolonging a war for political ends that could in no way justify or excuse the loss of one life. We know that after 'psychiatric treatment' which was the government's reply to Sassoon's formal protest, he went back to the war because he felt he could not remain separate from its other victims. Yet we are inclined to scale down the scathing, exact attack he made on those at home insensible to the suffering of the soldiers on the front: insensible partly because of the 'noble' welter of patriotism and valour-worship, insensible finally because it was easier to mug up an emotional, hero-worshipping attitude to the soldier in abstract than think about his position, locally, as he experienced it, in fear and in pain. Yet the moral censure of what Joseph Cohen calls the angry prophet is inescapable.[1] . . . [Quotes lines 1, 7–13 of 'Counter-Attack'.]

What is remarkable here is, firstly, the cool way in which the dead, in putrefaction, are represented. The 'sodden buttocks' and 'clotted heads' are abruptly, and brilliantly, contrasted with the human, living perception of something (ironically) non-human – non-human that is in contrast with the human dead. But when the perception comes, it is given an ironic turn – 'the jolly old rain'. One cannot speak the phrase 'jolly old rain' without evoking the hearty, almost lunatic, back-slapping camaraderie endemic in a society insensible to human pain, insensible therefore to the grotesque dead here. And thus, characteristically, Sassoon makes one of his lunges at the establishment he held responsible for the prolonged sufferings of the soldiers. Equally characteristic is this attack, more compressed, directed at the well-meaning but futile 'after-care' of the disabled by those at home.

> Does it matter? – losing your sight? . . .
> There's such splendid work for the blind . . .
> ('Does it Matter?')

It is part of his attack on the insensibility of those at home:

> The boys came back. Bands played and flags were flying,
> And Yellow-Pressmen thronged the sunlit street
> To cheer the soldiers who'd *refrained* from dying . . .
> ('Fight to a Finish')

The italics are mine. Sassoon is suggesting that there was a conspiracy on the part of the government to carry on the war, which resulted in the murdering of soldiers. How impolite (he seems to suggest) these surviving soldiers are. There is a delicious, grim politeness about the word in context.

Sassoon's use of language derived from Keats; his pastoral verses are sensuous but conventional. In his war poetry he incorporated (the point is obvious) the language and rhythms of speech with all its vividness – wheezed, goggle-eyed, guzzling, gulping, glum (glum heroes) – and either expelled the Keatsean mode or, more subtly, juxtaposed the two elements so that the everyday word created a satirical gap between itself and the prevailing 'poetic' norm. 'Glum heroes' is a fair example of this technique. And this method demonstrates what he was about. He wanted to jar those at home into a realisation of what was happening to the men at the front. He wanted to cut through the humbug and cant of a generation that could glorify war, and he did this by juxtaposing (through language) the attitudes of two generations further complicated by the divisions of class. In the film 'Colonel Blimp', the hero (the colonel of course) is puzzled by the techniques of a new warfare. He does not understand the machines, but more significantly, he cannot comprehend the young men, their attitudes and feelings, their detachment, their unpatriotic 'commitment', not to their country, nor to their allies, but merely to their job – the war. Their attitude is a long heave away from those attitudes of protest found in the first-war poets, but they have in common the 'feel' of their time, a feel that meant the discarding of patrotic, Victorian cant. Sassoon's contribution was this brilliant juxtaposition of savage, raw experience with elderly bewilderment and insensibility.

> If I were fierce, and bald, and short of breath,
>   I'd live with scarlet majors at the Base,
> And speed glum heroes up the line to death.
>   You'd see me with my puffy petulant face,
> Guzzling and gulping in the best hotel,
>   Reading the Roll of Honour. 'Poor young chap,'
> I'd say – 'I used to know his father well;
>   Yes, we've lost heavily in this last scrap.'
> And when the war is done and youth stone dead,
> I'd toddle safely home and die – in bed.
>
> ('Base Details')

SOURCE: 'Keeping The Home Fires Burning', *Stand*, IV, no. 3 (1960), pp. 37–8.

NOTE

1. Joseph Cohen, 'The Three Roles of Siegfried Sassoon', *Tulane Studies in English*, VII (1957).

Bernard Bergonzi   'Counter-Attack and Other Poems' (1965)

. . . In [*Counter-Attack and Other Poems*] Sassoon completes the transformation of documentary realism into an angry didactic outcry. Although he was never a poetic modernist or even, like Owen, a conscious experimenter, Sassoon was forced by the need

for exactness in registering front-line experience into a degree of
colloquial language and a conversational tone that was still a
novelty in contemporary verse. The quality of his realism, in
language and subject-matter, is evident in the first stanza of the
title-poem:

> We'd gained our first objective hours before
> While dawn broke like a face with blinking eyes,
> Pallid, unshaved and thirsty, blind with smoke.
> Things seemed all right at first. We held their line,
> With bombers posted, Lewis guns well placed,
> And clink of shovels deepening the shallow trench.
> The place was rotten with dead; green clumsy legs
> High-booted, sprawled and grovelled along the saps
> And trunks, face downward, in the·sucking mud,
> Wallowed like trodden sand-bags loosely filled;
> And naked sodden buttocks, mats of hair,
> Bulged, clotted heads slept in the plastering slime.
> And then the rain began, – the jolly old rain!

There is an immediate contrast between the two parts of the
stanza: in the opening lines the stress is on action; the attacking
troops, though possibly exhausted, are alert and prepared:

> We held their line,
> With bombers posted, Lewis guns well placed.

Tone and diction have a marked colloquial bareness: 'Things
seemed all right at first.' But this patch of local military activity is
seen to be literally resting on the dead; the larger point emerges
that the war is being fought on a foundation of corpses. In the
opening phrase of the second part, 'The place was rotten with
dead', the colloquial tone is continued, with a suggestion that the
dead are now equated with infesting vermin or some form of
loathsome corruption. But then the manner changes, and the
remaining extended description of the accumulated corpses is
written in a complex, almost Miltonic syntax which creates a
tension with the continued brutal realism of the diction and
subject: the dead, the literal foundation of the activity of the
living, are described with a kind of gruesome ritualism that sets

them apart from the modest, brisk activity of the still-living. There is a sharp return to the colloquial in the final phrase, 'the jolly old rain!' Jon Silkin has commented on this phrase [see previous extract–Ed.]:

One cannot speak the phrase 'jolly old rain' without evoking the hearty, almost lunatic, back-slapping camaraderie endemic in a society insensible to human pain, insensible therefore to the grotesque dead here. And thus, characteristically, Sassoon makes one of his lunges at the establishment he held responsible for the prolonged suffering of the soldiers.

This is a plausible interpretation, though it is possible that Silkin is making these words bear too large a weight of meaning: the larger context is not satirical, and a phrase like 'the jolly old rain' may be no more than an instance of the soldier's inevitable tendency to reduce the phenomena of front-line life to something like acceptable proportions by the use of familiar and contemptuous terms; one can compare the song about corpses 'hanging on the old barbed wire'.

    The description of the huddled corpses is also reminiscent of a work that must have had a certain influence on the poems in *Counter-Attack* – Henri Barbusse's *Le Feu*. This novel appeared in France in 1916, and the English translation, *Under Fire*, came out the following year. Barbusse is a realist in the tradition of Zola; his novel is a series of loosely connected sketches of trench life, based, it appears, on his own diaries; it is a work of violent protest against the war and the destruction of values that it involved, and it is marked by a harrowing and emphatic stress on death, mutilation and corruption, both moral and physical. Like the English war poets, Barbusse is concerned to shatter the traditional image of the hero:

'How will they regard this slaughter, they who'll live after us, to whom progress – which comes as sure as fate – will at last restore the poise of their conscience? How will they regard these exploits which even we who perform them don't know whether one should compare them with those of Plutarch's and Corneille's heroes or with those of hooligans and apaches?'

Le Feu, being written so close to the experiences which inspired it, is a novel of violent feeling and no detachment. In many respects, it is a work of intensive documentary realism; but in some ways Barbusse seems to have distorted, or at least formalised, his narrative in order to construct significant and didactic patterns. Unlike his English contemporaries, he betrays a strong political commitment; he was well to the Left, and in later years became an active Communist. One should also mention here that a French critic, Jean Cru, subsequently questioned much of the accuracy of Barbusse's detail, and was very critical of the authenticity of the total picture conveyed by the novel (see Cru's *Témoins*, Paris, 1929). Nevertheless, Sassoon and Owen both responded very favourably to *Le Feu* when they read it at Craiglockhart in 1917, and herein lies its significance for a study of English war poetry. Sassoon lent *Le Feu* to Owen, 'which set him alight as no other war book had done', and a paragraph from the novel about the brutalising effect of war appears as an epigraph to *Counter-Attack*.

In this collection Sassoon brought to perfection the hard, punchy, epigrammatic style that had already served him as an apt instrument for satire. We also see a certain extension of his range, as in the bitter pathos of 'Does it Matter?'

> Does it matter? – losing your sight? . . .
> There's such splendid work for the blind;
> And people will always be kind,
> As you sit on the terrace remembering
> And turning your face to the light.
>
> Do they matter? – those dreams from the pit? . . .
> You can drink and forget and be glad,
> And people won't say that you're mad;
> For they'll know that you've fought for your country,
> And no one will worry a bit.

Or consider, again, the blend of complex feelings in 'To Any Dead Officer':

> Good-bye, old lad! Remember me to God,
>   And tell Him that our Politicians swear
> They won't give in till Prussian Rule's been trod

> Under the Heel of England . . . Are you there? . . .
> Yes . . . and the War won't end for at least two years;
> But we've got stacks of men . . . I'm blind with tears,
>   Staring into the dark. Cheero!
> I wish they'd killed you in a decent show.

Here Sassoon makes a compelling use of colloquialism and the relaxed understatements of casual conversation. One might mention, again, 'Repression of War Experience', where the movement of the verse enacts a collapse from precarious serenity to shell-shocked nightmare; or 'Suicide in the Trenches', in which Sassoon, like other war poets, discovers the possibilities for ironical effect in a Housmanesque vehicle:

> You smug-faced crowds with kindling eye
> Who cheer when soldier lads march by,
> Sneak home and pray you'll never know
> The hell where youth and laughter go.

Yet despite the extended range in *Counter-Attack*, Sassoon remains fundamentally a poet of narrow but direct effects: his language is hard, clear, sharply defined, rather than suggestive or capable of the associative effects of a poet of larger resources. On the whole, Sassoon remained aware of his limitations and did not attempt a profundity that was beyond him: his gifts were, pre-eminently, those of a satirist, and it was in satire that he excelled; some of his epigrams have achieved a permanent status, like 'The General' – ' "He's a cheery old card", grunted Harry to Jack. . . . But he did for them both by his plan of attack.' The principal target for Sassoon's satire was the civilian population, and in particular, figures like politicians and journalists, who issued exhortations or encouragements to the troops without having any real conception of what they were enduring. And in one harsh poem, 'Glory of Women', Sassoon seems to attack the female sex in general: 'You love us when we're heroes, home on leave, Or wounded in a mentionable place. . . .' The feeling of being alienated from the women at home, who were fixated in civilian ignorance and conventional heroic responses, was expressed by a number of writers who went through the war; they felt themselves thrown back on the deeper and more authentic camaraderie of their fellows in arms. Sassoon's animus was given horrifying, crisp expression in 'Fight to a Finish':

> The boys came back. Bands played and flags were flying,
>   And Yellow-Pressmen thronged the sunlit street
> To cheer the soldiers who'd refrained from dying,
>   And hear the music of returning feet.
> 'Of all the thrills and ardours War has brought,
> This moment is the finest.' (So they thought.)
>
> Snapping their bayonets on to charge the mob,
>   Grim Fusiliers broke ranks with glint of steel,
> At last the boys had found a cushy job.
>
> .   .   .   .
>
>   I heard the Yellow-Pressmen grunt and squeal;
> And with my trusty bombers turned and went
> To clear those Junkers out of Parliament.

In such a poem as this – whose verbal accomplishment seems to me admirable – one is, I think, made aware of the inherent limits of Sassoon's (and perhaps of any) satirical approach: the complexities of actual experience are reduced to a single satisfying gesture (and a phrase like 'the soldiers who'd refrained from dying' suggests that the anti-heroic mode, just as much as the heroic, can achieve its effects too easily). In fact, although Sassoon's political sympathies at this time were vaguely on the Left (but not in the committed manner of Barbusse), this poem gives a revealing indication of a state of mind that could lead to fascism in its early, idealistic phase: the Italian *fascisti*, after all, were disillusioned ex-servicemen who considered that they had been betrayed by the corrupt institutions of a decadent par- liamentary society (their anti-proletarian bias had been anti- cipated by the feelings of the English Tommy that munition- workers were 'shirkers'; Graves remarked to a shocked Bertrand Russell during the war that his men loathed munition-workers and would be only too glad of the chance to shoot a few). Fortunately there was to be no native growth of ex-service fascism, save in the Black-and-Tans and the mythology of the Bulldog Drummond stories.

Counter-Attack secured Sassoon's reputation as a poet. By 1918 the public mood was ready for what he had to say, and his attacks on the Nation at Home were accepted with a possibly masochistic fervour. It found admirers in unexpectedly high places; Winston Churchill, at that time Minister of Munitions, was one: he learnt by heart some of the poems in *Counter-Attack*, and approved of them because, he claimed, they would finally bring home to the civilian population what the troops at the Front had to endure. Thus, Sassoon's anti-war outcry had been transformed, by a more agile mind than he could have foreseen, into a subtler form of pro-war propaganda. The Establishment has always been adept at incorporating rebels, and Sassoon – now once more a serving officer – saw something of the process when he was invited to meet Churchill and good-humouredly treated to a set speech on the militaristic virtues.

There is a significant passage in Henry Williamson's novel, *A Test to Destruction*: the hero, Phillip Maddison, has heard *Counter-Attack* discussed by some other young officers whilst he was in hospital, and later he asks his Colonel about it:

'Have you read, by any chance, the poems called *Counter Attack*, sir?'
'Oh yes. I read them in course of duty. I'm Intelligence at the War House, for my sins.'
'What do you think of them, sir?'
'Oh, I think we've all felt like that, at one time or another. I'm no judge of poetry, but I heard Winston Churchill at White's talkin' about them the other day. "Cries of pain wrung from soldiers during a test to destruction", were his words.'

If the poems in *Counter-Attack* were, in fact, regarded as inspired shell-shock symptoms, as psychological evidence rather than moral statements, then it seems as if Sassoon's public protest was blunted, just as his attempt at a personal protest had been. Nevertheless these poems, expressing a mood of anti-heroic revolt with such fervour and harsh wit, strike a new and incisive note in the literature of war.

Throughout the 'twenties, when he continued to have left-wing leanings, Sassoon wrote sharp, epigrammatic verses that sniped at authority and conventional attitudes. In this respect he was at one with his age (one can compare the more concentrated satirical observations of Edgell Rickword), and sometimes these poems rise to an unusual level of poetic intensity, as in 'On Passing the New Menin Gate':

> Here was the world's worst wound. And here with pride
> 'Their name liveth for ever,' the Gateway claims.
> Was ever an immolation so belied
> As these intolerably nameless names?
> Well might the Dead who struggled in the slime
> Rise and deride this sepulchre of crime.

As with other writers who narrowly survived the Great War, it was to remain Sassoon's one authentic subject; it, or the emotions stemming from it, inspired his best poems, and his admirable prose works. When Sassoon attempted to write straightforward poems on subjects remote from the war, he dwindled to the stature of a minor Georgian survival: the bulk of his later poetry, sententious or laxly pastoral, is carefully written and overpower-ingly dull. He continued to write pungently satirical poems into the 'thirties, but in 1940 he commemorated the feelings of the time in one or two flatly conventional patriotic poems. 'Silent Service', for instance, begins,

> Now, multifold, let Britain's patient power
> Be proven within us for the world to see.
> None are exempt from service in this hour;
> And vanquished in ourselves we dare not be.

This has been aptly described by D. J. Enright as 'a dash of Winston Churchill in an ocean of water'; he suggests the necessarily damaging comparison with Herbert Read's 'To a Conscript of 1940'.[1] (There were more reasons for *feeling* like this in 1940 than in 1914, but less excuse for writing like it.) In such pieces the mood is close to that of Sassoon's early exalted war poems of 1915; the wheel has swung full circle. But it is the poems of 1916–18 that count, and that represent Sassoon's ineradicable contribution both to English poetry and the records of the Great War.

SOURCE: extract from *Heroes' Twilight* (London, 1965), pp. 102–8.

NOTE

1. D. J. Enright, *The Modern Age* (vol. 7 of *The Pelican Guide to English Literature*, ed. Boris Ford, 1961), p. 161.

7. ON CHARLES SORLEY

John Press   'A Spirit of Stern and Stoic Feature' (1966)

Charles Sorley's *Marlborough and Other Poems* was published in 1916, a year after the author had been killed by a sniper's bullet through the head in the battle of Loos. By 1919 it had run through four editions; a fifth appeared in 1922; when it was reprinted in the Cambridge Miscellany series in 1932 it was reissued in the same year. In *A Survey of Modernist Poetry* (1926), Robert Graves and Laura Riding remarked that 'of the War poets whose works were temporarily advertised by their death in action, only three can be regretted as poets: Sorley, Rosenberg and Owen'.

Sorley's fame appeared secure, yet in the past thirty years his reputation has steadily declined. Yeats left him out of the *Oxford Book of Modern Verse* (1936) and Michael Roberts omitted him from his influential anthology, although naming him, together with de la Mare, Blunden, Muir, Plomer and Campbell, as one of those who 'seem to me to have written good poems without having been compelled to make any notable development of poetic technique'.[1] By 1943 he was completely forgotten. Robert Nichols's anthology of war poetry contains a preface in the form of a dialogue between himself and Julian Tennyson, in which the following passage occurs:

Tennyson: 'Who was Charles Sorley?'
Nichols: 'Probably the most clear-sighted English poet killed in that war.'[2]

Nichols's tribute has not served to rescue Sorley from oblivion. His poems are seldom included in anthologies, and even his name is scarcely known to poets and critics, let alone to the general reader.

Moreover, those critics who consider him worthy of mention have unwittingly given a false impression of his significance and of his development.[3] Thus D. J. Enright, in his essay 'The Literature of the First World War', after dealing with the shortcomings of Rupert Brooke's sonnet-sequence *1914*, refers to his death and observes that Sorley 'died six months later but those months had been spent on the Western Front'.[4] He then quotes with approval a short prose extract about poets and men of letters; a judgement on Brooke; and portions of two poems. Although Enright does not date these extracts, the reader would assume that Sorley wrote them during his service on the Western Front, which is presumed to have opened his eyes to the true nature of war. In fact, Sorley was at the Western Front only from 30 May 1915 until his death four and a half months later. The prose extract is from a paper on John Masefield given by Sorley to his school Literary Society in 1912 when he was seventeen; the judgement on Rupert Brooke was written in April 1915 when Sorley was still in England; and while one of the verse extracts is from what may well have been his last poem, written in France, the other is from a sonnet written probably as early as August 1914 and certainly before he had left for France.

Enright acknowledges his debt to a chapter on the trench poets in de Sola Pinto's *Crisis in English Poetry*. Admirable though this chapter is, it nonetheless contrives to be misleading about Sorley, while paying tribute to his originality and perceptiveness. Professor Pinto argues that Sorley broke away from the conventionally 'heroic' attitude of Brooke and Grenfell:

The poems that [Sorley] wrote in the last years of his life express new attitudes to the war which are quite different from those of Brooke and Grenfell. They are the attitudes of men who have known the horror and boredom of modern warfare at first hand.[5]

He then quotes immediately after this passage the following stanza:

A hundred thousand million mites we go
Wheeling and tacking o'er the eternal plain,
Some black with death – and some are white with woe.
Who sent us forth? Who takes us home again?

But this comes from a poem written in September 1914, the month in which Sorley became a soldier, eight months before he had begun to know at first hand the horror and boredom of modern war.

It may seem pedantic to harp on these trifling errors, but they spring from what seems to me a misplaced view of Sorley. Both Enright and de Sola Pinto are voicing the current orthodox belief about the poetry of the First World War, which may be summarised as follows: young men of the upper-middle classes, such as Brooke and Grenfell, knowing nothing of modern war, indulged in sentimental heroics on the outbreak of fighting in 1914; Siegfried Sassoon, having experienced the horror of actual warfare, began to describe its true nature in his satirical poems; Owen and Rosenberg, more profoundly and intensely than Sassoon, explored the tragedy and the pity of war, and wrote the finest poetry inspired by the conflict of 1914–18. It is tempting to believe that Sorley fits neatly into this pattern, that he is, as it were, a stepping-stone from Brooke to Sassoon. Thus, since he clearly does not echo the sentiments of Brooke or of the patriotic versifiers of 1914, it is assumed that his eyes must have been opened by his experience of war on the Western Front. And since he obviously felt no hatred of the Germans, but declared that the British and the German soldiers were linked in a common tragedy, it seems natural to suppose that he was anticipating the emotional responses of Owen and of Rosenberg, and foreshadowing their beliefs about the pity of war.

These assumptions, however, are not borne out by the evidence of his verse or his prose. His attitude to the war was, from the very outset, remarkably mature and perceptive; he was not disillusioned by his experience of fighting, because he had no illusions to shed. At the same time, his feelings about the war were complex, even ambiguous: to think of him as groping towards the beliefs of Owen and of Rosenberg is to oversimplify matters, to misread the intellectual and spiritual development of a most unusual character, to blur the distinctive nature of his achievement.

Charles Hamilton Sorley, who was born on 19 May 1895, was the elder twin son of William Ritchie Sorley, Professor of Moral

Philosophy at Aberdeen University, who became Knightsbridge
Professor at Cambridge in 1900. The young Sorley received his
early education at home, where he was taught by his mother.
Much of this education was devoted to reading aloud from the
Bible and *The Pilgrim's Progress*, and to learning by heart a wide
variety of poetry – Blake, Scott, Macaulay, Shakespeare and
ballads. At about the age of ten he wrote a poem, 'The Tempest',
which is interesting in that it foreshadows his preference for wind
and rain, and his sense of impending doom.

After a spell at King's College Choir School, he won an open
scholarship to Marlborough, thus becoming the first member of
his family to go to a public school. To the very end of his life
Sorley loved the countryside around Marlborough, and references to it occur in many of his poems. 'The Song of the Ungirt
Runners' is an attempt to convey something of the mystical
exhilaration which he experienced during his long solitary runs
over the Downs:

> We swing ungirded hips,
> And lightened are our eyes,
> The rain is on our lips,
> We do not run for prize.
> We know not whom we trust
> Nor whitherward we fare,
> But we run because we must
>   Through the great wide air.

Yet, despite his love for Marlborough, Sorley was severely
critical of the public-school system and of the values which it
inculcated. There are half a dozen references to this in his letters,
two of which may be quoted as typical of them all:

The penalty of belonging to a public school is that one plays before a
looking-glass all the time and has to think about the impression one is
making. And as public schools are run on the worn-out fallacy that
there can't be progress without competition, games as well as everything degenerate into a means of giving free play to the lower instincts of
man.[6]

What now seems to me such a pity was the way the public school
atmosphere deliberately overdevelops the nasty tyrannical instincts.

One is positively encouraged to confuse strength of character with petty self-assertion, and conscientiousness with Phariseeism.

And in a letter to A. E. Hutchinson, dated 7 February 1914, Sorley encloses a light-hearted but satirical poem about Marlborough, which contains such passages as these:

> And is there still a Folly called the corps
> Allowed out twice a week and thinking then
> It's learning how to kill its fellow-men? . . .
>
> And is the Chapel still a house of sin
> Where smiling men let false Religion in?

One can trace in his *Letters* the development of his literary tastes, and can discern there the values by which he set most store. He refers on several occasions to his dislike of Tennyson: 'A paltry poet in general, Tennyson is most pre-eminently paltry and superficial when he sings about nature and earth. He was not long in hedging her in with the shapely corsets of alliterative verbiage.' He praises Masefield because 'he does not, like Tennyson, shut off the world he has to write about, attempting to imagine shipwrecks from the sofa or battles in his bed.'

Sorley's youthful admiration for Masefield (which he soon outgrew) now seems excessive; but it is linked with his unremitting search for truth, and with his desire to get beyond the conventional prejudices of his class. He regrets that 'poetry up till now has been mainly by and for and about the Upper Classes'. Sometimes his zest for truth may seem faintly comic, as when he refuses to sing Latin hymns because he feels the use of an ancient tongue to be an affectation, savouring of unreality. It is, however, this passion for truth which gives his literary judgements a precision and an authority remarkable in a schoolboy. In his paper on Housman given to the school Literary Society in May 1913 Sorley notes that Housman's 'fine hall-mark is his cold bare truth' and proclaims that 'all true poets (that is, poets who insist on truth) have been consciously or unconsciously in revolt'. His verdict on the writers of his day is calm but damning:

The voice of our poets and men of letters is finely trained and sweet to hear; it teems with sharp saws and rich sentiment: it is a marvel of delicate technique: it pleases, it flatters, it charms, it soothes: it is a living lie.

Sorley at one point wanted to leave Marlborough and become an elementary school-teacher, but was persuaded by a master to sit for a scholarship at Oxford, so that he might take a degree before going on to teach at a Working Men's College. He duly won his scholarship, left Marlborough at Christmas 1913 and in the New Year went to live in Germany. He stayed with a lawyer's family at Schwerin in Mecklenberg from 20 January 1914 until the end of April, when he became a student at the University of Jena, remaining there until the outbreak of war.

His letters from Germany show how much he enjoyed himself there. Even during the war he remembered with pleasure his days in Germany, especially those in Jena 'where I was first on my own and found freedom'. Most of the letters are brimming over with high spirits, and although his wit is seldom malicious it is sometimes keen:

Dr. B. is a tall fat hearty man with moustaches. If he was English he might be a bounder, but being a German he is perfectly delightful.

German soldiers have an unfortunate way of marching as if there were somebody in front whom they had to kick.

In contrast to the priggish sermon of—about the Pagan Hedonism of Cannes I should say that [in Berlin] dowdy Christian Hedonism seemed to me the chief note.

Despite these critical comments it is plain that Sorley developed a deep affection for Germany. He admired the light-hearted spirit in which the Germans played games, their readiness to make fools of themselves, their energy, idealism, and lack of sophisticated cynicism:

Cynicism is a vice that doesn't exist here. That's why one's driven into it oneself for pure need of vinegar with the salad. In England there is so much vinegar that it is difficult to find the cucumber at all.

His intellectual development in these months was rapid. Hardy and Goethe took the place once occupied by Masefield; he read *John Gabriel Borkman* with profound admiration, rating it far above Ibsen's other plays; he discovered Hölderlin and Rilke (whom he called the best modern German poet): 'Their language is colossally beautiful and they are egoists to their finger nails – both of which traits I like.' He comments un-favourably on the English attitude to 'immoral' literature:

In Germany Wilde and Byron are appreciated as authors: in England they still go pecking about their love-affairs. Anyone who calls a book 'immoral' or 'moral' should be caned. A book by itself can be neither. It is only a question of the morality or immorality of the reader.

Yet he never lost his love of the English countryside, or jettisoned the best of the values which it fostered:

In the midst of my setting up and smashing of deities – Masefield, Hardy, Goethe – I always fall back on Richard Jefferies wandering about in the background. I have at least the tie of locality with him.

Nor was he blind to the sinister aspects of German life, expressing a detestation for the corps students and for the widely prevalent anti-Semitism. In view of the turn taken by events, it is curious to read Sorley's description of a couple of German companies of military, on their return from a field day:

They were roaring – something glorious and senseless about the Fatherland (in England it would have been contemptible Jingo: it wasn't in Deutschland) . . . when the tempest of the singing was at its loudest, I felt that perhaps I could die for Deutschland – and I have never had an inkling of that feeling about England and never shall.

On 2 August 1914 Sorley was arrested and kept in prison at Trier for a few hours before being released and making his way home. He blamed himself for lacking the courage to enlist as a private soldier in the regular army, and was about to do so when he received in late August a commission in the Seventh Battalion of the Suffolk Regiment. From the very outset he utterly rejected all false patriotism, heroics, sentimentality and optimism. In October 1914 he reckoned that the war would last three years and end in stalemate. He regarded Germany as a bigot rather than as a bully, and in a letter dated 14 November 1914 expresses his views about the war:

Goliath and Caiaphas – the Philistine and the Pharisee – pound these together and there you have Suburbia and Westminster and Fleet Street. And yet we have the impudence to write down Germany (who with all their bigotry are at least seekers) as 'Huns', because they are doing what every brave man ought to do and making experiments in morality. Not that I approve of the experiment in this particular case. Indeed I think that after the war all brave men will renounce their country and confess that they are strangers and pilgrims on the earth. . . . But all these convictions are useless for me to state since I have not had the courage of them. . . . I might have been giving my mind to fight against Sloth and Stupidity: instead, I am giving my body (by a refinement of cowardice) to fight against the most enterprising nation in the world.

He never changed his conviction that the war was a disaster, and that although Germany had to be crushed England was partly responsible for the outbreak of war. Nor did he care for talk of a just war: 'There is no such thing as a just war. What we are doing is casting out Satan by Satan.' His poetry and his prose are both explicitly clear in their hostility to jingoism and in their avoidance of high-sounding moralising:

Our friends and correspondents don't seem to be able to give up physical luxuries without indulging in emotional luxuries in compensation. But I'm thankful to see that Kipling hasn't written a poem yet.

Even his beloved Hardy comes in for criticism. While defending many of the poems in *Satires of Circumstance* against his parents' strictures, he remarks that

'Men who march away' is the most arid poem in the book, besides being untrue of the sentiments of the ranksman going to war: 'Victory crowns the just' is the worst line he ever wrote – filched from a leading article in *The Morning Post*.

His own reaction to the war comes out most clearly in the octet of his sonnet 'To Germany', probably written in August 1914:

> You are blind like us. Your hurt no man designed,
> And no man claimed the conquest of your land.

But gropers both through fields of thought confined
We stumble and we do not understand.
You only saw your future bigly planned
And we, the tapering paths of our own mind,
And in each other's dearest ways we stand,
And hiss and hate. And the blind fight the blind.

These lines display Sorley's chief weakness as a poet: a con-
ventionality of diction which, together with the absence of a
strong personal rhythm, prevents him from rivalling Owen or
Rosenberg in poetic intensity and force. Yet it displays also some
of his characteristic virtues: a clarity of mind, an attempt to set
down without equivocation the feelings and thoughts which were
agitating him, a desire to follow the truth wherever it might lead.
    Whereas 'To Germany' mirrors the meditative, brooding
strain in Sorley's nature, another poem written about the same
time embodies the harsher, more savage impulses which animated him:

All the hills and vales along
Earth is bursting into song,
And the singers are the chaps
Who are going to die perhaps.

This poem has some affinities with Grenfell's 'Into Battle', but it
is a darker, more ironical poem, owing much to Housman's
concept of Nature as hostile or indifferent to man:

Earth that never doubts nor fears,
Earth that knows of death, not tears,
Earth that bore with joyful ease
Hemlock for Socrates,
Earth that blossomed and was glad
'Neath the cross that Christ had,
Shall rejoice and blossom too
When the bullet reaches you.

Sorley's experience of army life confirmed his pre-war doubts
about the values inculcated by the public schools. He contrasted
the kindness and unselfishness of the other ranks with the

spitefulness and the spirit of rivalry which he had observed in the mèn of his own class. His comments on the death of Rupert Brooke are less a condemnation of Brooke himself than of the culture which fostered him, overvalued his sonnet-sequence *1914*, and elevated him to the status of hero-martyr. [See Sorley's assessment of Brooke, in Part One, above.]

One might have supposed that Sorley's experiences on the battlefield and in the trenches would have accentuated his revulsion from the war, and caused him to turn away still more decisively from the traditional values of his class and of his upbringing. Life and literary criticism would be much simpler if human beings were less complex and unpredictable: the writings of Sorley during the four and a half months left to him after he had landed in France display an attitude of mind that is, if not self-contradictory, at least highly ambiguous.

Much as he disliked certain aspects of public school morality, he never abandoned those elements in it which enjoined self-sacrifice, courage and devotion to duty. The poems inspired by these values are among his poorest, yet they are not the products of a thoughtless immaturity. The following stanza, for example, comes from 'Expectans Expectavi', written in May 1915 shortly before he left England for the trenches:

> With parted lips and outstretched hands
> And listening ears Thy servant stands,
> Call Thou early, call Thou late,
> To Thy great service dedicate.

An epistle in verse, 'I have not brought my Odyssey', dated 12 July 1915, contains such lines as these:

> And now the fight begins again,
> The old war-joy, the old war-pain.
> Sons of one school across the sea
> We have no fear to fight.

And as late as 8 September 1915, after fully experiencing the horror of war, he could write a commonplace epitaph on a school-fellow posthumously awarded the vc:

> There is no fitter end than this.
>   No need is now to yearn nor sigh.
> We know the glory that is his,
>   A glory that can never die.

Side by side with these poems are others which reveal an entirely different aspect of Sorley's nature. He had always been acutely sensitive to the poetry of the earth, loving wind and rain – 'Sorley's Weather', to quote the title of a poem by Robert Graves – and responding intuitively to the sadness and the mystery of human life. 'Stones', a poem written in July 1913, conveys with extraordinary vividness the emotions aroused in Sorley by a field covered with great white flints, glimpsed when he was walking with his parents on the downs one rainy afternoon:

> This field is almost white with stones
>   That cumber all its thirsty crust.
> And underneath, I know, are bones,
>   And all around is death and dust.[7]

His mother described how he 'stared at the field as if he saw something written on it'. What he discerned was a vision of those who lay buried there:

> Souls like the dry earth, hearts like stone,
>   Brains like that barren bramble-tree:
> Stern, sterile, senseless, mute, unknown –
>   .But bold, O bolder far than we!

This mystical sense of communion with the dead, this desire to make peace with the earth, recurs in both his letters and his poems. Thus in 'The River', dated February 1913, Sorley tries to explain the impulse which drove the protagonist of the poem to drown himself:

> He had a yearning for the strength
>   That comes of unity:
>
> The union of one soul at length

> With its twin-soul to lie:
> To be a part of one great strength
> That moves and cannot die.

A letter dated 14 November 1914 contains the phrase: 'The earth even more than Christ is the ultimate ideal of what man should strive to be.' His poem 'Lost', written in December 1914, is an attempt to describe the significance which the land round Marlborough held for him. Writing to a friend on 15 December 1914, he says of it: 'Simplicity, paucity of words, monotony almost, and mystery are necessary. I think I have got it at last here'.

When sending it home to his parents in April 1915, he calls it 'the last of my Marlborough poems'. It is perhaps the first of his poems which hints at the awareness of death overshadowing him and all his companions:

> Across my past imaginings
>   Has dropped a blindness silent and slow.
> My eye is bent on other things
>   Than those it once did see and know.
>
> I may not think on those dear lands
>   (O far away and long ago!)
> Where the old battered signpost stands
>   And silently the four roads go
>
> East, west, south and north,
>   And the cold winter winds do blow.
> And what the evening will bring forth
>   Is not for me nor you to know.

In two sonnets, dated 12 June 1915, Sorley writes more directly of death. The octet of the first sonnet is marred by lofty poeticisms and by slack phrases; the sestet has a fine bareness, and employs as an image of death's unfamiliar signpost the signpost of 'Lost':

> I think it like that signpost in my land,
> Hoary and tall, which pointed me to go
> Upward, into the hills, on the right hand,

Where the mists swim and the winds shriek and blow,
A homeless land and friendless, but a land
I did not know and that I wished to know.[8]

The second sonnet marks an even more willing acceptance of
death, both as the great leveller, and as the prelude to a richer
life:

Victor and vanquished are a-one in death:
Coward and brave: friend, foe. Ghosts do not say
'Come, what was your record when you drew breath?'
But a big blot has hid each yesterday
So poor, so manifestly incomplete.
And your bright Promise, withered long and sped,
Is touched, stirs, rises, opens and grows sweet
And blossoms and is you, when you are dead.

In a letter to the Master of Marlborough, dated 28 November
1914, Sorley had quoted a line spoken by Achilles in the *Iliad*:
'Died Patroclus too who was a far better man than thou', adding
that 'no saner and splendider comment on death has been made'.
This thought recurs in the poem found among his possessions
after his death, a poem which, it is worth repeating, does not
spring solely from his experience of war but is the culmination of
all those thoughts about the nature of the conflict that had begun
to germinate in the very early days of the war:

When you see millions of the mouthless dead
Across your dreams in pale battalions go,
Say not soft things as other men have said,
That you'll remember. For you need not so.
Give them not praise. For, deaf, how should they know
It is not curses heaped on each gashed head?
Nor tears. Their blind eyes see not your tears flow.
Nor honour. It is easy to be dead.
Say only this, 'They are dead.' Then add thereto,
'Yet many a better one has died before.'
Then, scanning all the o'ercrowded mass, should you
Perceive one face that you loved heretofore,
It is a spook. None wears the face you knew.
Great death has made all his for evermore.

Again, this is by no means a flawless poem: the poeticisms, the inversions, the general tone are not congenial to our present taste; the diction reveals a slackness and a floweriness which weaken the poem's impact. Yet it would have been astonishing if a man of twenty, isolated from the world of letters, had contrived to solve a problem which, in their different ways, Yeats, Pound, the Imagists and Eliot were still trying to master in 1915. And Sorley at least had learned to face with complete honesty the tragedy of war, the waste and the pity.

The pity of war. One thinks of Owen; yet one must resist the temptation to argue that Sorley was moving towards the attitudes that Rosenberg and Owen were to adopt in 1917 and 1918. In his introduction to the *Oxford Book of Modern Verse*, W. B. Yeats expresses his distaste for certain poems written during the war of 1914–18, on the grounds that 'passive suffering is not a theme for poetry. In all the great tragedies, tragedy is a joy to the man who dies; in Greece the tragic chorus danced.' Sorley, even on the battlefield, retained what his housemaster called 'an extraordinary thrust of life'. Before his first experience of battle he writes: 'I shall march hotly to the firing-line, by turn critic, actor, hero, coward and soldier of fortune: perhaps even for a moment Christian, humble, with "Thy will be done".' A few days later he describes how, in some ways, the war had liberated him:

Sorley is the Gaelic for wanderer. I have had a conventional education: Oxford would have corked it. But this has freed the spirit, glory be. Give me *The Odyssey*, and I return the New Testament to store. Physically as well as spiritually, give me the road.

Late in July a man in Sorley's platoon dropped a hand grenade under himself, and was carried dying to a shell-hole by Sorley – it was, he said, 'like carrying a piece of living pulp'. Sorley was slightly wounded, but was seen the next day walking along cheerfully, reading from his German pocket edition of *Faust*.[9] A letter dated 26 August 1915 shows how deeply he had been affected by this incident, and indeed by his whole experience of war:

Looking into the future one sees a holocaust somewhere: and at present there is – thank God – enough of 'experience' to keep the wits edged (a callous way of putting it, perhaps). But out in front at night in that no-man's land and long graveyard there is a freedom and a spur. Rustling of the grasses and grave-tapping of distant workers: the tension and silence of encounter, when one struggles in the dark for moral victory over the enemy patrol: the wail of the exploded bomb and the animal cries of wounded men. Then death and the horrible thankfulness when one sees that the next man is dead: 'We won't have to *carry* him in under fire, thank God; dragging will do': hauling in of the great resistless body in the dark, the smashed head rattling: the relief, the relief that the thing has ceased to groan: that the bullet or bomb that made the man an animal has now made the animal a corpse. One is hardened by now: purged of all false pity: perhaps more selfish than before. The spiritual and the animal get so much more sharply divided in hours of encounter, taking possession of the body by swift turns.

It is arguable that Sorley, having been purged of all false pity, would have discovered the true pity of war and, like Owen, would have made it the theme of his poetry. Yet this letter suggests that Sorley was near to embracing the joyous, tragic, heroic mood which Yeats advocates as the proper temper for poets writing of war.

On 5 October 1915 Sorley writes to the Master of Marlborough, expressing with a fine dignity his sense of relief in being a soldier:

I am now beginning to think that free thinkers should give their minds into subjection, for we who have given our actions and volitions into subjection gain such marvellous rest thereby. . . . Perhaps afterwards, I and my like will again become indiscriminate rebels. For the present we find high relief in making ourselves soldiers.

In the letter of 26 August already quoted he had spoken of his fellow-officers as men who had deliberately stifled their loneli-ness: 'They are surface wells. Not two hundred feet deep, so that you can see the stars at the bottom.' Sorley was too clear-sighted and courageous to seek any easy anodyne: knowing himself and mistrusting himself, he hoped only to behave well in the approaching battle. One of his three last letters, all dated 5 October 1915, begins by remarking that 'it is the eve of our crowning hour'. Then there comes a phrase (strangely re-miniscent of a line in 'Stones'): 'I am bleached with chalk.'

Finally, after recalling some of the most splendid meals of his life, Sorley acknowledges his fears and his self-mistrust:

I dread my own censorious self in the coming conflict – I also have great physical dread of pain. . . . Pray that I ride my frisky nerves with a cool and steady hand when the time arrives.

Eight days later he was dead.

Sorley wrote no poems comparable with the finest work of Owen or of Rosenberg, and in many ways his letters are more vigorous and penetrating than his verse. It is, however, only fair to remember that Sorley was barely twenty when he died in 1915; that Owen lived to be twenty-five and Rosenberg to be twenty-eight; that they both survived until 1918. The rapidity of their imaginative development suggests that a man of Sorley's gifts might have attained their stature had he been granted a few more years of life. Moreover, he himself knew that his poems needed revision before they were published, and rejected his mother's proposal that a volume of his verse should be printed.

It is fascinating, though unprofitable, to speculate what Sorley might have achieved had he survived the war:

The Poet Laureate once said to me that Sorley was potentially the greatest poet lost to us in that war, and that, had Sorley lived, he might have become our greatest dramatist since Shakespeare. . . . I think he would have become a very great dramatist . . . and that he would have been a dramatist of the stamp and stature – for he had the temperament – of a Corneille.[10]

Nichols then pays what seems to me a just tribute to Sorley, as

a spirit of stern and stoic feature – his early poems have a ring which recalls Emily Brontë – and this spirit appears steadfastly set upon subduing subjectivism and upon viewing what lay around as a whole and with himself and his poetry as only part of the whole.[11]

Even those who consider such praise extravagant may allow that Sorley deserves to be remembered for half a dozen true poems, and for a quality of mind which enabled him to see, from the beginning, the nature of the 1914–18 war, and thus preserved him from the illusions, and the subsequent disenchantment, to which so many of his contemporaries succumbed.

SOURCE: 'Charles Sorley', *Review of English Literature*, VII, 2 (April 1966), pp. 42–60.

NOTES

1. Michael Roberts (ed.), *Faber Book of Modern Verse* (London, 1936), p. 1.
2. Robert Nichols (ed.), *An Anthology of War Poetry* (London, 1943), p. 28.
3. This essay was written before the publication of J. H. Johnston, *English Poetry of the First World War* (Princeton, N.J., 1964) and of B. Bergonzi, *Heroes' Twilight* (London, 1965), which contain some scholarly and perceptive pages on Sorley.
4. D. J. Enright, *The Modern Age* (Harmondsworth, 1961), p. 156: vol. 7 of the Pelican Guide to English Literature.
5. V. de Sola Pinto, *Crisis in English Poetry, 1880–1940* (London, 1951), p. 141.
6. [Ed.] Prose quotations from Sorley are taken from *The Letters of Charles Sorley* (Cambridge, 1919).
7. Robert Graves, in *Poetic Unreason* (London, 1925), says that the beginning of this stanza 'makes me feel as if I had chalk in my mouth'.
8. When sending this sonnet to a friend, Sorley gave it the title 'Death – and the Downs'.
9. The incident is described in a letter by a brother-officer in *Letters*, pp. 294–5. It is typical of Sorley that he should have read both Goethe and Richard Jefferies in the trenches.
10. Robert Nichols, op. cit., p. 36.
11. Ibid., p. 37.

8. ON EDWARD THOMAS

William Cooke   Roads to France (1970)

As a war poet Thomas is virtually ignored. His poems are seldom included in anthologies of war poetry, and if his name is mentioned in critical studies it is largely for the sake of comprehensive appearances. The general feeling was summarised in 1947 by Athalie Bushnell:

Although the background to his writing was often an army hut or trench, yet very little of his poetry actually takes war or war incidents as its subject. His poetry is nature poetry, taking simplicity, wonder and longing as its keynotes.[1]

In *Edward Thomas* (1956), H. Coombes categorised 'between eighty and ninety' of his poems as 'nature poems' (this description is qualified) but found only 'six or seven war poems'.[2] John H. Johnston in *English Poetry of the First World War* (1964) dismissed him in a single reference: 'Unlike Francis Ledwidge and Edward Thomas, who refused to let the conflict interfere with their nostalgic rural visions, Blunden successfully adapted his talent for unpretentious landscape description to the scenes of war.'[3] Only a year later, in *Heroes' Twilight* (1965), Bernard Bergonzi compared Thomas with Blunden:

. . . like Blunden he found a therapeutic and sanative value in contemplating nature, or remembering rural England, in the midst of violence and destruction. But very few of Thomas's poems are actually about the war, even obliquely: in his loving concentration on the unchanging order of nature and rural society, the war exists only as a brooding but deliberately excluded presence.[4]

The inadequacy of these comments may be seen if they are considered alongside extracts from poems already discussed:

Bushnell: 'His poetry is nature poetry, taking simplicity, wonder and longing as its keynotes.'

                          wondering
    What of the lattermath to this hoar Spring?
                                      ('It Was Upon')

    Before the might,
    If you love it not, of night.   ('Out in the Dark')

Johnston: 'Edward Thomas . . . refused to let the conflict interfere with [his] nostalgic rural visions.'

    Tall reeds
    Like criss-cross bayonets . . .   ('Bright Clouds')

    Now all roads lead to France
    And heavy is the tread
    Of the living; but the dead
    Returning lightly dance. . . .   ('Roads')

Bergonzi: '. . . very few of Thomas's poems are actually about the war, even obliquely: in his loving concentration on the unchanging order of nature and rural society, the war exists only as a brooding but deliberately excluded presence.'

    And when the war began
    To turn young men to dung.   ('Gone, Gone Again')

    Helpless among the living and the dead,
    Like a cold water among broken reeds,
    Myriads of broken reeds all still and stiff . . .   ('Rain')

Even those anthologists who consider Thomas worthy of inclusion have unwittingly given a false impression of his significance and development. Brian Gardner includes 'No Case of Petty Right or Wrong' and 'No One Cares Less Than I' in his anthology *Up the Line to Death* (1964), and then makes this statement as part of his biographical note:

Joined the Artists' Rifles, *and was soon in the trenches*; transferred to the Royal Garrison Artillery. *He continued to write his favourite poems of nature and the countryside, even when in the front line, and he wrote few war poems.*[5]

The italicised lines (my italics) are inaccurate.

I. M. Parsons divides his anthology *Men Who March Away* (1965) into seven sections, each representative of a mood or a subject connected with the war. This allows him 'to try to reflect not only the chronological progress of the war, but also the changing attitude of poets to it'.[6] His first section, *Visions of Glory*, is introduced by Thomas's poem 'The Trumpet', which is followed by such poems as Julian Grenfell's 'Into Battle', Hardy's 'Men Who March Away' and Brooke's 'Peace'. This section represents

the mood of optimistic exhilaration with which so many writers, young and old, greeted the outbreak of war. This was the period of euphoria, when it was still possible to believe that war was a tolerably chivalrous affair, offering welcome opportunities for heroism and self-sacrifice, and to hope that this particular war would be over in six months.[7]

Afterward, four more of Thomas's poems are included in three other sections in order to reflect his 'changing' attitude to the war. 'There Was A Time' and 'As the Team's Head-Brass' appear in *The Pity of War*; 'A Private' appears among *The Dead*; and 'Lights Out' (the last poem but one) appears under *Aftermath*. The impression likely to be gained is that Thomas falls neatly into the familiar pattern of romantic idealist disillusioned by experiencing the horror of actual warfare. Though unintentional, this is a complete misrepresentation of his true development. His attitude to the war was, from the outset, remarkably mature and perceptive, and 'The Trumpet' is not one of those early chauvinistic poems – it is not even an early poem. It was written two years after that initial period of euphoria (when it was obvious that the war would not be over in six months) and only a month separates it from 'Lights Out'. So the circular movement of the anthology is misleading. So too is the apparent change in attitude from 'visions of glory' to 'the pity of war'. Thomas did not go through this process of disillusionment simply because he had no illusions to shed, and, in fact, 'There Was A Time', 'As the Team's Head-Brass' and 'A Private' were written *before* 'The Trumpet'. Finally, all his poetry was written between 1914 and 1916 *before he had been to France*. He wrote no poetry at all in the trenches, so quickly was he killed.[8]

Thus the above comments by various critics and anthologists are doubly misleading, since they are based on a fundamental error of approach. All of them wrongly assume that Thomas lived to become a trench poet. Athalie Bushnell speaks of the background to his writing as 'an army hut or trench'; Johnston dismisses him for his 'refusal' to adapt himself to 'the scenes of war'; Bergonzi imagines him writing therapeutically 'in the midst of violence and destruction'; both Gardner and Parsons refer to him explicitly as a front-line poet. A correct and more meaningful approach would be to explore his decision to enlist and volunteer for action in France. The whole perspective of his poetry needs to be changed.

'If they also serve who only sit and write, poets are doing their work well. Several of them, it seems to me, with names known and unknown, have been turned into poets by the war, printing verse now for the first time. Whatever other virtues they show, courage at least is not lacking – the courage to write for oblivion.' With these words Thomas began a review entitled 'War Poetry' in December 1914. He himself was one of those who had been turned into a poet by the war, but he had no desire to write for oblivion by complying with what the age demanded. Already he was writing 'Deceased'[9] over many books . . . [Quotes extracts from the review-article reproduced in Part One above.]

The review establishes beyond doubt his attitude to the 'rage of gladness' that greeted the outbreak of war. He restated it succinctly in 'No Case of Petty Right or Wrong':

> I hate not Germans, nor grow hot
> With love of Englishmen, to please newspapers.

The review also explains why he was to remain unpublished during his lifetime (and why he is still read today):

I need hardly say that by becoming ripe for poetry the poet's thoughts may recede far from their original resemblance to all the world's, and may seem to have little to do with daily events. They may retain hardly any colour from 1798 or 1914, and the crowd, deploring it, will naturally not read the poems.[10]

His own poetry had nothing in common with the rampant patriotism of the 'bardic' phase, and, indeed, seemed to have little to do with the events that were its inspiration. As a result he met with the neglect he foresaw. 'He offered some of these poems to various editors', his wife recalled, 'but no one had any room for such quiet meditative verse, in which the profound love and knowledge of his country were too subtle in their patriotism for the nation's mood.'[11]

The distinction between subtle (private) patriotism and deliberate (public) patriotism was one that Thomas himself drew several times. In a second review of 1914 he wrote:

The worst of the poetry being written today is that it is too deliberately, and not inevitably, English. It is for an audience: there is more in it of the shouting of rhetorician, reciter, or politician than of the talk of friends and lovers.[12]

In his essay 'England', he declared that *The Compleat Angler* was for him the most patriotic of books:

Since the war began I have not met so English a book, a book that filled me so with a sense of England, as this, though I have handled scores of deliberately patriotic works. There, in that sort of work, you get, as it were, the shouting without the crowd, which is ghastly. In Walton's book I touched the antiquity and sweetness of England – English fields, English people, English poetry, all together.[13]

It was this 'inevitable' English quality that he looked for when he compiled his *This England: An Anthology from her Writers* in 1915:

Building round a few most English poems like 'When icicles hang by the wall' – excluding professedly patriotic writing because it is generally bad and because indirect praise is sweeter and more profound – never aiming at what a committee from Great Britain and Ireland might call complete – I wished to make a book as full of English character and country as an egg is of meat. If I have reminded others, as I did myself continually, of some of the echoes called up by the name of England, I am satisfied.[14]

Into that anthology he slipped 'Haymaking' and 'The Manor Farm' by Edward Eastaway. They were among the first of his poems that he ever saw in print, and the occasion was never more suitable. For their inclusion was not a mischievous act by which 'he had his own back'[15] for his numerous rejections. He was rather placing himself in the tradition of writers who had celebrated England, in peace and war. Even the position he gave to his poems is significant. They appear immediately after Coleridge's 'Fears in Solitude', which he described in his earlier review as 'one of the noblest of patriotic poems' though 'no newspaper or magazine, then or now, would print such a poem, since a large part of it is humble.' The same applied to his own instinctive patriotism:

> The ages made her that made us from dust:
> She is all we know and live by, and we trust
> She is good and must endure, loving her so:
> And as we love ourselves we hate her foe.

His cool, tolerant assessment agreed with the spirit of the age no more than Coleridge's in 1798.

'Lob' is the apotheosis of all that he sought for his *This England* anthology and must surely be one of the most patriotic poems ever written. It is 'as full of English character and country as an egg is of meat':

> This is tall Tom that bore
> The logs in, and with Shakespeare in the hall
> Once talked, when icicles hung by the wall.
> (Chaucer – Wordsworth and all true poets were
> His friends, and Cobbett, Bunyan and Latimer . . .)[16]

> He is English as this gate, these flowers, this mire.
> And when at eight years old Lob-lie-by-the-fire
> Came in my books, this was the man I saw.
> He has been in England as long as dove and daw,
> Calling the wild cherry tree the merry tree,
> The rose campion Bridget-in-her-bravery;
> And in a tender mood he, as I guess,
> Christened one flower Love-in-idleness . . .

From him old herbal Gerard learnt, as a boy,
To name wild clematis the Traveller's-Joy.
Our blackbirds sang no English till his ear
Told him they called his Jan Toy 'Pretty dear' . . .
'Twas he first called the Hog's Back the Hog's Back.
That Mother Dunch's Buttocks should not lack
Their name was his care. He too could explain
Totteridge and Totterdown and Juggler's Lane:
He knows, if anyone. Why Tumbling Bay,
Inland in Kent, is called so, he might say . . .

The poem readily assimilates the line 'when icicles hang by the wall' from *Love's Labour's Lost*, around which he wished to 'build' his anthology. There was also a good reason why Cobbett's name should have been included. 'It was an altogether English name to begin with', Thomas had written in his introduction to *Rural Rides* in 1912, 'thoroughly native and rustic; and English it remains, pure English, old English, merry English . . . he is one of the few thorough-going countrymen in our literature. . . . His open-air scenes take us back to Chaucer.'[17] The fructifying association of such writers and poets with Lob was closely foreshadowed in *The Country*, where, extolling the lore of one old countryman, Thomas averred: 'You may be sure there were hundreds like him in Shakespeare's time and in Wordsworth's, and if there aren't a good sprinkling of them, generation after generation, I do not know what we shall come to, but I have my fears.'

Such fears are groundless in the poem, for Lob's wisdom is seen to be passed down the ages. In *This England*, Thomas had anthologised an extract from John Gerard's *The Herball* naming Traveller's-Joy: 'It is called commonly *Viorna quasi vias ornans*, of decking and adorning ways and hedges, where people travel, and thereupon I have named it the Traveller's-Joy.'[18] In the poem Lob became that informing master spirit:

From him old herbal Gerard learnt, as a boy,
To name wild clematis the Traveller's-Joy.

The couplet immediately following –

> Our blackbirds sang no English till his ear
> Told him they called his Jan Toy 'Pretty dear'

– alludes to the work of another countryman whom Thomas greatly admired, his contemporary Thomas Hardy. His poem 'The Spring Call' was also chosen for *This England:*

> Down Wessex way, when spring's a-shine,
>   The blackbird's 'pret-ty de-urr!'
> In Wessex accents marked as mine
>   Is heard afar and near . . .
>
> Yes, in this clime at pairing time,
>   As soon as eyes can see her
> At dawn of day, the proper way
>   To call is 'pret-ty de-urr!'[19]

Another latter-day inheritor was the eighteenth-century antiquarian William Stukeley. In his introduction to Isaac Taylor's *Words and Places* in 1911, Thomas wrote of him:

These were the men who made England great, fearing neither man nor God nor philology. There are some such still with us. . . . we have need of men like that to explain 'Eggpie' Lane near the village of Sevenoaks Weald, or Tumbling Bay in a neighbouring parish far inland.[20]

The last name was enshrined in the poem:

> He too could explain
> Totteridge and Totterdown and Juggler's Lane:
> He knows, if anyone. Why Tumbling Bay,
> Inland in Kent, is called so, he might say.

The other names to which Thomas refers had all previously appeared in his prose books. 'Totteridge' was mentioned in *A Literary Pilgrim*,[21] 'Totterdown' in *Richard Jefferies*,[22] and 'Juggler's Lane' in *The Icknield Way*.[23] More than any of his poems, 'Lob' was the *quintessence* of the best parts of his work.

Yet it is not a golden treasury of nostalgia. 'Lob' has such sardonic moments as:

> Hob being then his name,
> He kept the hog that thought the butcher came
> To bring his breakfast. 'You thought wrong', said Hob.

The 'hog' is perhaps an oblique reference to the 'fat patriot' in 'No Case of Petty Right or Wrong':

> Beside my hate for one fat patriot
> My hatred of the Kaiser is love true.

Wilfred Owen used the same image in 'The Calls':

> I see a food-hog whet his gold-filled tusk
> To eat less bread, and more luxurious rusk.

Owen too wished on them a savage retribution:

I wish the Boche would have the pluck to come right in and make a clean sweep of the pleasure boats, and the promenaders on the Spa, and all the stinking Leeds and Bradford war-profiteers now reading *John Bull* on Scarborough Sands.[24]

Lob carries out part of that wish. In all his exploits he shows an admirable sagacity and social conscience:

> And while he was a little cobbler's boy
> He tricked the giant coming to destroy
> Shrewsbury by flood . . .
>   . . . as Jack the giant-killer
> He made a name. He too ground up the miller,
> The Yorkshireman who ground men's bones for flour.

Thomas is not far from Owen's 'Leeds and Bradford war-profiteers' (or those at Sheffield whom he had discovered himself in 'Tipperary') in the last lines of this extract. Lob is the spirit which rises above such hypocrisy. It is he who faces the German threat, submerged in the image of the giant who comes with 'earth for damming Severn'. Thomas borrowed the fable from Charlotte S. Burne's *Shropshire Folk-Lore*[25] and gave it a 'new reality'.[26] In his essay 'It's a Long, Long Way', he reported that the countrypeople had made up their minds about invasion:

> They not only imagined themselves suffering like Belgian peasants, but being specially attacked in the Forest of Dean by German aeroplanes. Napoleon, a hundred years ago, was expected to sail up the Severn and destroy the Forest: now it was feared that the Germans were coming.[27]

On the next page, describing some of the adventures of the old shepherd 'Hobbe' against German spies and infiltrators, he wrote that before the war 'it was almost in vain that the newspapers had been erecting a *German Colossus* to terrify us.'[28] The image was to persist throughout the war, and 'The Prussian Bully 1857–1914' (a supplement of *Punch*) amply demonstrates how it was used.[29] The essence of these pages went into the image of 'the giant coming to destroy/Shrewsbury by flood', though by becoming ripe for poetry it seemed to have little to do with daily events.

These undertones of war resound in a final affirmation of English character and tradition that had outfaced danger on so many occasions:

> 'Do you believe Jack dead before his hour . . . ?
> One of the lords of No Man's Land, good Lob –
> Although he was seen dying at Waterloo,
> Hastings, Agincourt, and Sedgemoor too –
> Lives yet. He never will admit he is dead
> Till millers cease to grind men's bones for bread . . .'

Lob had to be both warrior and sage to protect what he held in trust. It was an example that his creator would inevitably follow.

The climax of 'Lob' is more deliberately patriotic than usual in Thomas's poetry. Ordinarily, he preferred that 'indirect praise' which he considered 'sweeter and more profound'. A starting-point for three of his poems was this excerpt from his essay 'England':

A writer in *The Times* on patriotic poetry said a good thing lately: 'There may be pleasanter places, there is no *word* like home.' A man may have this feeling even in a far quarter of England. One man said to

me that he felt it, that he felt England very strongly, one evening at
Stogumber under the Quantocks. His train stopped at the station which
was quite silent, and only an old man got in, bent, gnarled, and gross, a
Caliban; 'but somehow he fitted in with the darkness and the quietness
and the smell of burning wood, and it was all something I loved being
part of.' We feel it in war-time or coming from abroad, though we may
be far from home: the whole land is suddenly home.[30]

This feeling was the inspiration for 'Adlestrop', 'Home', and
'Good-Night', poems which are, in his own phrase, 'inevitably
English'; in Leavis's, they 'seem to happen';

> Yes. I remember Adlestrop –
> The name, because one afternoon
> Of heat the express-train drew up there
> Unwontedly. It was late June. . . .

> And for that minute a blackbird sang
> Close by, and round him, mistier,
> Farther and farther, all the birds
> Of Oxfordshire and Gloucestershire.   ('Adlestrop')

> Often I had gone this way before:
> But now it seemed I never could be
> And never had been anywhere else;
> 'Twas home; one nationality
> We had, I and the birds that sang,
> One memory.   ('Home')

> The friendless town is friendly; homeless, I am
>   not lost;
> Though I know none of these doors, and meet but
>   strangers' eyes.
> Never again, perhaps, after tomorrow, shall
> I see these homely streets, these church windows
>   alight,
> Not a man or woman or child among them all:
> But it is All Friends' Night, a traveller's good-night.
>   ('Good-Night')

A more complex response emerges from 'Tears', written on the same day as 'Adlestrop'. Like 'Swedes', the poem is composed of two disparate experiences which are fused in an unexpected relationship. The first is a vivid recollection of a fox-hunt:

> When twenty hounds streamed by me, not yet combed out
> But still all equals in their rage of gladness
> Upon the scent, made one, like a great dragon
> In Blooming Meadow that bends towards the sun
> And once bore hops . . .

The second, equally as English, is of the changing of the guard:

> They were changing guard,
> Soldiers in line, young English countrymen,
> Fair-haired and ruddy, in white tunics. Drums
> And fifes were playing 'The British Grenadiers'.
> The men, the music piercing that solitude
> And silence, told me truths I had not dreamed,
> And have forgotten since their beauty passed.

An incident which Charles Sorley described in a letter from Germany shortly before the war makes an interesting parallel to Thomas's poem:

I was coming back from a long walk with the Frau last night and we passed a couple of companies of military returning from a field day of sorts. It is truth that we could hear them a mile off. Were they singing? They were roaring – something glorious and senseless about the Fatherland (in England it would have been contemptible Jingo: it wasn't in Deutschland). . . . And when I got home, I felt I was a German, and proud to be a German: when the tempest of the singing was at its loudest, I felt that perhaps I could die for Deutschland – and I have never had an inkling of that feeling about England, and never shall. And if the feeling died with the cessation of the singing – well I had it, and it's the first time I have had the vaguest idea what patriotism meant – and that in a strange land.[31]

'Tears' offers an 'inkling' of that feeling for England without becoming the 'contemptible Jingo' that Sorley feared. It relies on the 'settled mystic patriotism' of Blake and Jefferies – indeed, a passage from Jefferies which Thomas had quoted in his study could stand as an epigraph to the poem: 'So subtle is the chord of life that sometimes to watch troops marching in rhythmic order, undulating along the column as the feet are lifted, brings tears into my eyes.[32]

That chord is struck in Thomas by the troops ('soldiers in line') *and* by the hounds ('still all equals') as they participate in their separate rituals. Yet not only do the two memories reflect in each other but *on* each other. For despite their superficial splendour, both hounds and soldiers also suggest a less attractive reality. The hounds are out to kill ('upon the scent') and merge into one menacing animal – 'a great dragon'; the troops have lost some of their individuality by being 'in line' and 'in white tunics', while it is a martial air that 'pierces' the silence. The profound ambiguity of the poem's basic emotion is caught in that astonishing paradox 'rage of gladness'.

'The Owl' (later re-titled 'Those Others') provides another mood, another step towards his enlistment:

> Downhill I came, hungry, and yet not starved;
> Cold, yet had heat within me that was proof
> Against the North wind; tired, yet so that rest
> Had seemed the sweetest thing under a roof.
>
> Then at the inn I had food, fire, and rest,
> Knowing how hungry, cold, and tired was I.
> All of the night was quite barred out except
> An owl's cry, a most melancholy cry
>
> Shaken out long and clear upon the hill,
> No merry note, nor cause of merriment,
> But one telling me plain what I escaped
> And others could not, that night, as in I went.
>
> And salted was my food, and my repose,
> Salted and sobered, too, by the bird's voice
> Speaking for all who lay under the stars,
> Soldiers and poor, unable to rejoice.

The impact of the poem lies in that repeated word 'salted', an example of 'the awkwardness and the irresistibleness of absolute sincerity'[33] in Thomas's verse. Firstly, the bird's voice 'salts' (i.e. flavours) his refuge at the inn by making him aware of his privileged position over others less fortunate. But almost immediately less comfortable connotations surface when the word is repeated. For 'salted' has that 'rich inheritance' which Thomas could not detect in Pater's 'sterilised words' nor in Swinburne's 'self-contained words'. It certainly means 'flavoured' or 'spiced', but it also evokes 'the harshness of salt, the salt in the wound, the taste of bitterness, and of tears.'[34] This self-chastening element introduces a sense of his own 'guilt' and pity for those 'unable to rejoice'. Their sacrifice was, for Thomas, the inescapable fact of war:

> 'Many a man sleeps worse tonight
> Than I shall.' 'In the trenches.' 'Yes, that's right . . .'
> ('Man and Dog')

> where now at last he sleeps
> More sound in France – that, too, he secret keeps.
> ('A Private')

> The flowers left thick at nightfall in the wood
> This Eastertide call into mind the men,
> Now far from home, who, with their sweethearts, should
> Have gathered them and will do never again.
> ('In Memoriam (Easter, 1915)')

> The cherry trees bend over and are shedding,
> On the old road where all that passed are dead,
> Their petals, strewing the grass as for a wedding
> This early May morn when there is none to wed.
> ('The Cherry Trees')

The 'unchanging order of . . . rural society' is not as unchanging as Bergonzi maintains; nor are these 'nostalgic rural visions' as remote from the conflict as Johnston would have us believe. Thomas was that rare poet for whom the division between the 'two Englands' did not exist, and he faced the tragedy of war, the waste and the pity, with an awareness beyond most of his contemporaries.[35] In reading his poetry we are reminded not of

Francis Ledwidge nor Edmund Blunden, but of Wilfred Owen. A friend of Owen's wrote that the keynote of his character was 'an intense pity for suffering humanity – a need to alleviate it, wherever possible, and an inability to shirk the sharing of it, even when this seemed useless'.[36] It is the keynote of such poems as 'The Owl', 'In Memoriam (Easter, 1915)' and 'The Cherry Trees'. 'The pity of war' entered Thomas's poetry before Owen had even enlisted.

'You have let me follow your thought in almost every twist and turn toward this conclusion', Frost replied, when Thomas acquainted him with his decision to enlist. 'I know pretty well how far down you have gone and how far off sideways.'[37] That decision culminates in a little-known poem called 'For These'. It was written at a time when Frost was urging him to go over to America, and it might almost have been on this theme. The first three stanzas depict a 'nostalgic rural vision' such as his critics have visualised:

> An acre of land between the shore and the hills,
> Upon a ledge that shows my kingdoms three,
> The lovely visible earth and sky and sea
> Where what the curlew needs not, the farmer tills:
>
> A house that shall love me as I love it,
> Well-hedged, and honoured by a few ash trees
> That linnets, greenfinches, and goldfinches
> Shall often visit and make love in and flit:
>
> A garden I need never go beyond,
> Broken but neat, whose sunflowers every one
> Are fit to be the sign of the Rising Sun:
> A spring, a brook's bend, or at least a pond:

A dream of retiring to 'the simple life' is typical of much Georgian verse (cf., e.g., W. H. Davies's 'Truly Great' or de la Mare's 'I Dream of a Place') – an impression that most people seem to retain of Thomas's poetry. Yet the title 'For These' is deceptive. The fourth and final stanza completely reverses our expectations:

For these I ask not, but, neither too late
Nor yet too early, for what men call content,
And also that something may be sent
To be contented with, I ask of Fate.

The poem ends with the mental urgency that Alun Lewis stressed
in 'To Edward Thomas'. For Thomas that 'hinted land' lay not
in America but in France. On the same day as he wrote 'For
These', he voluntarily enlisted. . . .

Thomas described his enlistment as 'the natural culmination of a
long series of moods and thoughts'. The same might be said of his
decision to volunteer for France, though these moods and
thoughts were perceptibly darker. The uncertainty of 'The Sign-
Post' was sharpened into foreboding in 'It Was Upon'; the
mental fretting towards his enlistment in 'This England' and 'For
These' was matched by the chafing of '"Home"' and 'Bright
Clouds'; pity for suffering humanity in 'The Owl' and 'In
Memoriam (Easter, 1915)' was more bleakly reflected in 'Rain'.
Finally, the need to participate in 'No Case of Petty Right or
Wrong' developed into a determination to prove himself and face
death if necessary in 'There Was A Time'. The very titles of the
poems – 'The Dark Forest', 'Out in the Dark', 'Lights Out' –
point only in one direction.

   In 'No Case of Petty Right or Wrong' Thomas had condemned
the futility of chauvinism and the murderous requirements of
war. At the same time he had asserted a willingness to accept
them by identifying himself with the Cause, thereby providing a
sanction for the same acceptance by those waiting to be
encouraged to commit themselves. 'The Trumpet' appears to be
that encouragement:

Rise up, rise up,
And, as the trumpet blowing
Chases the dreams of men,
As the dawn glowing
The stars that left unlit
The land and water,
Rise up and scatter

> The dew that covers
> The print of last night's lovers –
> Scatter it, scatter it!
>
> While you are listening
> To the clear horn,
> Forget, men, everything
> On this earth new-born,
> Except that it is lovelier
> Than any mysteries.
> Open your eyes to the air
> That has washed the eyes of the stars
> Through all the dewy night:
> Up with the light,
> To the old wars;
> Arise, arise!

It is not a good introduction to Thomas's poetry, yet it has retained its position as first poem in almost every collection of his work. Possibly it is for this reason that it is sometimes read as a poem of the 'visions of glory' category. It is, however, wholly different from such poems and testifies more to the ambiguity of Thomas's commitment. It was as if he had to pervert his own nature to adapt himself to the war, and the impotent climax of the first stanza

> Rise up and scatter
> The dew that covers
> The print of last night's lovers

amounts almost to an act of desecration against the lovers, who represent a norm of sanity in his other poems. In the second stanza he urges

> Forget, men, everything
> On this earth new-born,
> Except that it is lovelier
> Than any mysteries

– as if exhilaration in the Cause were to be had only at the

expense of thought. Even the poetry flags, and Thomas is guilty
of making the vaguest of gestures. Finally, in

> Up with the light,
> To the old wars;
> Arise, arise!

the long vowel sounds suggest a note of weary resignation rather
than joyful acceptance.

A phrase like 'the old wars' cuts right across any optimistic
belief in 'a war to end war'. Probably Thomas's historical
training had encouraged his healthy scepticism in this regard. 'I
have read a great deal of history', he wrote in *The South Country*,
'in fact, a university gave me a degree out of respect for my
apparent knowledge of history – but I have forgotten it all, or it
has got into my blood and is present in me in a form which defies
evocation or analysis.'[38] It is not wholly beyond analysis in 'The
Sun Used to Shine':

> The war
> Came back to mind with the moonrise
> Which soldiers in the east afar
> Beheld then. Nevertheless, our eyes
> Could as well imagine the Crusades
> Or Caesar's battles.

At first he seems to infer the impossibility of imagining the present
war – or any war. However, his *Marlborough* had shown him quite
capable of imagining its true condition, and a second reading
emerges from the lines which is not so innocent. His apparently
casual reference to the 'Crusades' reminds us that the First War
had been welcomed as a modern 'crusade'. He then ironically
juxtaposes the Holy Wars with 'Caesar's battles', implying that
they could as well imagine those old wars as this 'new' one, since
war was basically the same whether it was waged to reclaim
under the cross or subjugate under the imperial standard. Out of
this context came Thomas's version of the millennium in
'February Afternoon':

Men heard this roar of parleying starlings, saw,
   A thousand years ago even as now,
   Black rooks with white gulls following the plough
So that the first are last until a caw
Commands that last are first again – a law
   Which was of old when one, like me, dreamed how
   A thousand years might dust lie on his brow
Yet thus would birds do between hedge and shaw.

Time swims before me, making as a day
   A thousand years, while the broad ploughland oak
   Roars mill-like and men strike and bear the stroke
   Of war as ever, audacious or resigned,
And God still sits aloft in the array
   That we have wrought him, stone-deaf and stone-blind.

The ageless 'roar' of the starlings is associated with the 'roar' of
the oak, and both suggest peaceful activities of man ('following
the plough', 'Roars mill-like'). Yet both in turn are contrasted
with the impulse in man's nature to wage war. The natural
rhythm of the rooks and gulls ('so that first are last') is reflected in
the unnatural rhythm of the human world ('men strike and bear
the stroke'); this is simultaneously contrasted with the nature of
the oak through internal rhyme ('mill-like'/'strike') and end
rhyme ('oak'/'stroke'). The last two lines utterly refute any
misplaced faith in the war as a crusade, watched over by a
benevolent deity.

No less sceptical is a companion-piece to 'The Trumpet' called
'No One Cares Less Than I':

'No one cares less than I,
Nobody knows but God,
Whether I am destined to lie
Under a foreign clod,'
Were the words I made to the bugle call in the
   morning.

But laughing, storming, scorning,
Only the bugles know

What the bugles say in the morning,
And they do not care, when they blow
The call that I heard and made words to early this
    morning.

John Moore's superficial consideration of the poem is less than
helpful:

In September he was transferred for further training to the Royal
Artillery Barracks at Trowbridge, where 'the trumpet blew for
everything' and where one day he set some more words to the brave
bugle-call . . . [Quotes first stanza, as above.] These were the words he
made to the bugle-call in the morning.[38]

The impression which is conveyed (and which is* certainly
intended from that transferred epithet 'brave') is that Thomas
was careless of personal risk and eager to join the fray. In fact he is
saying no such thing. The romantic response of the first stanza is
deliberately undercut by the heavy 'God'/'clod' rhyme.
Significantly, it is 'a foreign clod', which may have been
Thomas's personal reaction to Brooke's 'corner of a foreign field/
That is for ever England'. The second stanza points to the
possible discrepancy (in the conjunction 'But') between the
words he makes to that call and what the bugles may really be
saying. Consequently, 'laughing, storming, scorning' may be
read not only as the stimulus for the cavalier attitude portrayed in
the first verse, but also as a criticism of it. For '*they*' do not care:
the single bugle of the earlier lines now includes all the morning
bugles, collectively referred to as 'they' – the pronoun used by the
common soldier to incriminate the politicians and generals
responsible for the war (Thomas used it in this way in his very
next poem). And that 'they' do not care what they are saying
when they make the call suggests their irresponsibility and the
ambiguous nature of that call, at once stimulating and hollow.

'As the Team's Head-Brass', written directly afterwards, gives
the lie to the 'no one cares less than I' attitude as far as Thomas
was concerned. His reply to a ploughman's question is exceptional for its common sense:

'Have you been out?' 'No.' 'And don't want to, perhaps?'
'If I could only come back again, I should.

> I could spare an arm. I shouldn't want to lose
> A leg. If I should lose my head, why, so,
> I should want nothing more . . .'

It is difficult to see how I. M. Parsons can read this as a trench poem. In *Men Who March Away*, his introductory comment to the section *The Pity of War* begins:

It was not necessary to have been in the trenches to appreciate 'the pity war distilled' or to understand, if one had the heart and wit, the larger implications of the conflict. Thus two of the most remarkable poems in this group – Hardy's 'I Looked Up From My Writing', and de la Mare's 'Motley' – are by older poets who wrote of it at a distance.[40]

It is in this context that Thomas's name should appear. But Parsons, after mentioning 'Tommies in the Train' and 'Bombardment' by the 'non-combatant' D. H. Lawrence (two other poems which are to be found in this section), goes on to make this distinction:

But it is still the front-line poets who, understandably, have most to say on this subject and who interpret it most diversely and movingly. Here the prevalent mood is meditative and reflective, rather than assertive or denunciatory. Typical of it are two gifted but very different poets, Edward Thomas and Edmund Blunden, who found it possible to construct, out of their varied experiences, if not 'something upon which to rejoice' at least something with which to solace themselves and others: poems like Thomas's 'As the Team's Head-Brass' or Blunden's 'Zillebeke Brook', whose quiet rhythms and perceptive insights create a sense of pastoral calm which, by antithesis, make their message all the more effective.[41]

Parsons seems to be reading 'As the Team's Head-Brass' as some sort of therapeutic activity ('to solace themselves and others') by which Thomas sustained himself in the front line. This is exactly what he was *not* doing. Blunden was the front-line poet for whom the muddy French stream suddenly recalled

> a glassy burn
> Ribanded through a brake of Kentish fern.
>
> ('Zillebeke Brook')

He was writing in France, in April 1917. Thomas's poem was written in England, in May 1916, and he is creating not a sense of 'pastoral calm' but a sense of the rural community undergoing serious disruption from the effects of the war:

> 'Have many gone
> From here?' 'Yes.' 'Many lost?' 'Yes, a good few.
> Only two teams work on the farm this year.
> One of my mates is dead. The second day
> In France they killed him . . .'

The 'pastoral calm' is not as prevalent as Parsons imagines. It is the sterility of the scene ('charlock', 'fallow', 'the fallen elm') that is most evident.

Even stranger is Hoxie N. Fairchild's discussion of the poem in *Religious Trends in English Poety* (1962). He begins by making the common mistake of regarding Thomas as a trench poet:

He wrote almost no 'war poetry' in the ordinary sense . . . the nature poems which he *stubbornly* continued to produce . . . were attempts to remind himself and his countrymen of what England was fighting to preserve.[42] (my italics.)

His subsequent exposition of 'As the Team's Head-Brass' may be quoted in full:

The war . . . is firmly kept in its place as an insane detour from the highway of the great eternal sanities.

> As the team's head-brass flashed out on the turn
> The lovers disappeared into the wood.

The observer talks about the war with the ploughman, who shows no awareness that it is more important than his ploughing. He would be willing enough to join up if he could be quite sure of coming back. Several men of the neighbourhood will never do so. 'One of my mates is dead.' But, adds the farmer, 'If we could see all all might seem good.' As if in corroboration of these words, the lovers emerge from the grove, while

> The horses started and for the last time
> I Watched the clods crumble and topple over
> After the ploughshare and the stumbling team.

That and the lovers are what really matter.

   More often, however, the war is kept in its place simply by writing as if it did not exist. . . .[43]

Fairchild confuses the dialogue as though it were the observer (obviously Thomas) who asks 'Have you been out?' Surely it is the ploughman, who shows more awareness than Fairchild credits him with. Moreover, it is not a question of 'joining up' but of 'going out' – to provoke the question the observer must *already* be in uniform. Finally, Fairchild insists that the ploughing and the lovers are what really matter. Yet the poem ends on an ominous note – 'for the last time' – which does not offer any of the consolation that he seemingly derives from it. His comments are more appropriate to Thomas Hardy's 'In Time of "The Breaking of Nations" ':

I

Only a man harrowing clods
   In a slow silent walk
With an old horse that stumbles and nods
   Half asleep as they stalk.

II

Only thin smoke without flame
   From the heaps of couch-grass;
Yet this will go onward the same
   Though Dynasties pass.

III

Yonder a maid and her wight
   Come whispering by:
War's annals will cloud into night
   Ere their story die.

The poem sets out to create Parson's sense of 'pastoral calm' and Bergonzi's 'unchanging order of nature and rural society'. The ploughman and lovers are, for Hardy, what really matter. But in Thomas's poem those 'great eternal sanities' are shown to be under pressure and actually disappearing.

In 'As the Team's Head-Brass' Thomas deliberated on the possibility of his own death. It is introduced so often in the poems, first as an intuition prior to his enlistment, then as a certainty as the time of his embarkation approached. In *Rose Acre Papers* in 1904, he wrote that 'sleep is a novitiate for the beyond'.[44] In 'Lights Out' in 1916, he faced that beyond. It is one of the quietest and most haunting of leave-takings:

> I have come to the borders of sleep,
> The unfathomable deep
> Forest where all must lose
> Their way, however straight,
> Or winding, soon or late;
> They cannot choose.
>
> Many a road and track
> That, since the dawn's first crack,
> Up to the forest brink,
> Deceived the travellers,
> Suddenly now blurs,
> And in they sink.
>
> Here love ends,
> Despair, ambition ends;
> All pleasure and all trouble,
> Although most sweet or bitter,
> Here ends in sleep that is sweeter
> Than tasks most noble.
>
> There is not any book
> Or face of dearest look
> That I would not turn from now
> To go into the unknown
> I must enter, and leave, alone,
> I know not how.
>
> The tall forest towers;
> Its cloudy foliage lowers
> Ahead, shelf above shelf;
> Its silence I hear and obey
> That I may lose my way
> And myself.

'His poetry is so brave,' wrote Frost after his friend's death, 'so unconsciously brave. He didn't think of it for a moment as war poetry, though that is what it is. It ought to be called Roads to France.'[45] His remark leaves no doubt as to the true origin of Thomas's poetry.

SOURCE: extracts from *Edward Thomas: A Critical Biography, 1878–1917* (London, 1970), pp. 209–25, 233–42.

NOTES

[These have been modified and renumbered from those in the original – Ed.]

1. Athalie Bushnell, 'Edward Thomas', *Poetry Review*, XXXVIII, 4 (1947), p. 251.
2. H. Coombes, *Edward Thomas* (London, 1956), pp. 187–8.
3. John H. Johnston, *English Poetry of the First World War* (Princeton, N.J., 1964), p. 128.
4. Bernard Bergonzi, *Heroes' Twilight* (London, 1965), p. 85.
5. Brian Gardner (ed.), *Up the Line to Death* (London, 1964), p. 182.
6. I. M. Parsons (ed.), *Men Who March Away* (London, 1965), p. 16.
7. Ibid.
8. [Ed.–This point is also made in the most recent anthology, Jon Silkin's *Penguin Book of First World War Poetry* (1979), p. 48. His selection from Thomas comprises 'A Private', 'Man and Dog', 'The Owl', 'In Memoriam (Easter, 1915)', 'Fifty Faggots', 'This is No Case of Petty Right or Wrong', 'Rain', 'Roads', 'February Afternoon', 'The Cherry Trees', 'As the Team's Head-Brass' and 'Gone, Gone Again'.]
9. 'I don't take the cigarette out of my mouth when I write Deceased over their letters. But one day I will write Deceased over many books': quoted in Edmund Blunden's 'Memoir' to *The Poems of Wilfred Owen* (London, 1960 edn), p. 36.
10. Edward Thomas, 'War Poetry', *Poetry and Drama*, II, 8 (Dec. 1914), pp. 341–5. [Included in Part One of this Casebook – Ed.]
11. Helen Thomas, *World Without End*, p. 165.
12. Edward Thomas, 'Anthologies and Reprints', *Poetry and Drama*, II, 8 (Dec. 1914), p. 384.
13. Edward Thomas, *The Last Sheaf*, p. 109.

14. Edward Thomas, Preface, *This England* (1915).

15. John Moore, *Letters*, p. 223.

16. The two lines in parenthesis are so marked on the MS. They were omitted from the printed version.

17. Edward Thomas, Introduction to his edition of Cobbett's *Rural Rides* (London, 1912), pp. vii–x.

18. *This England*, op. cit., p. 97.

19. Ibid., pp. 93–4.

20. Edward Thomas, Introduction, *Words and Places* (London, 1911), p. ix.

21. Edward Thomas, *A Literary Pilgrim in England* (London, 1917), p. 24.

22. Edward Thomas, *Richard Jefferies*, p. 11.

23. Edward Thomas, *The Icknield Way*, p. 3.

24. Quoted in Edmund Blunden's 'Memoir', op. cit., pp. 34–5.

25. See *This England*, pp. 68–9.

26. In *The Last Sheaf* (p. 139), Thomas related how many people were beginning to 'scent a new reality' in old prophecies and expressions as a result of the war and invasion scares.

27. *The Last Sheaf*, p. 136.

28. Ibid., p. 137.

29. Robert Graves's poem 'Goliath and David' is an offshoot of this idea. In his version David fails, and the giant moves in for the kill:

> spike-helmeted, grey, grim,
> Goliath straddles over him.

30. *The Last Sheaf*, op. cit., p. 108.

31. *The Letters of Charles Sorley* (London, 1919), p. 97.

32. Thomas, *Richard Jefferies*, op. cit., pp. 208–9.

33. C. Day Lewis, *Essays by Divers Hands*, p. 76.

34. Vernon Scannell, *Edward Thomas*, p. 20.

35. The date of 'In Memoriam (Easter 1915)' was the occasion when Brooke's sonnet 'The Soldier' was eulogised by Dean Inge in St Paul's Cathedral.

36. Quoted in Edmund Blunden's 'Memoir', op. cit., p. 29.

37. *Selected Letters of Robert Frost*, p. 184.

38. Edward Thomas, *The South Country*, pp. 4–5.

39. John Moore, *Letters*, p. 236.

40. I. M. Parsons (ed.), *Men Who March Away*, p. 20.

41. Ibid., p. 21.

42. H. N. Fairchild, *Religious Trends in English Poetry* (New York and London, 1962), vol. v, p. 339.

43. Ibid., p. 340.

44. Edward Thomas, *Rose Acre Papers* (London, 1904), p. 105.

45. *Selected Letters of Robert Frost*, p. 217.

SELECT BIBLIOGRAPHY

The following studies are recommended, in addition to those from which excerpts are reproduced in this Casebook:

Edmund Blunden, *The Mind's Eye* (London: Cape, 1934): the chapter on 'Siegfried Sassoon's War Poetry'.

Maurice Bowra, *Poetry and the First World War* (Oxford University Press, 1961): a useful introduction to the work of the principal non-British poets of the war.

David Daiches, *New Literary Values* (Edinburgh: Oliver and Boyd, 1936): the chapter on 'The Poetry of Wilfred Owen'.

John Gould Fletcher, 'On Subject-Matter and War Poetry', *The Egoist*, III, no. 12 (December 1916).

Frederick Grubb, *A Vision of Reality: A Study in Liberalism in Twentieth-Century Verse* (London: Chatto and Windus, 1965): the chapter on Owen and Rosenberg.

Philip Hobsbaum, *Tradition and Experiment in English Poetry* (London: Macmillan, 1979): the chapter on 'The Growth of English Modernism'.

Arthur E. Lane, *An Adequate Response: The War Poetry of Wilfred Owen and Siegfried Sassoon* (Wayne State University Press, 1972).

Robert Nichols (ed.), *Anthology of War Poetry, 1914–1918* (London: Nicholson and Watson, 1943): Nichols provides a long preface.

Ian Parsons, 'The Poems of Wilfred Owen (1893–1918)', *Criterion*, X (July 1931).

Ian Parsons (ed.), *Men Who March Away: Poems of the First World War* (London: Chatto and Windus, 1968): an anthology with an introduction.

Catherine W. Reilly, *English Poetry of the First World War: A Bibliography* (London: Prior, 1978).

Jon Silkin (ed.), *The Penguin Book of First World War Poetry* (Harmondsworth, 1979): an anthology with an introduction.

Stephen Spender, *The Destructive Element: A Study of Modern Writers and Beliefs* (London: Cape, 1935): the chapter on Owen.

Stand, IV, no. 3 (1960): in addition to the study on Sassoon by Jon Silkin, excerpted in Part Three above, this issue of the magazine also contains articles, by other critics, on Owen, Brooke and Blunden.

NOTES ON CONTRIBUTORS

JOHN BAYLEY: Thomas Warton Professor of English Literature, University of Oxford; his publications include *The Characters of Love: A Study in the Literature of Personality* (1960; new edition 1968) and *The Uses of Division: Unity and Disharmony in Literature* (1976).

BERNARD BERGONZI: Professor of English Literature, University of Warwick; his publications include studies of H. G. Wells (1961), T. S. Eliot (1972) and *Heroes' Twilight* (1965), and he is editor of the Casebook on T. S. Eliot's *Four Quartets*.

EDMUND BLUNDEN (1896–1974): poet and scholar; he recorded his war experiences in *Undertones of War* (1928) and in many poems, and wrote a number of essays on First War poetry.

WINSTON S. CHURCHILL (1874–1965): statesman and man of letters; he was First Lord of the Admiralty in 1915 and Rupert Brooke, as an officer in the Royal Naval Division, came under his supreme command.

WILLIAM COOKE: poet, tutor in English at Stoke-on-Trent Sixth Form College, and author of *Edward Thomas: A Critical Biography* (1970).

DONALD DAVIE: Professor of English at Vanderbilt University, having previously taught at Dublin, Cambridge, Essex and Stanford; his books include studies of Hardy (1972) and Ezra Pound (1976), and his *Collected Poems* were published in 1972.

BASIL DE SELINCOURT (1876–1966): author of books on Blake (1909), Whitman (1914) and other subjects, and literary journalist.

T. S. ELIOT (1888–1965): poet, dramatist and critic.

PAUL FUSSELL: Professor of English Literature, Rutgers University; his publications include *The Rhetorical World of Augustan Humanism* (1965) and *Samuel Johnson and the Life of Writing* (1971).

DOUGLAS GOLDRING (1887–1960): author of many books on travel,

literature and other subjects, including *James Elroy Flecker* (1922) and
The Nineteen-Twenties (1945).

SIR EDMUND GOSSE (1849–1928): man of letters and Librarian of the
House of Lords, he wrote *Father and Son* (1907) and numerous literary
essays.

D. W. HARDING: Emeritus Professor of Psychology, University of
London, and a former editor of *Scrutiny*; his publications include
Experience into Words: Essays on Poetry (1963) and *Words into Rhythm:
English Speech Rhythm in Verse and Prose* (1976).

PHILIP HOBSBAUM: Senior Lecturer in English, University of
Glasgow; his publications include *A Theory of Communication* (1970) and
Tradition and Experiment in English Poetry (1979).

JOHN H. JOHNSTON: Associate Professor of English, West Virginia
University; his publications include *English Poetry of the First World War*
(1964).

GALLOWAY KYLE (1875–1967): editor of the *Poetry Review* for thirty-
eight years and founder of the Poetry Society.

C. DAY LEWIS (1904–72): poet and critic, appointed Poet Laureate in
1968; with Spender, Auden and others, he was one of the group of left-
wing poets active in the 1930s.

H. W. MASSINGHAM (1860–1924): journalist and editor, particularly
remembered for his distinguished editorship of the *Nation* from 1907 to
1923.

J. MIDDLETON MURRY (1899–1957): literary critic and influential
journalist, editor of the *Athenaeum* (1919–21) and the *Adelphi* (1923–48).

SIR HENRY NEWBOLT (1862–1936): poet, best known for his patriotic verses.

WILFRED OWEN (1893–1918): poet; he gave up a private tutorship in
order to enlist in 1915 and was killed in action just before the Armistice;
the first collection of his poems was published in 1920.

DAVID PERKINS: Professor of English, Harvard University; his publications include *Wordsworth and the Poetry of Sincerity* (1964) and *A History
of Modern Poetry* (1976).

JOHN PRESS: poet and critic, regional director for the British Council in the South Midlands; his publications include *A Map of Modern English Verse* (1969) and *The Lengthening Shadows: Observations on Poetry and Its Enemies* (1971).

TIMOTHY ROGERS: Principal of Bosworth College, Leicestershire; editor of *Rupert Brooke: A Reappraisal and Selection* (1971) and of *Georgian Poetry, 1911–1922: The Critical Heritage* (1977).

ISAAC ROSENBERG (1890–1918): painter and poet; a student at the Slade School of Art before he enlisted, he was killed in action in April 1918; his *Collected Works* were published in 1937.

SIEGFRIED SASSOON (1886–1967): poet and autobiographer; he served as officer throughout the First War, writing many poems about it and, in later years, several volumes of reminiscences, including *Memoirs of an Infantry Officer* (1930).

JON SILKIN: poet, critic and editor of *Stand*, the literary magazine; he is author of *Out of Battle* (1972) and editor of two anthologies: *Poetry of the Committed Individual* (1973) and *The Penguin Book of First World War Poetry* (1979).

CHARLES SORLEY (1895–1915): poet and student, he wrote some remarkable letters from the Front before he was killed in action; his *Marlborough and Other Poems* came out in 1916.

DYLAN THOMAS (1914–53): poet, dramatist and broadcaster.

EDWARD THOMAS (1878–1917): known now as a poet but in his lifetime mainly as literary critic and journalist, he was killed by a shell-blast in 1917; his *Collected Poems* were published in 1922.

ARTHUR WAUGH (1866–1943): critic, chairman of Chapman and Hall, the publishers, and father of Evelyn and Alec Waugh.

DENNIS WELLAND: Professor of American Literature, University of Manchester, his publications include *Wilfred Owen: A Critical Study* (1960; new edition 1978), *Mark Twain in England* (1978) and the edited volume *United States: A Companion to American Studies* (1974).

VIRGINIA WOOLF (1882–1941): novelist and critic.

W. B. YEATS (1865–1939): poet, playwright and essayist.

INDEX

References to sections on individual poets are given in **bold type**.

Waugh, Arthur 14–15, 34–7, 244
Welland, Dennis 19, 21, 135–
53, 244
Woolf, Virginia 45–6, 244

Yeats, W. B.   12, 16, 21 n.4, 31–
2, 75, 80, 82, 108–10, 137, 153–
4, 158–60, 162, 164, 197, 210–
11, 244